KU-522-982

THE QUEEN'S CLASSICS
CERTIFICATE BOOKS

★

ALEXANDER POPE
Selected Poems and Letters

SELECTED
POEMS AND LETTERS OF
ALEXANDER POPE

Edited
with an Introduction and Notes
by

R. P. C. MUTTER

Reader in English,
Dean of the School of English and American Studies,
University of Sussex

and

M. KINKEAD-WEEKES

Senior Lecturer in English
University of Kent, Canterbury

Chatto and Windus
LONDON

Published by
Chatto & Windus (Educational) Ltd
42 William IV Street
London WC2

★

Clarke, Irwin & Co. Ltd
Toronto

First published 1962
Second impression 1966
Third impression 1970

ISBN 0 7010 0254 9

Reproduced and Printed in Great Britain by
Redwood Press Limited
Trowbridge & London

Preface

The text of the poems in this book is based on that of *The Twickenham Edition of the Poems of Alexander Pope* (general editor, John Butt), by kind permission of the publishers, Messrs Methuen and Co. We have made certain slight changes with the idea of promoting easier reading. The late Professor Butt afforded us the particular courtesy of allowing us to use the proofs of Volume I, and of the revised edition of Volume III ii. The text of the letters is that of *The Correspondence of Alexander Pope*, edited by George Sherburn (Oxford University Press); that of Spence's *Anecdotes* is from S.W. Singers's edition of 1820.

Our aim in the selection of poems has been, simply, to present as much as possible of the work of a great poet. With the *Essay on Criticism* we have tried to offer a guide rather than a mere anthology of purple passages, something which may lead the reader to study that poem more fully with the help of the Twickenham Edition. We have not been able to include a selection from Pope's 'grandest assault on Parnassus', the *Essay on Man*, but we stress its importance in our Introduction, and hope that the reader will be encouraged to test our remarks for himself. The extracts from the Letters seek to present in the best possible way the relevant biographical information, and to correct the conception of Pope as, in Lytton Strachey's words, 'a fiendish monkey', ladling out 'spoonfuls of boiling oil . . . upon such of the passers-by whom the wretch had a grudge against.' The Notes have been designed to provide as much information as is necessary to prevent the reader's mind being caught on the snags of obscure reference as he reads; perhaps more important, they try to turn the reader's attention continually back to the poetry itself, which is what matters.

Our general indebtedness to Pope scholars and critics is indicated by the reading-list on p. 250.

R. P. C. M.
M. K-W.

Contents

INTRODUCTION

IN many ways, English poetry of the earlier eighteenth century was a last flowering of the Renaissance. It retained a lively relationship with the classical poetry of Greece and Rome, which still seemed as fresh and meaningful as it had to the humanists of the sixteenth century, but there is a no less creative relationship with the whole of English Renaissance poetry too. In Pope, not only Homer and Virgil, Ovid and Horace, but also Chaucer, Spenser, Shakespeare, Donne, Milton and Dryden all continue to live. Pope was a traditional poet in the best sense, building his own poetry on a foundation of centuries of English and European achievement.

This involved certain attitudes to the writing of poetry that are no longer wholly familiar. It would seem a matter of course and common sense to a young poet beginning his career in the early eighteenth century to learn to write by studying what the poets of the past had done. Critics from Aristotle onwards had fostered the idea that there were a number of poetic *Kinds*— different types of poem, treating different subjects in different ways—and that for each of these there was a proper *Decorum*, an appropriate style, which would also partly depend on the kind of person or persons one was addressing. Having decided what kind of poem one wanted to write, one would turn quite naturally to a poet who had attempted the same kind, and try to learn all one could from him.

Wordsworth gave very different advice to a young poet: 'You feel strongly; trust to those feelings, and your poem will take its shape and proportions as a tree does from the vital principle that actuates it. I do not think that great poems can be cast in a mould.' Seen from such an angle, the theory of the Kinds might seem mechanical, with too little room for originality, spontaneity, inspiration. This would, however, be much too narrow and simple a view. The theory recognises, as Wordsworth's remark does not, that poetry is a craft as well as an art. It suggests a common-sense approach to craftsmanship, dictated by humility, not arrogance. Above all it is concerned with far more than the mere learning of technique. What was really important about the great poets was that they had found ways of illuminating the truth about nature, society, and the human heart and mind; the theory of the kinds was simply a way of formulating this achievement in order to make it available for others to use. Any 'rules' that were made were only a methodising of what men had already done in poetry: they were not inviolable. A modern poet had to beware of thinking he knew better than the masters, but the way was always open for genius to go beyond all rules, to 'snatch a Grace'—the word is significant—'beyond the reach of Art'. Of course small minds could then, as now, make stultifying systems out of living thought, but if they do the fault does not lie with the original ideas—and Pope's was not a small mind. Moreover, there is nothing second-hand about the idea of 'Imitation'. Having studied the wisdom and mastery of the past, the great Augustans sought not to reproduce, but to *use* it, to write in the present. Far from being second-hand, the literature that resulted was highly inventive; and Pope is the most inventive of its poets, not least when he is most closely in touch with the past.

Finally, the real strength of poetry founded on this creative relationship with the past goes well beyond questions of apprenticeship. T. S. Eliot's words become literally true of poetic experience: 'All time is eternally present'. We do not arrange our bookshelves chronologically, implying that the past is over and done with, superseded by the present. For Pope, Virgil and Dryden stand side by side, as do Horace, Marvell, Boileau; the whole legacy of poetry is felt to be part of the situation *now*, and in Pope's own writing the wisdom and power of centuries can be brought to bear on eighteenth-century man. But only a great poet can fully harness such power.

Pope trained himself to be a great poet as deliberately as Virgil, Spenser and Milton had done. His smiling account to Spence of his precocious boyhood (see p. 30) is amusing; but it reveals also a formidable strength of purpose. Starting with Homer in translation at the age of eight, he had studied all the greatest English poets, most of the classical and French ones in the original, Tasso and Ariosto in translation, and 'all the best critics' by the age of sixteen. He had begun to write ('am ashamed to say how soon') by the age of twelve, and what he wrote was epic and tragedy, nothing but the best. More important, he left these high flights behind and learnt, more humbly, to translate—completing over a quarter of Ovid's *Metamorphoses* and a part of Statius that was good enough to publish later. High aspiration meets here with its complement of humility, as the remark to Spence about 'my first taking to Imitating' shows. The past was an inspiration and a challenge, and not, as Wordsworth was to feel, a set of shackles holding one back; yet this did not mean that there was nothing left to do. Pope's mentor Walsh told him that 'though we had several great poets, we never had any one great poet that was correct, and he desired me to make that my study and aim'. To aim at absolute 'correctness', again, was not to aim at a slavish following of 'rules' or a mere superficial polish; it was to long for perfection of art, the complete appropriateness and mastery of all the resources of language, imagery, sound, rhythm and tone.

Pope was lucky, as Wordsworth was not, in having to hand a poetic idiom, a way of writing, that was already in a state of vigorous growth. His multiple apprenticeship finally set itself in one specific direction, so that he was to tell Spence that he had 'learned versification wholly from Dryden's works'. One of the great instances of the handing on of a literary torch occurred when Pope, before the age of twelve, persuaded some friends to take him to Dryden's favourite coffee-house so that he could gaze at the great man. Out of the confusion of late seventeenth-century styles Dryden had selected and improved one that seemed capable of almost unlimited development. From Dryden's extremely varied achievement in the heroic couplet Pope learnt how it could be made flowing and easy, or packed and concise, how it could spit like a firecracker or soar with eloquence, how it could be wittily antithetical or tenderly elegiac. The couplet may look monotonous as we see it on the page; but when we read it with attention as the poet's art directs us, it is a highly flexible style. Pope used it for nearly all his poetry—for all his greatest—because he could do anything with it that he wanted. Moreover, the heroic couplet demanded from a poet who tried to use its full resources a control and precision of language that would force him ever nearer to the goal of perfection. Wordsworth at the outset of his career had to struggle to free himself from the same idiom grown obsolete and mechanical, apparently incapable of expressing his new kind of perception; but for Pope, Dryden's couplet was exciting and liberating—a revelation of what could be done.

What is most revealing about Pope's apprenticeship, however, is the depth of his epic ambition. The reason for dedicating himself to poetry at such an early age, and for carrying through such an arduous, though enjoyable, self-education, was that he had determined to become the greatest kind of poet. Though he left behind his juvenile attempts at epic and tragedy, and set out on a humbler course, he never lost his ambition to write an epic. He actually started one late in life, of which only the plan and a fragment or two survive. We need not be too sorry that he never finished it: it seems unlikely for several reasons that a great epic could have been written in the eighteenth century, even by Pope. Milton's is the last in our literature. Yet we may never understand Pope's poetic career if we fail to see that its central shaping force was this desire to write heroic poetry—the greatest of all Kinds because the heroic writer fulfils the highest function of poetry, acting as the spokesman for a whole civilisation, enshrining its deepest values. That is why the heroic poet had to be a dedicated spirit.

So when Pope set out to write seriously for publication, he followed the road that had been marked out for the epic poet by Virgil. He began with *Pastorals*, seeking not just to copy but to recreate Virgil's *Eclogues* in English, as an essential preliminary to greater things, and in a highly successful attempt to master the couplet in the proper decorum for this minor Kind. In the *Essay on Criticism*, which is also an Art of Poetry, he tried to summarise and concentrate the critical wisdom he had gained from his reading and clarify his own thoughts about poetry. In *Windsor Forest* he went further along Virgil's path, in a poem that looks back clearly to the *Georgics*. It is still a young man's

poem, but it is the first broadening of his vision, his first attempt
to deal directly with some of the basic human concerns of his
society; and after it we find him writing three poems which
spring, in their different ways, directly out of his love and regard
for the heroic: the *Rape of the Lock*, *Eloisa to Abelard* and the
Elegy. With them he comes of age as a poet. Though none of
them is an epic proper, they all show the depth of insight, the
universal significance, the deep moral seriousness of the epic
poet; the *Rape* is in fact a whole epic scaled down for comic
purposes, but retaining the epic's searching criticism of Man—
or rather Woman—and Society. The gathering of these into the
collected *Works* of 1717 marks an already major achievement,
with Pope not yet thirty. He was inclined to depreciate these
poems from the standpoint of his later work—'A painted
Mistress, or a purling Stream'—but for all his right to judge his
own achievement, we should not let him persuade us to regard
them as works of 'Fancy' rather than of 'Truth'.

Ironically enough, he then gave to Homer himself the energy
that might have gone into the writing of an original epic; he
spent from 1715 to 1726 translating the *Iliad* and the *Odyssey*,
as well as editing Shakespeare. 'If I had not undertaken that
work, the translation of Homer, I should certainly have writ an
epic'; yet if he had not produced his Homer he might never have
gained the financial independence he prized so dearly, and of
which he was so justly proud. He was the first non-dramatic
poet in our literature who managed to make enough out of
poetry to live on—'Un-plac'd, un-pension'd, no Man's Heir, or
Slave'—and his later work would have been impossible if he had
had to depend on patronage. Independence is fundamental to
Pope's satiric position. It was hard earned: eleven years, nearly
a fifth of a life which never seemed likely to be a long one. Yet
it was a loving servitude, and the translation still further deepened
his understanding of epic form and style. His second mock-epic,
the *Dunciad* of 1728, shows this understanding put to good use.

The most marked deepening of his work, however, came
about not through the writing of an epic but through the creation
of what could be called an 'epic substitute'—the four lofty
didactic epistles of the *Essay on Man*, which he began about the

end of 1729 and worked on steadily till it was published in 1733-4. In this poem he tried to work out a fundamental analysis of Man in himself, in Society, and in relation to God. Pope chose to do this directly in the form of a treatise, rather than through an epic 'myth' such as Milton's, and this in itself indicates a change in intellectual climate; but his poem stands in the same relationship to his century as *Paradise Lost* had to the seventeenth. If it is not a great poem, it is a very important one; and its significance for us lies particularly in the way it helps us to understand the new depth and profoundly organic thinking, fusing literary, political, social and moral values into a single harmony, that the act of writing it enabled Pope to develop and use in the magnificent poems that appeared from 1733 to 1738. The *Epistles to Several Persons* are not as closely connected with the *Essay* as Pope's editor Warburton, and even Pope himself, later suggested; but they do use the *Essay*'s insights, with a vivid re-orchestration of some of its themes, to analyse man and society in new and detailed ways, while the *Imitations of Horace* are the most widely ranging and varied applications of his organic thinking to the world in which he found himself. All these poems came out interspersed with one another, as a glance at their publication dates will show. Together, though they look back in form and style to Horace rather than to Homer or Virgil, they make up a total analysis of great depth and power, continually stressing the lofty nature of the poet's calling. Pope does take as his province nothing less than the nature of man and the critique of a whole civilisation, and though the Kind of these poems is not epic, the total achievement certainly is. At the last epic itself floods back in Pope's most sombre, and most sublime, vision of human decadence—the *New Dunciad* of 1742.

The young poet of the *Pastorals* was already a fine technician, as we can see from the passage in *Summer* that Handel made famous by his setting:

> Where'er you walk, cool gales shall fan the glade,
> Trees, where you sit, shall crowd into a shade:
> Where'er you tread, the blushing flow'rs shall rise,
> And all things flourish where your turn your eyes.

Pope's first attempt at this might have been written by almost any poet of the day:

> While you your presence to the grove deny,
> Our flowers are faded, and our brooks are dry;
> Though with'ring herbs lay dying on the plain,
> At your return they shall be green again.

Everything about this is trite; the rhythms are flat and monotonous; the language generally lifeless. As Pope got to work on it however, ideas came and life began to quicken.* First, the hint of a more complex rhythm appears:

> Winds, where you walk, shall gently fan the glade . . .

Next, by *feeling*, it seems, the relationship between the *w*, *f* and *g* sounds of this line a new stage is reached: a softer, subtler movement for the beginning, followed by the more broken rhythm he had just hit upon:

> Where'er you walk, fresh gales shall fan the glade,
> Trees, where you sit, shall crowd into a shade . . .

Then:

> Flowers, where you tread, in painted pride shall rise . . .

But this is clumsy and repetitive. The rhythm of the first line would be better:

> Where'er you tread, the purple flowers shall rise,

and with this the conclusion also leaps to mind—summing up, quite simply, the central idea of the whole passage:

> And all things flourish where you turn your eyes.

With two more changes, the lines reach their final form. Pope substitutes the evocative 'cool' for 'fresh'; and 'blushing' as softer than 'purple', in pleasing consonance with 'flourish', 'shall', and 'shade', and also capturing the sense of colour flooding into something relatively colourless, delicately in keeping

---

* We owe our knowledge of these variants to C. V. Deane's *Aspects of 18th Century Nature Poetry*, but he should not be held responsible for our arguments.

with the central theme. The material is still generalised, the language still in a sense conventional; but the lines are now instinct with life, their beauty and music undeniable. Yet it is not simply a musical beauty: the life Pope has given is an embodiment, through the sensuous texture of poetry, of the idea he was trying to express—that the summery fulfilment of love *gives* life to everything. Even here, at the start of his work, we cannot speak merely of 'technique', or separate 'ideas' from 'texture'. The 'prose' concept of the first version and the last is the same; what is different is the whole difference between poetic language and a prosaic or doggerel use of words.

Poetry does involve a delicate and subtle command of the resources of rhythm and sound, and one can never point too often to Pope's achievement in these directions alone. But poetry is much more than this, and as Pope grew in maturity he began to turn his technical mastery to ever deeper, more complex, and more meaningful use. Here is another landscape—this time from *Windsor Forest*:

> The Groves of Eden, vanish'd now so long,
> Live in description, and look green in Song . . .
> Here Hills and Vales, the Woodland and the Plain,
> Here Earth and Water seem to strive again,
> Not *Chaos*-like together crush'd and bruis'd,
> But as the World, harmoniously confus'd:
> Where Order in Variety we see,
> And where, tho' all things differ, all agree.
> Here waving Groves a chequer'd Scene display,
> And part admit and part exclude the Day . . .
> There, interspers'd in Lawns and op'ning Glades,
> Thin Trees arise that shun each other's Shades.
> Here in full Light the russet Plains extend;
> There wrapt in Clouds the blueish Hills ascend:
> Ev'n the wild Heath displays her purple Dies,
> And 'midst the Desart fruitful Fields arise,
> That crown'd with tufted Trees and springing Corn,
> Like verdant Isles the sable Waste adorn.

8

As letter 3 (p. 18) shows, Pope has been studying painting, and merely as description his artful variation of colour, of light and shade, of density and openness, of distant and near perspective, makes a finely designed appeal to the senses. There is, moreover, the same emphasis on life springing from barrenness. But this time the picture is meaningful in a new sense that sets it much further beyond simple description and appeal to the eye and ear. As Eden was Nature in the first Creation out of Chaos, the setting and the symbol of Innocence and Peace, so now the Forest seems to recapture the possibility of harmony and fruitfulness after the chaos Man has made for himself through tyranny and war. *Windsor Forest* is a poem about war and peace, and this passage is Pope's first attempt to realise the difference between harmony, which allows diverse energies to combine into creative growth, and discord which produces only chaos and destruction. Pope uses Nature to write about Man.

Yet this is only a first step toward the depth of meaning Pope develops in his later work. The heart of discord is Pride—man's readiness to mutilate the work of God in nature, in society, and in the human heart and mind, in order to magnify himself. Pride is a theme of the *Essay on Criticism*, the *Rape of the Lock*, the *Elegy*; it might be called *the* theme of the later works. It receives one of its finest expressions in the *Epistle to Burlington*: the wealthy Timon sees in nature only the opportunity to build a grotesque and meaningless monument—to himself:

> To compass this, his building is a Town,
> His pond an Ocean, his parterre a Down:
> Who but must laugh, the Master when he sees,
> A puny insect, shiv'ring at a breeze!
> Lo, what huge heaps of littleness around!
> The whole, a labour'd Quarry above ground . . .
> No pleasing Intricacies intervene,
> No artful wildness to perplex the scene;
> Grove nods at grove, each Alley has a brother,
> And half the platform just reflects the other.
> The suff'ring eye inverted Nature sees,
> Trees cut to Statues, Statues thick as trees;

With here a Fountain, never to be play'd;
And there a Summer-house, that knows no shade . . .

But—

Another Age shall see the golden Ear
Imbrown the Slope, and nod on the Parterre,
Deep Harvests bury all his pride has plann'd,
And laughing Ceres re-assume the land.

Instead of the lively and varied harmony between man's work and God's of the *Windsor Forest* passage, we have the costly and useless perversion of nature in dead formality and empty show. God's creation is good, with its own innate harmony that man must discover and develop. If he fails, or worse, perverts this harmony, what he builds can never be fruitful. It must make way for nature again; any 'civilisation' that cuts its link with God's earth and the needs of humanity must crumble away into dirt for wiser men to cultivate. To sin against nature is for Pope to sin ultimately against both God and Man. What his mature work does, is to try to understand and body forth the proper harmonies of all human life, for by this alone could civilisation hope to *grow* in creativity, virtue, good sense, and love.

'Love' may well seem a word that has little to do with satire. Pope of course was not only a satirist, yet it is as our greatest satiric poet that he is justly remembered; and there lingers in the minds of many people the feeling that satire is something negative, unpleasant, unhealthy, something which sets out to hurt and destroy. It has too much to do with anger, envy, malice, hatred. Pope moreover used his poetry to attack specific people who had offended him, not only rogues and cheats, and often his victims were not really as black as he painted them. How can this be reconciled with his constant professions of virtue, his insistence indeed that poetry should be a sacred thing? So the picture grew up, in the nineteenth century especially, of Pope as the vicious wasp of Twickenham. We might retort with a more sympathetic account of how much Pope had to be bitter about: he was dwarfish, hunchbacked (probably from a tubercular ailment of the spine), and barred, as a Roman Catholic, from the universities and many opportunities in public life. His first publication was greeted by the formidable John Dennis with 'there is nothing so stupid and so impotent as a hunch-backed toad' and 'it [is] impossible that his outward Form, tho' it should be that of downright Monkey, should differ so much from human Shape, as his immaterial unthinking part does from human Understanding', and this set the tone for a lifetime of abuse. We should not be surprised if Pope's character had a bitter streak.

Yet this is not the important point, for no kind of art depends for its value on the personality of the artist; art can only be judged on its own intrinsic evidence. The eighteenth-century poets, in particular, did not think of poetry as 'self-expression'; they insisted that it should illustrate universal truth. Pope attacks Atticus, Bufo and Sporus in *To Arbuthnot* precisely *because* they make poetry the servant of personality (see p. 214 below). We must therefore look at the value of satirical poetry in itself. We must not of course sentimentalise satire. It is made from the darker passions; yet to say this is still to say nothing of fundamental importance, for art cannot be reduced to its raw materials either. Greek vases are no less beautiful and significant because they are made of mud. We have to go on to ask *why* the satirist is angry, and what he makes out of his anger. We have already found the answer to the first question: it is because Pope feels so deeply about harmony and health in people and society that he is filled with anger and disgust at chaos and moral disease. It is only if we do not care very much about these things that we can treat bad writing, bad politics and bad men simply as a joke. The great satirist is great because he takes his values so seriously that the perversion of them fills him with a loathing that demands expression in art. As to the second question—what happens to the raw materials of satire, the poet's victims and his feelings about them?—the answer is that they change. The essence of Pope's careful distinction between satire and lampoon is that satire can transcend its origins while lampoon cannot; the latter remains merely personal hatred. True satire transforms its materials because the poet is no longer merely attacking a person. As his imagination fires, he is attacking what that person stands for, creating a symbol of certain values, going behind the 'real-life' man to hit out at vice in the cause of virtue. Of course Pope pays off old grudges, and can be unfair to 'real' people; but what matters about his satire is the no less real characters that the *poetry* creates, and the impersonal nature of the standards and feelings by which and for which they are pilloried.

Those standards, as Pope builds them up poem by poem over thirty years, are essentially creative and constructive. Never does he allow an attack to stand without stating or creating the positive values he is appealing to. Even the experience of reading the attacks themselves is a constructive one, because we are brought to realise imaginatively the nature of the true by being made to hate and reject the false. The poetry works predominantly in the cause of virtue and health: it is a defence as well as an attack. It is a defence of standards for which the poet feels a deep and abiding love, and both the poetry and the letters reveal a capacity for loving the people who seemed to Pope to embody those standards, that is just as important as his hatred of those that he thought negated them. He earned the right to proclaim the moral seriousness of his poetry, to hail Satire as a

> . . . Sacred weapon! left for Truth's defence . . .
> To all but Heav'n-directed hands deny'd,
> The Muse may give thee, but the Gods must guide.

The only remaining question is whether personal satire was the best way for Pope to achieve his end. Here we can only point to the poems, especially the second *Epilogue* and *To Fortescue*, or to letter 11 (p. 25), where he argues just this point. He had written deeply meaningful general satire in *To Burlington*, only to find it misconstrued and dirtied by ignorant or malicious gossip, his creation blotted out by a smoke-screen of scandal. The first duty of a didactic poet is to be understood, and Pope came to believe that it was only by hunting out and exposing specific examples that he could have any effect in an age of corruption. It was necessary to produce evidence, and this led him to the logical conclusion of naming everyone, giving no quarter high or low, from the King to Japhet Crook. Pope was a courageous man—not least because poetry and morality were always more important to him than his own 'crazy carcass'.

Pope is a complete master of the resources of language, and his poetry is a constant appeal to the full range of our senses and our intelligence. But his final greatness lies in the fact that he makes us *care*—care for poetry, for intelligence, for morality, for love, for life.

EXTRACTS FROM THE LETTERS

APPRECIATION of Pope's letters has been too much coloured by righteous indignation at his methods of securing their publication, and at his habit of 'editing' them by omission, conflation and alteration. Critics have tended to feel that there is a shameful conceit in publishing one's private correspondence, although there is nothing wrong in printing verse epistles, however intimate, or in the publication of letters after the writer's death. Certainly Pope was aware that this construction might be placed on him, and hence he had to resort to a roundabout and disingenuous way of publishing. He took advantage of the fact that his enemy Edmund Curll, a disreputable bookseller who had already got hold of and published some of Pope's letters to Henry Cromwell in 1726, was advertising for materials towards a biography of him—presumably with no very high-minded intentions. Pope anonymously placed some of his letters into Curll's hands and, when the edition appeared in 1735, indignantly repudiated it and set about securing an 'authorized' edition in 1737. Later Pope had to resort to more chicanery in order to publish his correspondence with Swift.

The element of trickery employed hardly matters now: it hardly mattered in the nineteenth century either, but too many writers then chose to see in Pope simply the warped, vicious satirist, a *mens curva in corpore curvo*, and, having given the dog a bad name, were determined to hang, draw and quarter him. What matters more is that we should understand and appreciate the letters themselves, and Pope's motives for publication. The alterations spoken of are not very important: they mainly amount to giving the letters a wash and brush-up, so to speak, before sending them into polite company. That, apart from the occasional turn of phrase, they are substantially genuine is no longer to be doubted.

We must remember, in the first place, that to Pope and his contemporaries letter-writing was itself a form of art, to which the principles of decorum applied: 'It is idle', Pope remarked to Spence, 'to say that letters should be written in an easy familiar style: that, like most other general rules, will not hold. The style, in letters as in all other things, should be adapted to the subject.' The letters, in fact, whether originally written with an eye to publication or not (and it is worth remembering that Pope published only about a tenth of the letters that have survived), could be considered part of the writer's Works. In the 1730s Pope had been increasingly subjected to personal attack, both on him-

self and his family, and to hostile criticism as poet and satirist; the letters
were to provide additional testimony to the sincerity of his motives and
beliefs—of, he told Caryll in 1726, 'my own love for good men, or
theirs for me', and would be 'more to my reputation than all my works
put together'. They are to be seen in the context of such poems as the
Epistles to *Arbuthnot* and *Fortescue*, and the *Epilogue to the Satires*—as
a defence of his position both as Satirist and as private individual.
Moreover, they might serve to remind his attackers that he had powerful and devoted friends.

Pope's remark to Spence, quoted above, should put us on our guard
against thinking that his letters will be like those of Keats, or even like
those of such eighteenth-century writers as Gray, Cowper and Horace
Walpole. The style was to be adapted to the subject and the recipient.
Thackeray, who had no love for Pope, was able to praise the majority
of those letters which were, in 1851, available: 'you live in them in the
finest company in the world', he says. 'A little stately, perhaps; a little
apprêté and conscious that they are speaking to whole generations who
are listening; but in the tone of their voices—pitched, as no doubt they
are, beyond the mere conversation key—in the expression of their
thoughts, their various views and natures, there is something generous,
and cheering, and ennobling. . . . He who reads these noble records of
a past age, salutes and reverences the great spirits who adorn it.' Many
of Pope's letters were not available to Thackeray, particularly the less
'stately' ones, and we are better able than he was to see Pope in his
more relaxed moments, and to appreciate his essential humanity, kindli-
ness, and charm.

For it is these qualities which, above all else, show through the
letters: Spence records Lord Bolingbroke as saying, just before Pope's
death, 'I never in my life knew a man that had so tender a heart for his
particular friends, or a more general friendship for mankind!' If Pope
was insincere, he deceived a great many remarkable people; it is easier,
and wiser, to assume that, when he spoke of friendship, of his love for
virtue and hatred of vice, of his moral purpose in writing poetry, Pope
meant what he said. It is impossible to read through his letters in Professor Sherburn's great edition, or in the admirable World's Classics
selection by Professor Butt, without feeling that one has been in touch
with a great and noble man. Of the more than 1600 letters printed by
Sherburn, it is possible to give only a very small sample here; but this
sample may give an indication of their quality, and justify the phrases
of David Mallet quoted in letter 16.

Alexander Pope was born in London on 21 May 1688, the only

child of middle-aged Roman Catholic parents. His earliest letters, dating from the end of 1704, show us a young man writing somewhat earnestly, somewhat self-consciously, somewhat priggishly, always gracefully and with a studied wit, to his elders in the literary world: to Wycherley the dramatist, now in his sixties, who calls him affectionately 'My great Little Friend . . . My Deare Little Infallible'; to the critic William Walsh, who had known Dryden; to Henry Cromwell, another middle-aged poet and critic. The letters to Cromwell are the most relaxed; those to Walsh and Wycherley tend to be 'set-pieces', re-worked by Pope for his later printing; but they all throw light on the seriousness with which Pope approached his chosen career of poetry. Like Wordsworth at the same age, Pope knew himself to be 'a dedicated spirit'.

1. To William Walsh, 2 July 1706 (extract)

I cannot omit the first opportunity of making you my acknowledgments for reviewing those Papers of mine. You have no less right to correct me, than the same hand that rais'd a Tree has to prune it. I am convinc'd as well as you, that one may correct too much; for in Poetry as in Painting, a Man may lay Colours one upon another, till they stiffen and deaden the Piece. Besides to bestow heightening on every part is monstrous: Some parts ought to be lower than the rest; and nothing looks more ridiculous, than a Work, where the Thoughts, however different in their own nature, seem all on a level: 'Tis like a Meadow newly mown, where *Weeds*, *Grass*, and *Flowers* are all laid even, and appear undistinguish'd. I believe too that sometimes our first Thoughts are the best, as the first squeezing of the Grapes makes the finest and richest Wine. . . .

I wou'd beg your opinion too as to another point: It is how far the liberty of *Borrowing* may extend? I have defended it sometimes by saying, that it seems not so much the Perfection of Sense, to say things that have *never* been said before, as to express those *best* that have been said *oftenest*; and that Writers in the case of borrowing from others, are like Trees which of themselves wou'd produce only one sort of Fruit, but by being grafted upon others, may yield variety. A mutual commerce makes Poetry flourish; but then Poets like Merchants, shou'd repay with something of their own what they take from others;

not like Pyrates, make prize of all they meet. I desire you to tell me sincerely, if I have not stretch'd this Licence too far in these Pastorals? I hope to become a Critic by your Precepts, and a Poet by your Example. . . .

At this time, as throughout his life, Pope mixes an unbuttoned, carpet-slippers style of writing with his graver, more formal manner. He tells Cromwell: 'I resume my old liberty of throwing out my self upon paper to you, and making what thoughts float uppermost in my head, the subject of a letter' (30 December 1710). This extract gives some idea of his familiar style at this time:

2. To Cromwell, 10 April 1710 (Easter) (extract)

I had written to you sooner but that I made some Scruple of sending Profane Things to You in Holy week. Besides Our Family wou'd have been Scandalizd to see me write, who take it for granted I write nothing but ungodly Verses; and They say here so many Pray'rs, that I can make but few Poems: For in this point of Praying, I am an Occasional Conformist. So just as I am drunk or Scandalous in Town, according to my Company, I am for the same reason Grave & Godly here. I assure you I am look'd upon in the Neighbourhood for a very Sober & well-disposd Person, no great Hunter indeed, but a great Esteemer of the noble Sport, & only unhappy in my Want of Constitution for that, & Drinking. They all say 'tis pitty I am so sickly, & I think 'tis pitty They are so healthy: But I say nothing that may destroy their good opinion of me. I have not quoted one Latin Author since I came down, but have learn'd without book a Song of Mr Tho: Durfey's, who is your only Poet of tolerable Reputation in this Country. He makes all the Merriment in our Entertainments, & but for him, there wou'd be so miserable a Dearth of Catches, that I fear they wou'd (sans ceremonie) put either the Parson or Me upon making some for 'em. . . .

By his middle twenties Pope had already achieved fame as a poet, and his acquaintance was extending to include such eminent men as Steele, Addison and Gay, partly through his friendship with the prominent Catholic gentleman, John Caryll (at whose request Pope wrote *The Rape of the Lock*.) His correspondence with both Gay and Caryll lasted until their death. At this time, as he tells Gay, he was taking lessons from Charles Jervas, the portrait-painter.

3. To John Gay, 23 August 1713 (extract)

... I have been near a week in *London*, where I am like to remain, till I become by Mr *Jervas*'s help, *Elegans Formarum Spectator*. I begin to discover Beauties that were till now imperceptible to me. Every Corner of an Eye, or Turn of a Nose or Ear, the smallest degree of Light or Shade on a Cheek, or in a dimple, have charms to distract me. ... You may guess in how uneasy a state I am, when every day the performances of others appear more beautiful and excellent, and my own more despicable. I have thrown away three Dr *Swift*'s, each of which was once my Vanity, two Lady *Bridgwaters*, a Dutchess of *Montague*, besides half a dozen Earls, and one Knight of the Garter. I have crucify'd *Christ* over-again in effigie, and made a *Madona* as old as her mother St *Anne*. Nay, what is yet more miraculous, I have rival'd St *Luke* himself in Painting, and as 'tis said an Angel came and finish'd his Piece, so you would swear a Devil put the last hand to mine, 'tis so begrim'd and smutted. However I comfort my self with a christian Reflection, that, I have not broken the Commandment, for my Pictures are not the likeness of any thing in heaven above, or in earth below, or in the waters under the earth. ...

From this time, too, dates Pope's acquaintanceship with Martha ('Patty') Blount, who was Caryll's god-daughter, and her sister Teresa. His friendship later cooled with Teresa for some reason, but his affection for Martha continued till his death, and she was the principal beneficiary under his will. That Pope was in love with Martha can hardly be doubted; but at the beginning of the correspondence Pope flirts charmingly with both sisters.

4. To Martha Blount, after 24 November 1714 (extract)

... That Heart must have abundance of Flames which is at once warm'd by Wine and You; Wine awakens and refreshes the lurking Passions of the Mind, as Varnish does the Colours that are sunk in a Picture, and brings them out in all their natural Glowings. My good Qualities have been so frozen and lockd up in a dull Constitution at all my former Sober hours, that it is very astonishing to me, now I am drunk, to find so much Virtue in me.

In these Overflowings of my heart I pay you my thanks for those two obliging Letters you favord me with. . . . That which begins with Dear Creature, and my charming Mr Pope, was a Delight to me beyond all Expression. You have at last entirely gaind the Conquest over your fair Sister; 'tis true you are not handsome, for you are a Woman and think you are not; but this Good humor and Tenderness for me has a charm that cannot be resisted. That Face must needs be irresistible which was adorned with Smiles even when it could not see the Coronation. . . .

I do suppose you will not show this Epistle out of Vanity, as I doubt not your said Sister does all I writ to her. Indeed to correspond with Mr Pope may make any one proud who lives under a Dejection of Heart in the Country. Every one values Mr Pope, but every one for a different reason. One for his firm adherence to the Catholic Faith, another for his Neglect of Popish Superstition, one for his grave behavior, another for his Whymsicalness. Mr Tydcomb for his pretty Atheistical Jests, Mr Caryl for his moral and christian Sentences, Mrs Teresa for his Reflections on Mrs Patty, and Mrs Patty for his Reflections on Mrs Teresa. . . .

Poor Parnelle is now on the briny Ocean which he increases with his briny Tears for the Loss of You &c. Pray for him, if you please, but not for me. Don't so much as hope I may go to Heaven: tis a place I am not very fond of, I hear no great good of it: All the Descriptions I ever heard of it amount to no more than just this: It is eternal singing, & piping, and sitting in Sunshine. Much good may it do the Saints; and those who intend to be Saints. For my part I am better than a Saint, for I am/Madam /Your most faithful Admirer, Friend, Servant,/any thing . . .

The first books of Pope's Homer came out in June 1715, and in 1716 Pope was engaged on *Eloisa*. In 1717 his collected *Works* appeared, and later that year we find him off on one of the 'rambles' which gave him so much pleasure in his earlier life, and occasionally in his later. His letters describing these show his flair for humorous description, as well as the element of 'romantic melancholy' in his make-up. From this period, too, dates Pope's romantic attachment—later to collapse in such bitterness—to Lady Mary Wortley Montagu.

5. To Teresa and Martha Blount, 13 September 1717 (extract)

... I'll content myself by giving you as plain a History of my Pilgrimage as Mr Purchas himself, or as John Bunyan could do, of his Walking thro' the Wilderness of this world, &c.

First then I went by water to Hampton Court, unattended by all but my own Virtues, which were not of so modest a nature as to keep themselves, or me, conceald from the Courtiers. For I met the Prince with all his Ladies (tho few or none of his Lords) on horseback coming from Hunting. Mrs Bellendine & Mrs Lepell took me into protection (contrary to the Laws against harbouring Papists), & gave me a Dinner, with something I liked better, an opportunity of conversation with Mrs Howard. We all agreed that the life of a Maid of Honor was of all things the most miserable; & wished that every Woman who envyd it had a Specimen of it. To eat Westphalia Ham in a morning, ride over Hedges & ditches on borrowed Hacks, come home in the heat of the day with a Feavor, & what is worse a hundred times, a red Mark in the forehead with a Beaver hatt; all this may qualify them to make excellent Wives for Fox-hunters, & bear abundance of ruddy-complexion'd Children. As soon as they can wipe off the Sweat of the day, they must simper an hour, & catch cold, in the Princesses apartment; from thence *To Dinner, with what appetite they may*—And after that, till midnight, walk, work, or think, which they please? I can easily believe, no lone House in Wales, with a Mountain & a Rookery, is more contemplative than this Court; and as a proof of it I need only tell you Mrs Lepell walk'd all alone with me three or 4 hours, by moonlight; and we mett no Creature of any quality, but the King, who gave audience all alone to the Vice-chamberlen, under the Garden-wall. ...

6. To Teresa and Martha Blount (September 1717) (extract)

... I came from Stonor (its Master not being at home) to

Oxford the same night. Nothing could have more of that Melancholy which once us'd to please me, than that day's journey: For after having passd thro' my favorite Woods in the forest, with a thousand Reveries of past pleasures; I rid over hanging hills, whose tops were edgd with Groves, & whose feet water'd with winding rivers, listening to the falls of Cataracts below, & the murmuring of Winds above. The gloomy Verdure of Stonor succeeded to these, & then the Shades of the Evening overtook me, the Moon rose in the clearest Sky I ever saw, by whose solemn light I pac'd on slowly, without company, or any interruption to the range of my thoughts. About a mile before I reachd Oxford, all the Night bells toll'd, in different notes; the Clocks of every College answerd one another; & told me, some in a deeper, some in a softer voice, that it was eleven a clock. . . .

The early and middle 1720s saw the completion of Pope's work on Homer, and his edition of Shakespeare. His health was indifferent, and as time went on the illness of his aged mother kept him more or less tied to Twickenham. By now Pope's circle of friends was wide and distinguished, including Lord Bolingbroke, the Earl of Burlington, Lord Bathurst, the Earl of Oxford, the Bishop of Rochester (Atterbury), the Earl of Peterborough and Jonathan Swift. Pope and Swift resumed correspondence in 1723 after a lapse of some years. In 1726 and 1727 Swift visited Pope at Twickenham: some idea of the depth of their friendship—their love, in fact—can be gauged from the following letter.

7. To Swift, 22 August 1726 (extract)

Many a short sigh you cost me the day I left you, and many more you will cost me, till the day you return. I really walk'd about like a man banish'd, and when I came home, found it no home. 'Tis a sensation like that of a limb lopp'd off, one is trying every minute unawares to use it, and finds it is not. I may say you have used me more cruelly than you have done any other man; you have made it more impossible for me to live at ease without you: Habitude itself would have done that, if I had less friendship in my nature than I have. Besides my natural memory of you, you have made a local one, which presents you to me in every place I frequent: I shall never more think of Lord Cobham's, the woods of Ciceter, or the pleasing prospect of Byberry, but your Idea must be join'd with 'em; nor see one seat in my own garden, or one room in my own house, without a Phantome of you, sitting or walking before me. I travell'd with you to Chester, I felt the extream heat of the weather, the inns, the roads, the confinement and closeness of the uneasy coach, and wish'd a hundred times I had either a Deanery or a horse in my gift. In real truth, I have felt my soul peevish ever since with all about me, from a warm uneasy desire after you. I am gone out of myself to no purpose, and cannot catch you. . . .

The end of this decade, and the early 1730s, show Pope engaged on the *Dunciad*, the *Essay on Man*, the 'Epistles to Several Persons', and the first Imitations of Horace; but his own ill-health, the illness of his friends and his mother, and his increasingly sombre view of the state of the country, give a darker colour to his letters. In 1732 Gay died; in 1733 Mrs Pope, at the age of 93. Pope was more free to travel now, but less physically able to do so; the danger of sea-sickness to one in his condition prevented him from visiting Swift in Ireland. 1735 saw the death of Arbuthnot and the Earl of Peterborough.

8. To Gay (late 1728/early 1729)

Dear Gay,—No words can tell you the great concern I feel for you; I assure you it was not, and is not lessen'd, by the immediate apprehension I have now every day lain under of losing my Mother. Be assur'd, no Duty less than that, should have kept me one day from attending your condition: I would come and take a room by you at *Hampstead*, to be with you daily, were she not still in danger of death. I have constantly had particular accounts of you from the Doctor, which have not ceas'd to alarm me yet. God preserve your life, and restore your health. I really beg it for my own sake, for I feel I love you more than I thought, in health, tho' I always lov'd you a great deal. If I am so unfortunate as to bury my poor Mother, and yet have the good fortune to have my prayers heard for you, I hope we may live most of our remaining days together. If, as I believe, the air of a better clime as the Southern Part of *France* may be thought useful for your recovery, thither I would go with you infallibly; and it is very probable we might get the Dean* with us, who is in that abandon'd state already in which I shall shortly be, as to other Cares and Duties. Dear *Gay* be as chearful as your Sufferings will permit: God is a better friend than a Court: Even any honest man is a better. I promise you my entire friendship in all events, heartily praying for your recovery./Your, &c.

Do not write, if you are ever so able: The Doctor tells me all.

9. To Caryll, 27 September 1732 (extract)

. . . I was so disappointed in not having a few entire days of your company that I can't find it in my heart to give you any account of my studies: It would be tedious to do it at length (for a few words will not suffice to let you into the design of them), and to do it imperfectly and consequently unsatisfactorily would be worse than not doing it at all. Let it suffice to tell you that they are directed to a good end, the advancement of moral and religious vertue, and the discouragement of vicious and corrupt hearts. As to the former, I treat it with the uttmost seriousness and respect; as to the latter, I think any means are fair and any method equal, whether preaching or laughing, whatever will do best. My work is systematical and proceeds in order; yet that does not hinder me from finishing some of the particular parts, which may be published at any time, when I judge particular vices demand them. And I believe you'll see one or two of these next winter, one especially of the Use of Riches, which seems at present to be the favorite, nay, the only, mistress of mankind, to which all their endeavours are directed, thro' all the paths of corruption and luxury. My satire will therefore be impartial on both extremes, avarice and profusion. I shall make living examples, which inforce best, and consequently put you once more upon the defence of your friend against the roar and calumny, which I expect, and am ready to suffer in so good a cause. . . .

10. To Swift, ? 20 April 1733 (extract)

You say truly, that death is only terrible to us as it separates us from those we love, but I really think those have the worst of

* ·Swift.

it who are left by us, if we are true friends. I have felt more (I fancy) in the loss of poor Mr Gay, than I shall suffer in the thought of going away myself into a state that can feel none of this sort of losses. I wish'd vehemently to have seen him in a condition of living independent, and to have lived in perfect indolence the rest of our days together, the two most idle, most innocent, undesigning Poets of our age. I now as vehemently wish, you and I might walk into the grave together, by as slow steps as you please, but contentedly and chearfully: Whether that ever can be, or in what country, I know no more, than into what country we shall walk out of the grave. But it suffices me to know it will be exactly what region or state our Maker appoints, and that whatever *Is*, is *Right*. . . .

That I am an Author whose characters are thought of some weight, appears from the great noise and bustle that the Court and Town make about any I give: and I will not render them less important or interesting, by sparing Vice and Folly, or by betraying the cause of Truth and Virtue. I will take care they shall be such as no man can be angry at but the persons I would have angry. You are sensible with what decency and justice I paid homage to the Royal Family, at the same time that I satirized false Courtiers, and Spies, &c. about 'em. I have not the courage however to be such a Satyrist as you, but I would be as much, or more, a Philosopher. You call your satires, Libels; I would rather call my satires, Epistles: They will consist more of morality than wit, and grow graver, which you will call duller. I shall leave it to my Antagonists to be witty (if they can) and content myself to be useful, and in the right. . . .

I have met with some complaints, and heard at a distance of some threats, occasion'd by my satires: I sent fair messages to acquaint them where I was to be found in town, and to offer to call at their houses to satisfy them, and so it dropp'd. It is very poor in any one to rail and threaten at a distance, and have nothing to say to you when they see you.—I am glad you persist and abide by so good a thing as that Poem, in which I am immortal for my Morality: I never took any praise so kindly, and yet I think I deserve that praise better than I do any other. . . . I have but last week finished another of my Epistles, in the order of the system; and this week . . . I have translated, or rather parody'd, another of Horace's, in which I introduce you advising me about my expences, house-keeping, &c. But these things shall lye by, till you come to carp at 'em, and alter rhymes, and grammar, and triplets, and cacaphonies of all kinds. . . .

. . . you use to love what I hate, a hurry of politicks, &c. Courts I see not, Courtiers I know not, Kings I adore not, Queens I compliment not; so I am never like to be in fashion, nor in dependance.

Several other letters of 1734 and 1735 are concerned with statements to his friends of his satiric position: 'it is Truth and a clear Conscience that I think will set me above all my Enemies, and make no Honest man repent of having been my Friend' (to Arbuthnot, September 1734). One of the clearest statements of his position is contained in the following letter:

11. To Dr Arbuthnot, 2 August (1734) (extract)

. . . I thank you dear Sir for making That your Request to me which I make my Pride, nay my Duty; 'that I should continue my Disdain & abhorrence of Vice, & manifest it still in my writings'. I would indeed do it with more restrictions, & less personally; it is more agreeable to my nature, which those who know it not are greatly mistaken in: But General Satire in Times of General Vice has no force, & is no Punishment: People have ceas'd to be ashamed of it when so many are joind with them; and tis only by hunting One or two from the Herd that any Examples can be made. If a man writ all his Life against the Collective Body of the Banditti, or against Lawyers, would it do the least Good, or lessen the Body? But if some are hung up, or pilloryed, it may prevent others. And in my low Station, with no other Power than this, I hope to deter, if not to reform.

It would be wrong, though, to give the impression that these years were filled with gloom. 'I am glad to hear Mr Pope is grown a Rambler', wrote Swift, and, despite his indifferent health, Pope was able to get away from London for extended visits to the country. This letter is written from Bevis Mount, near Southampton; Pope was staying with the Earl of Peterborough, who died the following year.

12. To the Earl of Oxford, 1 September 1734 (extract)

. . . You cannot think how happy we are here; I wish, my
Lord, you Saw it: If you did, you would be very well pleas'd,
very well fed, and very Merry, if I am not very much mistaken:
We have the best Sea fish & River fish in the world, much
tranquillity, some Reading, no Politiques, admirable Melons, an
excellent Bowling-green & Ninepin alley, Besides the amuse-
ment of a Witch in the parish. I have an incomparable Story to
tell you on the last of these, but it would fill 2 sheets of paper.
I have been at the Ruins of the finest Abbey & Castle I ever
saw, within five miles of this place, which I am surprised to find
Camden take no notice of.

'Increase of years', wrote Pope to Swift in August 1736, 'makes men
more talkative but less writative.' He goes on: 'I now write no letters
but of plain business, or plain how-d'ye's, to those few I am forced to
correspond with, either out of necessity, or love: And I grow Laconic
even beyond Laconicisme; for sometimes I return only Yes, or No, to
questionary or petitionary Epistles half a yard long. You and Lord
Bolingbroke are the only men to whom I write, and always in folio.
You are indeed almost the only men I know, who either can write in
this age, or whose writings will reach the next: Others are mere mortals.'
It is far from true that Bolingbroke & Swift were Pope's only corre-
spondents at this time; but the following letter indicates Pope's state
of mind at this time, and demonstrates his continuing love for Swift,
now approaching seventy and in failing health.

13. To Swift, 25 March 1736 (extract)

If ever I write more Epistles in Verse, one of them shall be
address'd to you. I have long concerted it, and begun it, but I
would make what bears your name as finished as my last work
ought to be, that is to say, more finished than any of the rest.
The subject is large, and will divide into four Epistles, which
naturally follow the Essay on Man, viz. 1. Of the Extent and
Limits of Human Reason, and Science, 2. A view of the useful
and therefore attainable, and of the un-useful and therefore
un-attainable, Arts. 3. Of the nature, ends, application, and the
use of different Capacities. 4. Of the use of *Learning*, of the

Science of the *World*, and of *Wit*. It will conclude with a Satire against the misapplication of all these, exemplify'd by pictures, characters, and examples.

But alas! the task is great, and *non sum qualis eram*! My understanding indeed, such as it is, is extended rather than diminish'd: I see things more in the whole, more consistent, and more clearly deduced from, and related to, each other. But what I gain on the side of philosophy, I lose on the side of poetry: the flowers are gone, when the fruits begin to ripen, and the fruits perhaps will never ripen perfectly. The climate (under our Heaven of a Court) is but cold and uncertain: the winds rise, and the winter comes on. I find myself but little disposed to build a new house; I have nothing left but to gather up the reliques of a wreck, and look about me to see what friends I have! Pray whose esteem or admiration should I desire now to procure by my writings? whose friendship or conversation to obtain by 'em? I am a man of desperate fortunes, that is a man whose friends are dead: for I never aimed at any other fortune than in friends. . . .

I wish you had any motive to see this kingdom. I could keep you, for I am rich, that is, I have more than I want. I can afford you room for your self and two servants; I have indeed room enough, nothing but myself at home! the kind and hearty house-wife is dead! the agreeable and instructive neighbour is gone! yet my house is inlarg'd, and the gardens extend and flourish, as knowing nothing of the guests they have lost. I have more fruit-trees and kitchen-garden than you have any thought of; nay I have good Melons and Pine-apples of my own growth. I am as much a better Gardiner, as I'm a worse Poet, than when you saw me: But gardening is near a-kin to Philosophy, for Tully says *Agricultura proxima sapientiæ*. For God's sake, why should not you, (that are a step higher than a Philosopher, a Divine, yet have too much grace and wit to be a Bishop) e'en give all you have to the Poor of Ireland (for whom you have already done every thing else) so quit the place, and live and die with me? And let *Tales Animæ Concordes* be our Motto and our Epitaph.

Pope's last years saw the writing of the *Epilogue to the Satires*

(1738), the unfinished *One Thousand Seven Hundred and Forty*, the *New Dunciad* in 1742, and the making of the four-book *Dunciad* in 1743; but, doubtless in the knowledge that he had not long to live, his main concerns at this time include the publication of the 'authentic' edition of the letters (1737), of the correspondence with Swift (1741), and the gathering together, with Warburton, of his complete works. He 'rambles' whenever possible, and spends a good deal of pleasant time on his grotto at Twickenham; his friendships are undiminished, and include new acquaintances; but the later letters are shot through with wry references to his health, the loss of friends, and the view of the world so powerfully recorded in the last book of the *Dunciad*.

14. To Allen (? 1 December 1742) (extract)

. . . Indeed my Heart is sick of This bad World, (as Cato said.) and I see it daily growing worse. If there were to be Another Deluge, I protest I don't know more than One Noah; and his Wife, (for he happens to have no children) whom I could expect God would save. . . .

15. To Lords Marchmont and Bolingbroke (January 1744)

My dear Lords,—Yes, I would see you as long as I can see you, & then shut my eyes upon the world, as a thing worth seeing no longer. If your charity would take up a small Bird that is half dead of the frost, and set it a-chirping for half an hour, I'll jump into my Cage, & put myself into your hands to morrow, at any hour you send. Two horses will be enough to draw me, (& so would two Dogs if you had them) but even the fly upon the chariot wheel required some bigger animal than itself, to set it a going. *Quadrigis petimus benè vivere*, is literally true when one cannot get into good Company without Horses, & such is my case. I am faithfully, to you both, a most Cordial, Entire Servant.

He ends a letter to Fortescue (15 March 1744), 'I am faithfully Yours, while I live, but God forbid it should be too long!' Two months later he was dead of an asthmatical dropsy: the last extract is from David Mallet's letter to the Earl of Orrery, 1 June 1744—two days after Pope's death.

16. At last, my Lord, we have lost that excellent Man! His Person I loved, his Worth I knew, & shall ever cherish his Memory with all the Regard of Esteem, with all the Tenderness of Friendship. . . .

. . . The same social Kindness, the same friendly Concern for those he loved, even in the minutest Instances, that had distinguished his Heart through Life, were uppermost in his Thoughts to the last.

He dyed on Wednesday, about the Middle of the Night, without a Pang, or a Convulsion, unperceived of those that watched him, who imagined he was only in a sounder Sleep than ordinary.—But I cannot go on. After the Loss of such a Friend, what can I think of but those very few I have left?

EXTRACTS FROM SPENCE'S *ANECDOTES*

THE Rev. Joseph Spence (1699-1768) met Pope in 1727 and became
one of his closest friends. Spence, who was Professor of Poetry at
Oxford from 1728 to 1738, had written an Essay on Pope's *Odyssey*,
which led to their meeting. Perhaps with the intention of writing a
biography of Pope, he took down notes of conversations they had
together. Some of these were used in early biographies of Pope; a
selection, supplemented by records of Spence's conversation with
other members of Pope's circle, was published in 1819. Dr Johnson describes
Spence as 'a man whose learning was not very great, and whose mind
was not very powerful', but adds: 'his criticism, however, was com-
monly just; what he thought, he thought rightly, and his remarks were
recommended by coolness and candour'.

The following extracts have been arranged to illustrate Pope's early
reading and writing; remarks on some later works; and general observations on the art and purpose of poetry.

. . . Waller, Spenser, and Dryden, were Mr Pope's great
favourites, in the order they are named, in his first reading till
he was about twelve years old.

. . . I began writing verses of my own invention farther back
than I can well remember. . . . Ogilby's translation of Homer
was one of the first large poems that ever Mr Pope read; and he
still spoke of the pleasure it then gave him, with a sort of
rapture, only in reflecting on it. . . . 'It was that great edition
with pictures, I was then about eight years old. This led me to
Sandys' Ovid, which I liked extremely; and so I did a translation
of Statius, by some very bad hand.'

. . . When I was about twelve, I wrote a kind of play, which
I got to be acted by my schoolfellows. It was a number of
speeches from the Iliad; tacked together with verses of my own.
. . . The epic poem which I begun a little after I was twelve,
was Alcander, Prince of Rhodes: there was an under-water
scene in the first book, it was in the Archipelago. . . . I wrote
four books toward it, of about a thousand verses each; and had

the copy by me, till I burnt it, by the advice of the Bishop of Rochester, a little before he went abroad.

... I endeavoured, (said he, smiling), in this poem, to collect all the beauties of the great epic writers into one piece: there was Milton's style in one part, and Cowley's in another; here the style of Spenser imitated, and there of Statius; here, Homer and Virgil, and there Ovid and Claudian. . . . My next work, after my Epic, was my Pastorals.

... When I had done with my priests, I took to reading by myself, for which I had a very great eagerness and enthusiasm, especially for poetry: and in a few years, I had dipped into a great number of the English, French, Italian, Latin, and Greek poets. This I did without any design, but that of pleasing myself: and got the languages, by hunting after the stories in the several poets I read; rather than read the books to get the languages. I followed every where as my fancy led me, and was just like a boy gathering flowers in the fields and woods, just as they fall in his way. . . . These five or six years I still look upon as the happiest part of my life.

... In these rambles of mine through the poets; when I met with a passage, or story, that pleased me more than ordinary, I used to endeavour to imitate it, or translate it into English; and this gave rise to my Imitations published so long after.

.. My first taking to imitating was not out of vanity, but humility: I saw how defective my own things were; and endeavoured to mend my manner, by copying good strokes from others.

... It is easy to mark out the general course of our poetry. Chaucer, Spenser, Milton, and Dryden, are the great land-marks for it.

... When I had a fever, one winter in town, that confined me to my room for five or six days, Lord Bolingbroke, who came to see me, happened to take up a Horace that lay on the table; and in turning it over, dipped on the first satire of the second book. which begins *Sunt quibus in satira, &c.* He observed, how well that would hit my case, if I were to imitate it in English. After he was gone, I read it over; translated it in a morning or two, and sent it to the press in a week or fortnight after. And this was the occasion of my imitating some other of the satires and epistles afterwards.

. . . The things that I have written fastest, have always pleased the most. . . . I wrote the Essay on Criticism fast; for I had digested all the matter, in prose, before I began upon it in verse. The Rape of the Lock was written fast; all the machinery was added afterwards; and the making that, and what was published before, hit so well together, is, I think, one of the greatest proofs of judgment of any thing I ever did. I wrote most of the Iliad fast; a great deal of it on journeys, from the little pocket Homer on that shelf there; and often forty or fifty verses in a morning in bed. . . . The Dunciad cost me as much pains as any thing I ever wrote.

. . . I learned versification wholly from Dryden's works.

. . . Dryden always uses proper language; lively, natural, and fitted to the subject. It is scarce ever too high, or too low: never, perhaps, except in his plays.

. . . I have followed the significance of the numbers, and the adapting them to the sense, much more even than Dryden; and much oftener than any one minds it. Particularly in the translations of Homer, where 'twas most necessary to do so: and in the Dunciad, often, and indeed in all my poems.

. . . After writing a poem, one should correct it all over, with one single view at a time. Thus for language; if an elegy; 'these lines are very good, but are not they of too heroical a strain?' and so *vice versa*.

. . . The great rule of verse is to be musical.

. . . The great secret how to write well, is to know thoroughly what one writes about, and not to be affected.

. . . If I am a good poet? (for in truth I do not know whether

32

I am or not.) But if I should be a good poet, there is one thing I value myself upon, and which can scarce be said of any of our good poets: and that is, 'that I have never flattered any man, nor ever received any thing of any man for my verses'.

. . . I am in no concern, whether people should say this is writ well or ill, but that this was writ with a good design. . . . 'He has written in the cause of virtue, and done something to mend people's morals:' this is the only commendation I long for.

. . . No writing is good that does not tend to better mankind some way or other.

from AN ESSAY ON CRITICISM

'Tis hard to say, if greater Want of Skill
Appear in Writing or in Judging ill;
But, of the two, less dang'rous is th'Offence,
To tire our Patience, than mis-lead our Sense:
Some few in that, but Numbers err in this,
Ten Censure wrong for one who Writes amiss;
A Fool might once himself alone expose,
Now One in Verse makes many more in Prose.
   'Tis with our Judgments as our Watches, none
Go just alike, yet each believes his own.   10
In Poets as true Genius is but rare,
True Taste as seldom is the Critick's Share;
Both must alike from Heav'n derive their Light,
These born to Judge, as well as those to Write. . . .

Most possess at least the *seeds* of Judgment, but their growth is too
often stunted by false learning, folly, vanity, spite: the good critic must
know his own range:

(46-51)
   But you who seek to give and merit Fame,
And justly bear a Critick's noble Name,
Be sure your self and your own Reach to know,
How far your Genius, Taste, and Learning go;
Launch not beyond your Depth, but be discreet,
And mark that Point where Sense and Dulness meet. . . . 20

(68-91)
   First follow NATURE, and your Judgment frame
By her just Standard, which is still the same:
Unerring Nature, still divinely bright,
One clear, unchang'd, and Universal Light,
Life, Force, and Beauty, must to all impart,
At once the Source, and End, and Test of Art.

34

Art from that Fund each just Supply provides,
Works without Show, and without Pomp presides:
In some fair Body thus th'informing Soul
With Spirits feeds, with Vigour fills the whole,   30
Each Motion guides, and ev'ry Nerve sustains;
It self unseen, but in th'Effects, remains.
Some, to whom Heav'n in Wit has been profuse
Want as much more, to turn it to its use;
For Wit and Judgment often are at strife,
Tho' meant each other's Aid, like Man and Wife.
'Tis more to guide than spur the Muse's Steed;
Restrain his Fury, than provoke his Speed;
The winged Courser, like a gen'rous Horse,
Shows most true Mettle when you check his Course.   40
    Those RULES of old discover'd, not devis'd,
Are Nature still, but Nature Methodiz'd;
Nature, like Liberty, is but restrain'd
By the same Laws which first herself ordain'd. . . .

The great merit of the Classic writers was that they 'followed
Nature': the aspiring critic, then, should study them:

(118-129)
    You then whose Judgment the right Course wou'd steer,
Know well each ANCIENT's proper Character,
His Fable, Subject, Scope in ev'ry Page,
Religion, Country, Genius of his Age:
Without all these at once before your Eyes,
Cavil you may, but never Criticize.   50
Be Homer's Works your Study, and Delight,
Read them by Day, and meditate by Night,
Thence form your Judgment, thence your Maxims bring,
And trace the Muses upward to their Spring;
Still with It self compar'd, his Text peruse;
And let your Comment be the Mantuan Muse. . . .

The 'Rules' are not restrictive: the true Genius—but only he—can
at times overleap them, 'And snatch a Grace beyond the Reach of Art';

but the lesser writer does this at his peril. Some foolish critics have complained of the Ancients for 'breaking rules': the Ancients remain unmoved:

(181-200)

    Still green with Bays each ancient Altar stands,
Above the reach of Sacrilegious Hands,
Secure from Flames, from Envy's fiercer Rage,
Destructive War, and all-involving Age.   60
See, from each Clime the Learn'd their Incense bring;
Hear, in all Tongues consenting Pæans ring!
In Praise so just, let ev'ry Voice be join'd,
And fill the Gen'ral Chorus of Mankind.
Hail Bards Triumphant! born in happier Days;
Immortal Heirs of Universal Praise!
Whose Honours with Increase of Ages grow,
As Streams roll down, enlarging as they flow!
Nations unborn your mighty Names shall sound,
And Worlds applaud that must not yet be found!   70
Oh may some Spark of your Cœlestial Fire
The last, the meanest of your Sons inspire,
(That on weak Wings, from far, pursues your Flights;
Glows while he reads, but trembles as he writes)
To teach vain Wits a Science little known,
T'admire Superior Sense, and doubt their own!

What chiefly hinders true judgment is Pride:

(201-18)

    Of all the Causes which conspire to blind
Man's erring Judgment, and misguide the Mind,
What the weak Head with strongest Byass rules,
Is Pride, the never-failing Vice of Fools.   80
Whatev'r Nature has in Worth deny'd,
She gives in large Recruits of needful Pride;
For as in Bodies, thus in Souls, we find
What wants in Blood and Spirits, swell'd with Wind;
Pride, where Wit fails, steps in to our Defence,
And fills up all the mighty Void of Sense!

If once right Reason drives that Cloud away,
Truth breaks upon us with resistless Day;
Trust not your self; but your Defects to know,
Make use of ev'ry Friend—and ev'ry Foe.   90
    A little Learning is a dang'rous Thing;
Drink deep, or taste not the Pierian Spring:
There shallow Draughts intoxicate the Brain,
And drinking largely sobers us again. . . .

(233-6)
    A perfect Judge will read each Work of Wit
With the same Spirit that its Author writ,
Survey the Whole, nor seek slight Faults to find,
Where Nature moves, and Rapture warms the Mind; . . .

(243-6)
    In Wit, as Nature, what affects our Hearts
Is not th'Exactness of peculiar Parts;   100
'Tis not a Lip, or Eye, we Beauty call,
But the joint Force and full Result of all. . . .

(253-8)
    Whoever thinks a faultless Piece to see,
Thinks what ne'er was, nor is, nor e'er shall be.
In ev'ry Work regard the Writer's End,
Since none can compass more than they Intend;
And if the Means be just, the Conduct true,
Applause, in spite of trivial Faults, is due. . . .

But the lesser critics insist on judging a work by parts, not the whole.
Some confine their attention to Conceit, or 'False Wit', missing the true:

(297-302)
    True Wit is Nature to Advantage drest,
What oft was Thought, but ne'er so well Exprest,   110
Something, whose Truth convinc'd at Sight we find,
That gives us back the Image of our Mind:
As Shades more sweetly recommend the Light,
So modest Plainness sets off sprightly Wit. . . .

Some are concerned only with Style, not bothering about the Sense:

(309-23)

Words are like Leaves; and where they most abound,
Much Fruit of Sense beneath is rarely found.
False Eloquence, like the Prismatic Glass,
Its gawdy Colours spreads on ev'ry place;
The Face of Nature we no more Survey,
All glares alike, without Distinction gay: 120
But true Expression, like th'unchanging Sun,⎫
Clears, and improves whate'er it shines upon,⎬
It gilds all Objects, but it alters none.   ⎭
Expression is the Dress of Thought, and still
Appears more decent as more suitable;
A vile Conceit in pompous Words exprest,
Is like a Clown in regal Purple drest;
For diff'rent Styles with diff'rent Subjects sort,
As several Garbs with Country, Town, and Court. . . .

But most are concerned only with the mechanics of versification:

(337-373)

But most by Numbers judge a Poet's Song,   130
And smooth or rough, with them, is right or wrong;
In the bright Muse tho' thousand Charms conspire,
Her Voice is all these tuneful Fools admire,
Who haunt Parnassus but to please their Ear,   ⎫
Not mend their Minds; as some to Church repair ⎬
Not for the Doctrine, but the Musick there.   ⎭
These Equal Syllables alone require,
Tho' oft the Ear the open Vowels tire,
While Expletives their feeble Aid *do* join,
And ten low words oft creep in one dull Line,   140
While they ring round the same unvary'd Chimes,
With sure Returns of still expected Rhymes.
Where-e'er you find the cooling Western Breeze,
In the next Line, it whispers thro' the Trees;
If Chrystal Streams with pleasing Murmurs creep,
The Reader's threaten'd (not in vain) with Sleep.

Then, at the last, and only Couplet fraught
With some unmeaning Thing they call a Thought,
A needless Alexandrine ends the Song,
That like a wounded Snake, drags its slow length along.　150
Leave such to tune their own dull Rhimes, and know
What's roundly smooth, or languishingly slow;
And praise the Easie Vigor of a Line,
Where Denham's Strength, and Waller's Sweetness join.
True Ease in Writing comes from Art, not Chance,
As those move easiest who have learn'd to dance.
'Tis not enough no Harshness gives Offence,
The Sound must seem an Eccho to the Sense.
Soft is the Strain when Zephyr gently blows,
And the smooth Stream in smoother Numbers flows;　160
But when loud Surges lash the sounding Shore,
The hoarse, rough Verse shou'd like the Torrent roar.
When Ajax strives, some Rock's vast Weight to throw,
The Line too labours, and the Words move slow;
Not so, when swift Camilla scours the Plain,
Flies o'er th'unbending Corn, and skims along the Main.

Other dull critics confine themselves to one class of writers—
Ancient, Modern, English, foreign—and despise all others. Then there
are the parasites and flatterers, the flighty and inconsistent, the envious:
but true merit cannot be permanently harmed by these:

(466-75)
Envy will Merit as its Shade pursue,
But like a Shadow, proves the Substance true;
For envy'd Wit, like Sol Eclips'd, makes known
Th'opposing Body's Grossness, not its own.　170
When first that Sun too powerful Beams displays,
It draws up Vapours which obscure its Rays;
But ev'n those Clouds at last adorn its Way,
Reflect new Glories, and augment the Day.
Be thou the first true Merit to befriend;
His Praise is lost, who stays till All commend . . .

The writer has enough trouble with ignorant critics: let not the learned, through self-love and jealousy, also attack him. The critic should remember that he, and the poet, are human beings:

(520-5)

To what base Ends, and by what Abject Ways,
Are Mortals urg'd thro' Sacred Lust of Praise!
Ah ne'er so dire a Thirst of Glory boast,
Nor in the Critick let the Man be lost!   180
Good-Nature and Good-Sense must ever join;
To Err is Human; to Forgive, Divine.

Such perversions of literature as obscenity must, however, always be attacked. The critic is a guardian of morals: a teacher, who practises courtesy, diffidence, accessibility, freedom of advice. The poem moves into an attack on the scribblers, and their critical equivalents, then goes on to define the true critic:

(631-42)

But where's the Man, who Counsel can bestow,
Still pleas'd to teach, and yet not proud to know?
Unbiass'd, or by Favour or by Spite;
Not dully prepossest, nor blindly right;
Tho' Learn'd, well-bred; and tho' well-bred, sincere;
Modestly bold, and Humanly severe?
Who to a Friend his Faults can freely show,
And gladly praise the Merit of a Foe?   190
Blest with a Taste exact, yet unconfin'd;
A Knowledge both of Books and Humankind;
Gen'rous Converse; a Soul exempt from Pride;
And Love to Praise, with Reason on his Side?

This is what critics once were; and the poem praises the great writers of the past, and goes on to trace the history of criticism, through the Dark Ages and the Renaissance, to modern times. It concludes with a praise of Roscommon, and finally of the recently-dead William Walsh.

THE RAPE OF THE LOCK

An Heroi-comical Poem in five Cantos

CANTO I

What dire Offence from am'rous Causes springs,
What mighty Contests rise from trivial Things,
I sing—This Verse to *Caryll*, Muse! is due;
This, ev'n *Belinda* may vouchsafe to view:
Slight is the Subject, but not so the Praise,
If She inspire, and He approve my Lays.

    Say what strange Motive, Goddess! cou'd compel
A well-bred *Lord* t'assault a gentle *Belle*?
Oh say what stranger Cause, yet unexplor'd,
Cou'd make a gentle *Belle* reject a *Lord*?   10
In Tasks so bold, can Little Men engage,
And in soft Bosoms dwells such mighty Rage?

    Sol thro' white Curtains shot a tim'rous Ray,
And op'd those Eyes that must eclipse the Day;
Now Lapdogs give themselves the rowzing Shake,
And sleepless Lovers, just at Twelve, awake:
Thrice rung the Bell, the Slipper knock'd the Ground,
And the press'd Watch return'd a silver Sound.
Belinda still her downy Pillow prest,
Her Guardian *Sylph* prolong'd the balmy Rest.   20
'Twas he had summon'd to her silent Bed
The Morning-Dream that hover'd o'er her Head.
A Youth more glitt'ring than a *Birth-night Beau*,
(That ev'n in Slumber caus'd her Cheek to glow)
Seem'd to her Ear his winning Lips to lay,
And thus in Whispers said, or seem'd to say.

    Fairest of Mortals, thou distinguish'd Care
Of thousand bright Inhabitants of Air!
If e'er one Vision touch'd thy infant Thought,
Of all the Nurse and all the Priest have taught,   30

41

Of airy Elves by Moonlight Shadows seen,
The silver Token, and the circled Green,
Or Virgins visited by Angel-Pow'rs,
With Golden Crowns and Wreaths of heav'nly Flow'rs,
Hear and believe! thy own Importance know,
Nor bound thy narrow Views to Things below.
Some secret Truths from Learned Pride conceal'd,
To Maids alone and Children are reveal'd:
What tho' no Credit doubting Wits may give?
The Fair and Innocent shall still believe.   40
Know then, unnumber'd Spirits round thee fly,
The light *Militia* of the lower Sky;
These, tho' unseen, are ever on the Wing,
Hang o'er the *Box*, and hover round the *Ring*.
Think what an Equipage thou hast in Air,
And view with scorn *Two Pages* and a *Chair*.
As now your own, our Beings were of old,
And once inclos'd in Woman's beauteous Mold;
Thence, by a soft Transition, we repair
From earthly Vehicles to these of Air.   50
Think not, when Woman's transient Breath is fled,
That all her Vanities at once are dead:
Succeeding Vanities she still regards,
And tho' she plays no more, o'erlooks the Cards.
Her Joy in gilded Chariots, when alive,
And Love of *Ombre*, after Death survive.
For when the Fair in all their Pride expire,
To their first Elements their Souls retire:
The Sprights of fiery Termagants in Flame
Mount up, and take a *Salamander's* Name.   60
Soft yielding Minds to Water glide away,
And sip with *Nymphs*, their Elemental Tea.
The graver Prude sinks downward to a *Gnome*,
In search of Mischief still on Earth to roam.
The light Coquettes in *Sylphs* aloft repair,
And sport and flutter in the Fields of Air.
    Know farther yet; Whoever fair and chaste
Rejects Mankind, is by some *Sylph* embrac'd:

For Spirits, freed from mortal Laws, with ease
Assume what Sexes and what Shapes they please.   70
What guards the Purity of melting Maids,
In Courtly Balls, and Midnight Masquerades,
Safe from the treach'rous Friend, the daring Spark,
The Glance by Day, the Whisper in the Dark;
When kind Occasion prompts their warm Desires,
When Musick softens, and when Dancing fires?
'Tis but their *Sylph*, the wise Celestials know,
Tho' *Honour* is the Word with Men below.

    Some Nymphs there are, too conscious of their Face,
For Life predestin'd to the *Gnomes'* Embrace.   80
These swell their Prospects and exalt their Pride,
When Offers are disdain'd, and Love deny'd.
Then gay Ideas crowd the vacant Brain;
While Peers and Dukes, and all their sweeping Train,
And Garters, Stars, and Coronets appear,
And in soft Sounds, *Your Grace* salutes their Ear.
'Tis these that early taint the Female Soul,
Instruct the Eyes of young *Coquettes* to roll,
Teach Infant-Cheeks a bidden Blush to know,
And little Hearts to flutter at a *Beau*.   90

    Oft when the World imagine Women stray,
The *Sylphs* thro' mystick Mazes guide their Way,
Thro' all the giddy Circle they pursue,
And old Impertinence expel by new.
What tender Maid but must a Victim fall
To one Man's Treat, but for another's Ball?
When *Florio* speaks, what Virgin could withstand,
If gentle *Damon* did not squeeze her Hand?
With varying Vanities, from ev'ry Part,
They shift the moving Toyshop of their Heart;   100
Where Wigs with Wigs, with Sword-knots Sword-knots strive,
Beaus banish Beaus, and Coaches Coaches drive.
This erring Mortals Levity may call,
Oh blind to Truth! the *Sylphs* contrive it all.

    Of these am I, who thy Protection claim,
A watchful Sprite, and *Ariel* is my Name.

Late, as I rang'd the Crystal Wilds of Air,
In the clear Mirror of thy ruling *Star*
I saw, alas! some dread Event impend,
Ere to the Main this Morning Sun descend.   110
But Heav'n reveals not what, or how, or where:
Warn'd by thy *Sylph*, oh Pious Maid beware!
This to disclose is all thy Guardian can.
Beware of all, but most beware of Man!

    He said; when *Shock*, who thought she slept too long,
Leapt up, and wak'd his Mistress with his Tongue.
'Twas then *Belinda*! if Report say true,
Thy Eyes first open'd on a *Billet-doux*;
Wounds, *Charms*, and *Ardors*, were no sooner read,
But all the Vision vanish'd from thy Head.   120

    And now, unveil'd, the *Toilet* stands display'd,
Each Silver Vase in mystic Order laid.
First, rob'd in White, the Nymph intent adores
With Head uncover'd, the *Cosmetic* Pow'rs.
A heav'nly Image in the Glass appears,
To that she bends, to that her Eyes she rears;
Th'inferior Priestess, at her Altar's side,
Trembling, begins the sacred Rites of Pride.
Unnumber'd Treasures ope at once, and here
The various Off'rings of the World appear;   130
From each she nicely culls with curious Toil,
And decks the Goddess with the glitt'ring Spoil.
This Casket *India's* glowing Gems unlocks,
And all *Arabia* breathes from yonder Box.
The Tortoise here, and Elephant unite,
Transform'd to *Combs*, the speckled and the white.
Here Files of Pins extend their shining Rows,
Puffs, Powders, Patches, Bibles, Billet-doux.
Now awful Beauty puts on all its Arms;
The Fair each moment rises in her Charms,   140
Repairs her Smiles, awakens ev'ry Grace,
And calls forth all the Wonders of her Face;
Sees by Degrees a purer Blush arise,
And keener Lightnings quicken in her Eyes.

The busy *Sylphs* surround their darling Care;
These set the Head, and those divide the Hair,
Some fold the Sleeve, whilst others plait the Gown;
And *Betty*'s prais'd for Labours not her own.

Canto II

Not with more Glories, in th'Etherial Plain,
The Sun first rises o'er the purpled Main,
Than issuing forth, the Rival of his Beams
Launch'd on the Bosom of the Silver *Thames*.
Fair Nymphs, and well-drest Youths around her shone,
But ev'ry Eye was fix'd on her alone.
On her white Breast a sparkling *Cross* she wore,
Which *Jews* might kiss, and Infidels adore.
Her lively Looks a sprightly Mind disclose,
Quick as her Eyes, and as unfix'd as those: 10
Favours to none, to all she Smiles extends,
Oft she rejects, but never once offends.
Bright as the Sun, her Eyes the Gazers strike,
And, like the Sun, they shine on all alike.
Yet graceful Ease, and Sweetness void of Pride,
Might hide her Faults, if *Belles* had Faults to hide:
If to her share some Female Errors fall,
Look on her Face, and you'll forget 'em all.
    This Nymph, to the Destruction of Mankind,
Nourish'd two Locks, which graceful hung behind   20
In equal Curls, and well conspir'd to deck
With shining Ringlets the smooth Iv'ry Neck.
Love in these Labyrinths his Slaves detains,
And mighty Hearts are held in slender Chains.
With hairy Sprindges we the Birds betray,
Slight Lines of Hair surprize the Finny Prey,
Fair Tresses Man's Imperial Race insnare,
And Beauty draws us with a single Hair.
    Th'Adventrous *Baron* the bright Locks admir'd,
He saw, he wish'd, and to the Prize aspir'd: 30
Resolv'd to win, he meditates the way,
By Force to ravish, or by Fraud betray;

For when Success a Lover's Toil attends,
Few ask, if Fraud or Force attain'd his Ends.
  For this, ere *Phœbus* rose, he had implor'd
Propitious Heav'n, and ev'ry Pow'r ador'd,
But chiefly *Love*—to *Love* an Altar built,
Of twelve vast *French* Romances, neatly gilt.
There lay three Garters, half a Pair of Gloves;
And all the Trophies of his former Loves.   40
With tender *Billet-doux* he lights the Pyre,
And breathes three am'rous Sighs to raise the Fire.
Then prostrate falls, and begs with ardent Eyes
Soon to obtain, and long possess the Prize:
The Pow'rs gave Ear, and granted half his Pray'r,
The rest, the Winds dispers'd in empty Air.
  But now secure the painted Vessel glides,
The Sun-beams trembling on the floating Tydes,
While melting Musick steals upon the Sky,
And soften'd Sounds along the Waters die.   50
Smooth flow'd the Waves, the Zephyrs gently play,
Belinda smil'd, and all the World was gay.
All but the *Sylph*—With careful Thoughts opprest,
Th'impending Woe sate heavy on his Breast.
He summons strait his Denizens of Air;
The lucid Squadrons round the Sails repair:
Soft o'er the Shrouds Aerial Whispers breathe,
That seem'd but *Zephyrs* to the Train beneath.
Some to the Sun their Insect-Wings unfold,
Waft on the Breeze, or sink in Clouds of Gold.   60
Transparent Forms, too fine for mortal Sight,
Their fluid Bodies half dissolv'd in Light.
Loose to the Wind their airy Garments flew,
Thin glitt'ring Textures of the filmy Dew;
Dipt in the richest Tincture of the Skies,
Where Light disports in ever-mingling Dies,
While ev'ry Beam new transient Colours flings,
Colours that change whene'er they wave their Wings.
Amid the Circle, on the gilded Mast,
Superior by the Head, was *Ariel* plac'd;   70

His Purple Pinions opening to the Sun,
He rais'd his Azure Wand, and thus begun.

    Ye *Sylphs* and *Sylphids*, to your Chief give Ear,
Fays, Fairies, Genii, Elves, and *Dæmons* hear!
Ye know the Spheres and various Tasks assign'd,
By Laws Eternal, to th'Aerial Kind.
Some in the Fields of purest *Æther* play,
And bask and whiten in the Blaze of Day.
Some guide the Course of wandring Orbs on high,
Or roll the Planets thro' the boundless Sky.   80
Some less refin'd, beneath the Moon's pale Light
Pursue the Stars that shoot athwart the Night,
Or suck the Mists in grosser Air below,
Or dip their Pinions in the painted Bow,
Or brew fierce Tempests on the wintry Main,
Or o'er the Glebe distill the kindly Rain.
Others on Earth o'er human Race preside,
Watch all their Ways, and all their Actions guide:
Of these the Chief the Care of Nations own,
And guard with Arms Divine the *British Throne.*   90

    Our humbler Province is to tend the Fair,
Not a less pleasing, tho' less glorious Care.
To save the Powder from too rude a Gale,
Nor let th'imprison'd Essences exhale,
To draw fresh Colours from the vernal Flow'rs,
To steal from Rainbows ere they drop in Show'rs
A brighter Wash; to curl their waving Hairs,
Assist their Blushes, and inspire their Airs;
Nay oft, in Dreams, Invention we bestow,
To change a *Flounce,* or add a *Furbelo.*   100

    This Day, black Omens threat the brightest Fair
That e'er deserv'd a watchful Spirit's Care;
Some dire Disaster, or by Force, or Slight,
But what, or where, the Fates have wrapt in Night.
Whether the Nymph shall break *Diana's* Law,
Or some frail *China* Jar receive a Flaw,
Or stain her Honour, or her new Brocade,
Forget her Pray'rs, or miss a Masquerade,

Or lose her Heart, or Necklace, at a Ball;
Or whether Heav'n has doom'd that *Shock* must fall. 110
Haste then ye Spirits! to your Charge repair;
The flutt'ring Fan be *Zephyretta*'s Care;
The Drops to thee, *Brillante*, we consign;
And, *Momentilla*, let the Watch be thine;
Do thou, *Crispissa*, tend her fav'rite Lock;
Ariel himself shall be the Guard of *Shock*.

  To Fifty chosen *Sylphs*, of special Note,
We trust th'important Charge, the *Petticoat*:
Oft have we known that sev'nfold Fence to fail,
Tho' stiff with Hoops, and arm'd with Ribs of Whale. 120
Form a strong Line about the Silver Bound,
And guard the wide Circumference around.

  Whatever Spirit, careless of his Charge,
His Post neglects, or leaves the Fair at large,
Shall feel sharp Vengeance soon o'ertake his Sins,
Be stopt in *Vials*, or transfixt with *Pins*;
Or plung'd in Lakes of bitter *Washes* lie,
Or wedg'd whole Ages in a *Bodkin*'s Eye:
Gums and *Pomatums* shall his Flight restrain,
While clog'd he beats his silken Wings in vain; 130
Or Alom-*Stypticks* with contracting Power
Shrink his thin Essence like a rivell'd Flower.
Or as *Ixion* fix'd, the Wretch shall feel
The giddy Motion of the whirling Mill,
In Fumes of burning Chocolate shall glow,
And tremble at the Sea that froaths below!

  He spoke, the Spirits from the Sails descend;
Some, Orb in Orb, around the Nymph extend,
Some thrid the mazy Ringlets of her Hair,
Some hang upon the Pendants of her Ear; 140
With beating Hearts the dire Event they wait,
Anxious, and trembling for the Birth of Fate.

Canto III

  Close by those Meads for ever crown'd with Flow'rs,
Where *Thames* with Pride surveys his rising Tow'rs,

There stands a Structure of Majestick Frame,
Which from the neighb'ring *Hampton* takes its Name.
Here *Britain's* Statesmen oft the Fall foredoom
Of Foreign Tyrants, and of Nymphs at home;
Here Thou, Great *Anna*! whom three Realms obey,
Dost sometimes Counsel take—and sometimes *Tea*.

  Hither the Heroes and the Nymphs resort,
To taste awhile the Pleasures of a Court;   10
In various Talk th'instructive hours they past,
Who gave the *Ball*, or paid the *Visit* last:
One speaks the Glory of the *British Queen*,
And one describes a charming *Indian Screen*;
A third interprets Motions, Looks, and Eyes;
At ev'ry Word a Reputation dies.
Snuff, or the *Fan*, supply each Pause of Chat,
With singing, laughing, ogling, and all that.

  Mean while declining from the Noon of Day,
The Sun obliquely shoots his burning Ray;   20
The hungry Judges soon the Sentence sign,
And Wretches hang that Jury-men may Dine;
The Merchant from th'*Exchange* returns in Peace,
And the long Labours of the *Toilette* cease—
Belinda now, whom Thirst of Fame invites,
Burns to encounter two adventrous Knights,
At *Ombre* singly to decide their Doom;
And swells her Breast with Conquests still to come.
Strait the three Bands prepare in Arms to join,
Each Band the number of the Sacred Nine.   30
Soon as she spreads her Hand, th'Aerial Guard
Descend, and sit on each important Card:
First *Ariel*, perch'd upon a *Matadore*,
Then each, according to the Rank they bore;
For *Sylphs*, yet mindful of their ancient Race,
Are, as when Women, wondrous fond of Place.

  Behold, four *Kings* in Majesty rever'd,
With hoary Whiskers and a forky Beard;
And four fair *Queens* whose hands sustain a Flow'r,
Th'expressive Emblem of their softer Pow'r;   40

Four *Knaves* in Garbs succinct, a trusty Band,
Caps on their heads, and Halberds in their hand;
And Particolour'd Troops, a shining Train,
Draw forth to Combat on the Velvet Plain.
   The skilful Nymph reviews her Force with Care;
Let Spades be Trumps! she said, and Trumps they were.
   Now move to War her Sable *Matadores*,
In Show like Leaders of the swarthy *Moors*.
Spadillio first, unconquerable Lord!
Led off two captive Trumps, and swept the Board.   50
As many more *Manillio* forc'd to yield,
And march'd a Victor from the verdant Field.
Him *Basto* follow'd, but his Fate more hard
Gain'd but one Trump and one *Plebeian* Card.
With his broad Sabre next, a Chief in Years,
The hoary Majesty of Spades appears;
Puts forth one manly Leg, to sight reveal'd;
The rest his many-colour'd Robe conceal'd.
The Rebel-*Knave*, who dares his Prince engage,
Proves the just Victim of his Royal Rage.   60
Ev'n mighty *Pam* that Kings and Queens o'erthrew,
And mow'd down Armies in the Fights of *Lu*,
Sad Chance of War! now, destitute of Aid,
Falls undistinguish'd by the Victor *Spade*!
   Thus far both Armies to *Belinda* yield;
Now to the *Baron* Fate inclines the Field.
His warlike *Amazon* her Host invades,
Th'Imperial Consort of the Crown of *Spades*.
The *Club's* black Tyrant first her Victim dy'd,
Spite of his haughty Mien, and barb'rous Pride: 70
What boots the Regal Circle on his Head,
His Giant Limbs in State unwieldy spread?
That long behind he trails his pompous Robe,
And of all Monarchs only grasps the Globe?
   The *Baron* now his *Diamonds* pours apace;
Th'embroider'd *King* who shows but half his Face,
And his refulgent *Queen*, with Pow'rs combin'd,
Of broken Troops an easie Conquest find.

Clubs, *Diamonds*, *Hearts*, in wild Disorder seen,
With Throngs promiscuous strow the level Green.   80
Thus when dispers'd a routed Army runs,
Of *Asia's* Troops, and *Africk's* Sable Sons,
With like Confusion different Nations fly,
Of various Habit and of various Dye,
The pierc'd Battalions dis-united fall,
In Heaps on Heaps; one Fate o'erwhelms them all.
   The *Knave* of *Diamonds* tries his wily Arts,
And wins (oh shameful Chance!) the *Queen* of *Hearts*.
At this, the Blood the Virgin's Cheek forsook,
A livid Paleness spreads o'er all her Look;   90
She sees, and trembles at th'approaching Ill,
Just in the Jaws of Ruin, and *Codille*.
And now, (as oft in some distemper'd State)
On one nice *Trick* depends the gen'ral Fate.
An *Ace* of Hearts steps forth: The *King* unseen
Lurk'd in her Hand, and mourn'd his captive *Queen*.
He springs to Vengeance with an eager pace,
And falls like Thunder on the prostrate *Ace*.
The Nymph exulting fills with Shouts the Sky,
The Walls, the Woods, and long Canals reply.   100
   Oh thoughtless Mortals! ever blind to Fate,
Too soon dejected, and too soon elate!
Sudden these Honours shall be snatch'd away,
And curs'd for ever this Victorious Day.
   For lo! the Board with Cups and Spoons is crown'd,
The Berries crackle, and the Mill turns round.
On shining Altars of *Japan* they raise
The silver Lamp; the fiery Spirits blaze.
From silver Spouts the grateful Liquors glide,
While *China's* Earth receives the smoking Tyde.   110
At once they gratify their Scent and Taste,
And frequent Cups prolong the rich Repast.
Strait hover round the Fair her Airy Band;
Some, as she sip'd, the fuming Liquor fann'd,
Some o'er her Lap their careful Plumes display'd,
Trembling, and conscious of the rich Brocade.

Coffee, (which makes the Politician wise,
And see thro' all things with his half-shut Eyes)
Sent up in Vapours to the *Baron*'s Brain
New Stratagems, the radiant Lock to gain.   120
Ah cease rash Youth! desist ere 'tis too late,
Fear the just Gods, and think of *Scylla*'s Fate!
Chang'd to a Bird, and sent to flit in Air,
She dearly pays for *Nisus*' injur'd Hair!

    But when to Mischief Mortals bend their Will,
How soon they find fit Instruments of Ill!
Just then, *Clarissa* drew with tempting Grace
A two-edg'd Weapon from her shining Case;
So Ladies in Romance assist their Knight,
Present the Spear, and arm him for the Fight.   130
He takes the Gift with rev'rence, and extends
The little Engine on his Fingers' Ends,
This just behind *Belinda*'s Neck he spread,
As o'er the fragrant Steams she bends her Head:
Swift to the Lock a thousand Sprights repair,
A thousand Wings, by turns, blow back the Hair,
And thrice they twitch'd the Diamond in her Ear,
Thrice she look'd back, and thrice the Foe drew near.
Just in that instant, anxious Ariel sought
The close Recesses of the Virgin's Thought;   140
As on the Nosegay in her Breast reclin'd,
He watch'd th'Ideas rising in her Mind,
Sudden he view'd, in spite of all her Art,
An Earthly Lover lurking at her Heart.
Amaz'd, confus'd, he found his Pow'r expir'd,
Resign'd to Fate, and with a Sigh retir'd.

    The Peer now spreads the glitt'ring *Forfex* wide,
T'inclose the Lock; now joins it, to divide.
Ev'n then, before the fatal Engine clos'd,
A wretched *Sylph* too fondly interpos'd;   150
Fate urg'd the Sheers, and cut the *Sylph* in twain,
(But Airy Substance soon unites again)
The meeting Points the sacred Hair dissever
From the fair Head, for ever and for ever!

Then flash'd the living Lightning from her Eyes,
And Screams of Horror rend th'affrighted Skies.
Not louder Shrieks to pitying Heav'n are cast,
When Husbands, or when Lap-dogs breathe their last,
Or when rich *China* Vessels, fal'n from high,
In glittring Dust and painted Fragments lie!   160
   Let Wreaths of Triumph now my Temples twine,
(The Victor cry'd) the glorious Prize is mine!
While Fish in Streams, or Birds delight in Air,
Or in a Coach and Six the *British* Fair,
As long as *Atalantis* shall be read,
Or the small Pillow grace a Lady's Bed,
While *Visits* shall be paid on solemn Days,
When numerous Wax-lights in bright Order blaze,
While Nymphs take Treats, or Assignations give,
So long my Honour, Name, and Praise shall live!   170
   What Time wou'd spare, from Steel receives its date,
And Monuments, like Men, submit to Fate!
Steel cou'd the Labour of the Gods destroy,
And strike to Dust th'Imperial Tow'rs of *Troy*;
Steel cou'd the Works of mortal Pride confound,
And hew Triumphal Arches to the Ground.
What Wonder then, fair Nymph! thy Hairs shou'd feel
The conqu'ring Force of unresisted Steel?

Canto IV

   But anxious Cares the pensive Nymph opprest,
And secret Passions labour'd in her Breast.
Not youthful Kings in Battel seiz'd alive,
Not scornful Virgins who their Charms survive,
Not ardent Lovers robb'd of all their Bliss,
Not ancient Ladies when refus'd a Kiss,
Not Tyrants fierce that unrepenting die,
Not *Cynthia* when her *Manteau's* pinn'd awry,
E'er felt such Rage, Resentment, and Despair,
As Thou, sad Virgin! for thy ravish'd Hair.   10
   For, that sad moment, when the *Sylphs* withdrew,
And *Ariel* weeping from *Belinda* flew,

Umbriel, a dusky melancholy Spright,
As ever sully'd the fair face of Light,
Down to the Central Earth, his proper Scene,
Repair'd to search the gloomy Cave of *Spleen*.
  Swift on his sooty Pinions flitts the *Gnome*,
And in a Vapour reach'd the dismal Dome.
No cheerful Breeze this sullen Region knows,
The dreaded *East* is all the Wind that blows.   20
Here, in a Grotto, sheltred close from Air,
And screen'd in Shades from Day's detested Glare,
She sighs for ever on her pensive Bed,
Pain at her Side, and *Megrim* at her Head.
  Two Handmaids wait the Throne: Alike in Place,
But diff'ring far in Figure and in Face.
Here stood *Ill-nature* like an *ancient Maid*,
Her wrinkled Form in *Black* and *White* array'd;
With store of Pray'rs, for Mornings, Nights, and Noons,
Her Hand is fill'd; her Bosom with Lampoons.   30
  There *Affectation* with a sickly Mien
Shows in her Cheek the Roses of Eighteen,
Practis'd to Lisp, and hang the Head aside,
Faints into Airs, and languishes with Pride;
On the rich Quilt sinks with becoming Woe,
Wrapt in a Gown, for Sickness, and for Show.
The Fair-ones feel such Maladies as these,
When each new Night-Dress gives a new Disease.
  A constant *Vapour* o'er the Palace flies;
Strange Phantoms rising as the Mists arise;   40
Dreadful, as Hermit's Dreams in haunted Shades,
Or bright as Visions of expiring Maids.
Now glaring Fiends, and Snakes on rolling Spires,
Pale Spectres, gaping Tombs, and Purple Fires:
Now Lakes of liquid Gold, *Elysian* Scenes,
And Crystal Domes, and Angels in Machines.
  Unnumber'd Throngs on ev'ry side are seen
Of Bodies chang'd to various Forms by *Spleen*.
Here living *Teapots* stand, one Arm held out,
One bent; the Handle this, and that the Spout: 50

A Pipkin there like *Homer's Tripod* walks;
Here sighs a Jar, and there a Goose-pye talks;
Men prove with Child, as pow'rful Fancy works,
And Maids turn'd Bottels, call aloud for Corks.

   Safe past the *Gnome* thro' this fantastick Band,
A Branch of healing *Spleenwort* in his hand.
Then thus addrest the Pow'r—Hail wayward Queen!
Who rule the Sex to Fifty from Fifteen,
Parent of Vapors and of Female Wit,
Who give th'*Hysteric* or *Poetic* Fit,   60
On various Tempers act by various ways,
Make some take Physick, others scribble Plays;
Who cause the Proud their Visits to delay,
And send the Godly in a Pett, to pray.
A Nymph there is, that all thy Pow'r disdains,
And thousands more in equal Mirth maintains.
But oh! if e'er thy *Gnome* could spoil a Grace,
Or raise a Pimple on a beauteous Face,
Like Citron-Waters Matrons' Cheeks inflame,
Or change Complexions at a losing Game;   90
If e'r with airy Horns I planted Heads,
Or rumpled Petticoats, or tumbled Beds,
Or caused Suspicion when no Soul was rude,
Or discompos'd the Head-dress of a Prude,
Or e'er to costive Lap-Dog gave Disease,
Which not the Tears of brightest Eyes could ease:
Hear me, and touch *Belinda* with Chagrin;
That single Act gives half the World the Spleen.

   The Goddess with a discontented Air
Seems to reject him, tho' she grants his Pray'r.   80
A wondrous Bag with both her Hands she binds,
Like that where once *Ulysses* held the Winds;
There she collects the Force of Female Lungs,
Sighs, Sobs, and Passions, and the War of Tongues.
A Vial next she fills with fainting Fears,
Soft Sorrows, melting Griefs, and flowing Tears.
The *Gnome* rejoicing bears her Gifts away,
Spreads his black Wings, and slowly mounts to Day.

Sunk in *Thalestris*' Arms the Nymph he found,
Her Eyes dejected and her Hair unbound.   90
Full o'er their Heads the swelling Bag he rent,
And all the Furies issued at the Vent.
Belinda burns with more than mortal Ire,
And fierce *Thalestris* fans the rising Fire.
O wretched Maid! she spread her Hands, and cry'd,
(While *Hampton's* Ecchos, wretched Maid! reply'd)
Was it for this you took such constant Care
The *Bodkin*, *Comb*, and *Essence* to prepare;
For this your Locks in Paper-Durance bound,
For this with tort'ring Irons wreath'd around?   100
For this with Fillets strain'd your tender Head,
And bravely bore the double Loads of Lead?
Gods! shall the Ravisher display your Hair,
While the Fops envy, and the Ladies stare!
Honour forbid! at whose unrival'd Shrine
Ease, Pleasure, Virtue, All, our Sex resign.
Methinks already I your Tears survey,
Already hear the horrid things they say,
Already see you a degraded Toast,
And all your Honour in a Whisper lost!   110
How shall I, then, your helpless Fame defend?
'Twill then be Infamy to seem your Friend!
And shall this Prize, th'inestimable Prize,
Expos'd thro' Crystal to the gazing Eyes,
And heighten'd by the Diamond's circling Rays,
On that Rapacious Hand for ever blaze?
Sooner shall Grass in *Hide*-Park *Circus* grow,
And Wits take Lodgings in the Sound of *Bow*;
Sooner let Earth, Air, Sea, to *Chaos* fall,
Men, Monkies, Lap-Dogs, Parrots, perish all!   120
She said; then raging to *Sir Plume* repairs,
And bids her *Beau* demand the precious Hairs:
(*Sir Plume*, of *Amber Snuff-box* justly vain,
And the nice Conduct of a *clouded Cane*)
With earnest Eyes, and round unthinking Face,
He first the Snuff-box open'd, then the Case,

And thus broke out—'My Lord, why, what the Devil?
'Z—ds! damn the Lock! 'fore Gad, you must be civil!
'Plague on't! 'tis past a Jest—nay prithee, Pox!
'Give her the Hair'—he spoke, and rapp'd his Box.   130
   It grieves me much (reply'd the Peer again)
Who speaks so well shou'd ever speak in vain.
But by this Lock, this sacred Lock I swear,
(Which never more shall join its parted Hair,
Which never more its Honours shall renew,
Clipt from the lovely Head where late it grew)
That while my Nostrils draw the vital Air,
This Hand, which won it, shall for ever wear.
He spoke, and speaking, in proud Triumph spread
The long-contended Honours of her Head.   140
   But *Umbriel*, hateful *Gnome*! forbears not so;
He breaks the Vial whence the Sorrows flow.
Then see! the *Nymph* in beauteous Grief appears,
Her Eyes half-languishing, half-drown'd in Tears;
On her heav'd Bosom hung her drooping Head,
Which, with a Sigh, she rais'd; and thus she said.
   For ever curs'd be this detested Day,
Which snatch'd my best, my fav'rite Curl away!
Happy! ah ten times happy, had I been,
If *Hampton-Court* these Eyes had never seen!   150
Yet am not I the first mistaken Maid,
By Love of *Courts* to num'rous Ills betray'd.
Oh had I rather un-admir'd remain'd
In some lone Isle, or distant *Northern* Land;
Where the gilt *Chariot* never marks the Way,
Where none learn *Ombre*, none e'er taste *Bohea*!
There kept my Charms conceal'd from mortal Eye,
Like Roses that in Desarts bloom and die.
What mov'd my Mind with youthful Lords to rome?
O had I stay'd, and said my Pray'rs at home!   160
'Twas this, the Morning *Omens* seem'd to tell;
Thrice from my trembling hand the *Patch-box* fell;
The tott'ring *China* shook without a Wind,
Nay, *Poll* sate mute, and *Shock* was most Unkind!

A *Sylph* too warn'd me of the Threats of Fate,
In mystic Visions, now believ'd too late!
See the poor Remnants of these slighted Hairs!
My hands shall rend what ev'n thy Rapine spares:
These, in two sable Ringlets taught to break,
Once gave new Beauties to the snowie Neck.   170
The Sister-Lock now sits uncouth, alone,
And in its Fellow's Fate foresees its own;
Uncurl'd it hangs, the fatal Sheers demands;
And tempts once more thy sacrilegious Hands.
Oh hadst thou, Cruel! been content to seize
Hairs less in sight, or any Hairs but these!

CANTO V

She said: the pitying Audience melt in Tears,
But *Fate* and *Jove* had stopp'd the *Baron's* Ears.
In vain *Thalestris* with Reproach assails,
For who can move when fair *Belinda* fails?
Not half so fixt the *Trojan* cou'd remain,
While *Anna* begg'd and *Dido* rag'd in vain.
Then grave *Clarissa* graceful wav'd her Fan;
Silence ensu'd, and thus the Nymph began.
Say, why are Beauties prais'd and honour'd most,
The wise Man's Passion, and the vain Man's Toast?   10
Why deck'd with all that Land and Sea afford,
Why Angels call'd, and Angel-like ador'd?
Why round our Coaches crowd the white-glov'd Beaus,
Why bows the Side-box from its inmost Rows?
How vain are all these Glories, all our Pains,
Unless good Sense preserve what Beauty gains:
That Men may say, when we the Front-box grace,
Behold the first in Virtue, as in Face!
Oh! if to dance all Night, and dress all Day,
Charm'd the Small-pox, or chas'd old Age away;   20
Who would not scorn what Huswife's Cares produce,
Or who would learn one earthly Thing of Use?
To patch, nay ogle, might become a Saint,
Nor could it sure be such a Sin to paint.

But since, alas! frail Beauty must decay,
Curl'd or uncurl'd, since Locks will turn to grey,
Since painted, or not painted, all shall fade,
And she who scorns a Man, must die a Maid;
What then remains, but well our Pow'r to use,
And keep good Humour still whate'er we lose?   30
And trust me, Dear! good Humour can prevail,
When Airs, and Flights, and Screams, and Scolding fail.
Beauties in vain their pretty Eyes may roll;
Charms strike the Sight, but Merit wins the Soul.

So spoke the Dame, but no Applause ensu'd;
Belinda frown'd, *Thalestris* call'd her Prude.
To Arms, to Arms! the fierce Virago cries,
And swift as Lightning to the Combate flies.
All side in Parties, and begin th'Attack;
Fans clap, Silks russle, and tough Whalebones crack;   40
Heroes' and Heroins' Shouts confus'dly rise,
And base, and treble Voices strike the Skies.
No common Weapons in their Hands are found,
Like Gods they fight, nor dread a mortal Wound.

So when bold *Homer* makes the Gods engage,
And heav'nly Breasts with human Passions rage;
'Gainst *Pallas, Mars*; *Latona, Hermes* Arms;
And all *Olympus* rings with loud Alarms.
Jove's Thunder roars, Heav'n trembles all around;
Blue *Neptune* storms, the bellowing Deeps resound;   50
Earth shakes her nodding Tow'rs, the Ground gives way;
And the pale Ghosts start at the Flash of Day!

Triumphant *Umbriel* on a Sconce's Height
Clapt his glad Wings, and sate to view the Fight:
Propt on their Bodkin Spears, the Sprights survey
The growing Combat, or assist the Fray.

While thro' the Press enrag'd *Thalestris* flies,
And scatters Deaths around from both her Eyes,
A *Beau* and *Witling* perish'd in the Throng,
One dy'd in *Metaphor*, and one in *Song*.   60
O cruel Nymph! a living Death I bear,
Cry'd *Dapperwit*, and sunk beside his Chair.

A mournful Glance Sir *Fopling* upwards cast,
Those Eyes are made so killing—was his last:
Thus on *Meander's* flow'ry Margin lies
Th'expiring Swan, and as he sings he dies.

   When bold Sir *Plume* had drawn *Clarissa* down,
Chloe stept in, and kill'd him with a Frown;
She smil'd to see the doughty Hero slain,
But at her Smile, the Beau reviv'd again.   70

   Now *Jove* suspends his golden Scales in Air,
Weighs the Men's Wits against the Lady's Hair;
The doubtful Beam long nods from side to side;
At length the Wits mount up, the Hairs subside.

   See fierce *Belinda* on the *Baron* flies,
With more than usual Lightning in her Eyes;
Nor fear'd the Chief th'unequal Fight to try,
Who sought no more than on his Foe to die.
But this bold Lord, with manly Strength indu'd,
She with one Finger and a Thumb subdu'd: 80
Just where the Breath of Life his Nostrils drew,
A Charge of *Snuff* the wily Virgin threw;
The *Gnomes* direct, to ev'ry Atome just,
The pungent Grains of titillating Dust.
Sudden, with starting Tears each Eye o'erflows,
And the high Dome re-ecchoes to his Nose.

   Now meet thy Fate, incens'd *Belinda* cry'd,
And drew a deadly *Bodkin* from her Side.
(The same, his ancient Personage to deck,
Her great great Grandsire wore about his Neck   90
In three *Seal-Rings*; which after, melted down,
Form'd a vast *Buckle* for his Widow's Gown:
Her infant Grandame's *Whistle* next it grew,
The *Bells* she gingled, and the *Whistle* blew;
Then in a *Bodkin* grac'd her Mother's Hairs,
Which long she wore, and now *Belinda* wears.)

   Boast not my Fall (he cry'd) insulting Foe!
Thou by some other shalt be laid as low.
Nor think, to die dejects my lofty Mind;
All that I dread, is leaving you behind!   100

Rather than so, ah let me still survive,
And burn in *Cupid's* Flames,—but burn alive.
   Restore the Lock! she cries; and all around
Restore the Lock! the vaulted Roofs rebound.
Not fierce *Othello* in so loud a Strain
Roar'd for the Handkerchief that caus'd his Pain.
But see how oft Ambitious Aims are cross'd,
And Chiefs contend 'till all the Prize is lost!
The Lock, obtain'd with Guilt, and kept with Pain,
In ev'ry place is sought, but sought in vain: 110
With such a Prize no Mortal must be blest,
So Heav'n decrees! with Heav'n who can contest?
   Some thought it mounted to the Lunar Sphere,
Since all things lost on Earth, are treasur'd there.
There Heroes' Wits are kept in pondrous Vases,
And Beaus' in *Snuff-boxes* and *Tweezer-Cases.*
There broken Vows, and Death-bed Alms are found,
And Lovers' Hearts with Ends of Riband bound;
The Courtier's Promises, and Sick Man's Pray'rs,
The Smiles of Harlots, and the Tears of Heirs,   120
Cages for Gnats, and Chains to Yoak a Flea;
Dry'd Butterflies, and Tomes of Casuistry.
   But trust the Muse—she saw it upward rise,
Tho' mark'd by none but quick Poetic Eyes:
(So *Rome's* great Founder to the Heav'ns withdrew,
To *Proculus* alone confess'd in view.)
A sudden Star, it shot thro' liquid Air,
And drew behind a radiant *Trail of Hair.*
Not *Berenice's* Locks first rose so bright,
The Heav'ns bespangling with dishevel'd Light.   130
The *Sylphs* behold it kindling as it flies,
And pleas'd pursue its Progress thro' the Skies.
   This the *Beau-monde* shall from the *Mall* survey,
And hail with Musick its propitious Ray.
This, the blest Lover shall for *Venus* take,
And send up Vows from *Rosamonda's* Lake.
This *Partridge* soon shall view in cloudless Skies,
When next he looks thro' *Galilæo's* Eyes;

And hence th'Egregious Wizard shall foredoom
The Fate of *Louis*, and the Fall of *Rome*.   140
    Then cease, bright Nymph! to mourn thy ravish'd Hair
Which adds new Glory to the shining Sphere!
Not all the Tresses that fair Head can boast
Shall draw such Envy as the Lock you lost.
For, after all the Murders of your Eye,
When, after Millions slain, your self shall die;
When those fair Suns shall sett, as sett they must,
And all those Tresses shall be laid in Dust;
This Lock, the Muse shall consecrate to Fame,
And mid'st the Stars inscribe *Belinda's* Name!   150

ELOISA TO ABELARD

In these deep solitudes and awful cells,
Where heav'nly-pensive, contemplation dwells,
And ever-musing melancholy reigns;
What means this tumult in a Vestal's veins?
Why rove my thoughts beyond this last retreat?
Why feels my heart its long-forgotten heat?
Yet, yet I love!—From *Abelard* it came,
And *Eloisa* yet must kiss the name.

Dear fatal name! rest ever unreveal'd,
Nor pass these lips in holy silence seal'd.   10
Hide it, my heart, within that close disguise,
Where, mix'd with God's, his lov'd Idea lies.
Oh write it not, my hand—The name appears
Already written—wash it out, my tears!
In vain lost *Eloisa* weeps and prays,
Her heart still dictates, and her hand obeys.

Relentless walls! whose darksom round contains
Repentant sighs, and voluntary pains:
Ye rugged rocks! which holy knees have worn;
Ye grots and caverns shagg'd with horrid thorn!   20
Shrines! where their vigils pale-ey'd virgins keep,
And pitying saints, whose statues learn to weep!
Tho' cold like you, unmov'd, and silent grown,
I have not yet forgot myself to stone.
All is not Heav'n's while *Abelard* has part,
Still rebel nature holds out half my heart;
Nor pray'rs nor fasts its stubborn pulse restrain,
Nor tears, for ages, taught to flow in vain.

Soon as thy letters trembling I unclose,
That well-known name awakens all my woes.   30
Oh name for ever sad! for ever dear!
Still breath'd in sighs, still usher'd with a tear.
I tremble too where-e'er my own I find,
Some dire misfortune follows close behind.

Line after line my gushing eyes o'erflow,
Led thro' a sad variety of woe:
Now warm in love, now with'ring in thy bloom,
Lost in a convent's solitary gloom!
There stern religion quench'd th'unwilling flame,
There dy'd the best of passions, Love and Fame.   40
    Yet write, oh write me all, that I may join
Griefs to thy griefs, and eccho sighs to thine.
Nor foes nor fortune take this pow'r away.
And is my *Abelard* less kind than they?
Tears still are mine, and those I need not spare,
Love but demands what else were shed in pray'r;
No happier task these faded eyes pursue,
To read and weep is all they now can do.
    Then share thy pain, allow that sad relief;
Ah more than share it! give me all thy grief.   50
Heav'n first taught letters for some wretch's aid,
Some banish'd lover, or some captive maid;
They live, they speak, they breathe what love inspires,
Warm from the soul, and faithful to its fires,
The virgin's wish without her fears impart,
Excuse the blush, and pour out all the heart,
Speed the soft intercourse from soul to soul,
And waft a sigh from *Indus* to the *Pole*.
    Thou know'st how guiltless first I met thy flame,
When Love approach'd me under Friendship's name;   60
My fancy form'd thee of Angelick kind,
Some emanation of th'all-beauteous Mind.
Those smiling eyes, attemp'ring ev'ry ray,
Shone sweetly lambent with celestial day:
Guiltless I gaz'd; heav'n listen'd while you sung;
And truths divine came mended from that tongue.
From lips like those what precept fail'd to move?
Too soon they taught me 'twas no sin to love.
Back thro' the paths of pleasing sense I ran,
Nor wish'd an Angel whom I lov'd a Man.   70
Dim and remote the joys of saints I see,
Nor envy them, that heav'n I lose for thee.

How oft', when press'd to marriage, have I said,
Curse on all laws but those which love has made!
Love, free as air, at sight of human ties,
Spreads his light wings, and in a moment flies.
Let wealth, let honour, wait the wedded dame,
August her deed, and sacred be her fame;
Before true passion all those views remove,
Fame, wealth, and honour! what are you to Love?   80
The jealous God, when we profane his fires,
Those restless passions in revenge inspires;
And bids them make mistaken mortals groan,
Who seek in love for ought but love alone.
Should at my feet the world's great master fall,
Himself, his throne, his world, I'd scorn 'em all:
Not *Cæsar's* empress wou'd I deign to prove;
No, make me mistress to the man I love;
If there be yet another name more free,
More fond than mistress, make me that to thee!   90
Oh happy state! when souls each other draw,
When love is liberty, and nature, law:
All then is full, possessing and possest,
No craving Void left aking in the breast:
Ev'n thought meets thought ere from the lips it part,
And each warm wish springs mutual from the heart.
This sure is bliss (if bliss on earth there be)
And once the lot of *Abelard* and me.

Alas how chang'd! what sudden horrors rise!
A naked Lover bound and bleeding lies!   100
Where, where was *Eloise*? her voice, her hand,
Her ponyard, had oppos'd the dire command.
Barbarian stay! that bloody stroke restrain;
The crime was common, common be the pain.
I can no more; by shame, by rage supprest,
Let tears, and burning blushes speak the rest.

Canst thou forget that sad, that solemn day,
When victims at yon' altar's foot we lay?
Canst thou forget what tears that moment fell,
When, warm in youth, I bade the world farewell?   110

As with cold lips I kiss'd the sacred veil,
The shrines all trembled, and the lamps grew pale:
Heav'n scarce believ'd the conquest it survey'd,
And Saints with wonder heard the vows I made.
Yet then, to those dread altars as I drew,
Not on the Cross my eyes were fix'd, but you;
Not grace, or zeal, love only was my call,
And if I lose thy love, I lose my all.
Come! with thy looks, thy words, relieve my woe;
Those still at least are left thee to bestow.   120
Still on that breast enamour'd let me lie,
Still drink delicious poison from thy eye,
Pant on thy lip, and to thy heart be prest;
Give all thou canst—and let me dream the rest.
Ah no! instruct me other joys to prize,
With other beauties charm my partial eyes,
Full in my view set all the bright abode,
And make my soul quit *Abelard* for God.

    Ah think at least thy flock deserves thy care,
Plants of thy hand, and children of thy pray'r.   130
From the false world in early youth they fled,
By thee to mountains, wilds, and deserts led.
You rais'd these hallow'd walls; the desert smil'd,
And Paradise was open'd in the Wild.
No weeping orphan saw his father's stores
Our shrines irradiate, or emblaze the floors;
No silver saints, by dying misers giv'n,
Here brib'd the rage of ill-requited heav'n:
But such plain roofs as piety could raise,
And only vocal with the Maker's praise.   140
In these lone walls (their day's eternal bound)
These moss-grown domes with spiry turrets crown'd,
Where awful arches make a noon-day night,
And the dim windows shed a solemn light;
Thy eyes diffus'd a reconciling ray,
And gleams of glory brighten'd all the day.
But now no face divine contentment wears,
'Tis all blank sadness, or continual tears.

See how the force of others' pray'rs I try,
(Oh pious fraud of am'rous charity!)   150
But why should I on others' pray'rs depend?
Come thou, my father, brother, husband, friend!
Ah let thy handmaid, sister, daughter move,
And, all those tender names in one, thy love!
The darksom pines that o'er yon' rocks reclin'd
Wave high, and murmur to the hollow wind,
The wandring streams that shine between the hills,
The grots that eccho to the tinkling rills,
The dying gales that pant upon the trees,
The lakes that quiver to the curling breeze;   160
No more these scenes my meditation aid,
Or lull to rest the visionary maid;
But o'er the twilight groves, and dusky caves,
Long-sounding aisles, and intermingled graves,
Black Melancholy sits, and round her throws
A death-like silence, and a dread repose:
Her gloomy presence saddens all the scene,
Shades ev'ry flow'r, and darkens ev'ry green,
Deepens the murmur of the falling floods,
And breathes a browner horror on the woods.   170
    Yet here for ever, ever must I stay;
Sad proof how well a lover can obey!
Death, only death, can break the lasting chain;
And here ev'n then, shall my cold dust remain,
Here all its frailties, all its flames resign,
And wait, till 'tis no sin to mix with thine.
    Ah wretch! believ'd the spouse of God in vain,
Confess'd within the slave of love and man.
Assist me, heav'n! but whence arose that pray'r?
Sprung it from piety, or from despair?   180
Ev'n here, where frozen chastity retires,
Love finds an altar for forbidden fires.
I ought to grieve, but cannot what I ought;
I mourn the lover, not lament the fault;
I view my crime, but kindle at the view,
Repent old pleasures, and sollicit new:

Now turn'd to heav'n, I weep my past offence,
Now think of thee, and curse my innocence.
Of all affliction taught a lover yet,
'Tis sure the hardest science to forget!   190
How shall I lose the sin, yet keep the sense,
And love th'offender, yet detest th'offence?
How the dear object from the crime remove,
Or how distinguish penitence from love?
Unequal task! a passion to resign,
For hearts so touch'd, so pierc'd, so lost as mine.
Ere such a soul regains its peaceful state,
How often must it love, how often hate!
How often, hope, despair, resent, regret,
Conceal, disdain—do all things but forget.   200
But let heav'n seize it, all at once 'tis fir'd,
Not touch'd, but rapt; not waken'd, but inspir'd!
Oh come! oh teach me nature to subdue,
Renounce my love, my life, my self—and you.
Fill my fond heart with God alone, for he
Alone can rival, can succeed to thee.

How happy is the blameless Vestal's lot!
The world forgetting, by the world forgot.
Eternal sun-shine of the spotless mind!
Each pray'r accepted, and each wish resign'd;   210
Labour and rest, that equal periods keep;
'Obedient slumbers that can wake and weep';
Desires compos'd, affections ever ev'n,
Tears that delight, and sighs that waft to heav'n.
Grace shines around her with serenest beams,
And whisp'ring Angels prompt her golden dreams.
For her th'unfading rose of *Eden* blooms,
And wings of Seraphs shed divine perfumes;
For her the Spouse prepares the bridal ring,
For her white virgins *Hymenæals* sing;   220
To sounds of heav'nly harps, she dies away,
And melts in visions of eternal day.

Far other dreams my erring soul employ,
Far other raptures, of unholy joy:

When at the close of each sad, sorrowing day,
Fancy restores what vengeance snatch'd away,
Then conscience sleeps, and leaving nature free,
All my loose soul unbounded springs to thee.
O curst, dear horrors of all-conscious night!
How glowing guilt exalts the keen delight!   230
Provoking Dæmons all restraint remove,
And stir within me ev'ry source of love.
I hear thee, view thee, gaze o'er all thy charms,
And round thy phantom glue my clasping arms.
I wake—no more I hear, no more I view,
The phantom flies me, as unkind as you.
I call aloud; it hears not what I say;
I stretch my empty arms; it glides away:
To dream once more I close my willing eyes;
Ye soft illusions, dear deceits, arise!   240
Alas no more!—methinks we wandring go
Thro' dreary wastes, and weep each other's woe;
Where round some mould'ring tow'r pale ivy creeps,
And low-brow'd rocks hang nodding o'er the deeps.
Sudden you mount! you beckon from the skies;
Clouds interpose, waves roar, and winds arise.
I shriek, start up, the same sad prospect find,
And wake to all the griefs I left behind.
    For thee the fates, severely kind, ordain
A cool suspense from pleasure and from pain;   250
Thy life a long, dead calm of fix'd repose;
No pulse that riots, and no blood that glows.
Still as the sea, ere winds were taught to blow,
Or moving spirit bade the waters flow;
Soft as the slumbers of a saint forgiv'n,
And mild as opening gleams of promis'd heav'n.
    Come *Abelard*! for what hast thou to dread?
The torch of *Venus* burns not for the dead;
Nature stands check'd; Religion disapproves;
Ev'n thou art cold—yet *Eloisa* loves.   260
Ah hopeless, lasting flames! like those that burn
To light the dead, and warm th'unfruitful urn.

What scenes appear where-e'er I turn my view!
The dear Ideas, where I fly, pursue,
Rise in the grove, before the altar rise,
Stain all my soul, and wanton in my eyes!
I waste the Matin lamp in sighs for thee,
Thy image steals between my God and me,
Thy voice I seem in ev'ry hymn to hear,
With ev'ry bead I drop too soft a tear.   270
When from the Censer clouds of fragrance roll,
And swelling organs lift the rising soul;
One thought of thee puts all the pomp to flight,
Priests, Tapers, Temples, swim before my sight:
In seas of flame my plunging soul is drown'd,
While Altars blaze, and Angels tremble round.

While prostrate here in humble grief I lie,
Kind, virtuous drops just gath'ring in my eye,
While praying, trembling, in the dust I roll,
And dawning grace is opening on my soul: 280
Come, if thou dar'st, all charming as thou art!
Oppose thy self to heav'n; dispute my heart;
Come, with one glance of those deluding eyes,
Blot out each bright Idea of the skies.
Take back that grace, those sorrows, and those tears,
Take back my fruitless penitence and pray'rs,
Snatch me, just mounting, from the blest abode,
Assist the Fiends, and tear me from my God!

No, fly me, fly me! far as Pole from Pole;
Rise *Alps* between us! and whole oceans roll!   290
Ah come not, write not, think not once of me,
Nor share one pang of all I felt for thee.
Thy oaths I quit, thy memory resign,
Forget, renounce me, hate whate'er was mine.
Fair eyes, and tempting looks (which yet I view!)
Long lov'd, ador'd ideas! all adieu!
O grace serene! oh virtue heav'nly fair!
Divine oblivion of low-thoughted care!
Fresh blooming hope, gay daughter of the sky!
And faith, our early immortality!   300

Enter each mild, each amicable guest;
Receive, and wrap me in eternal rest!
   See in her Cell sad *Eloisa* spread,
Propt on some tomb, a neighbour of the dead
In each low wind methinks a Spirit calls,
And more than Echoes talk along the walls.
Here, as I watch'd the dying lamps around,
From yonder shrine I heard a hollow sound.
Come, sister come! (it said, or seem'd to say)
Thy place is here, sad sister come away!   310
Once like thy self, I trembled, wept, and pray'd,
Love's victim then, tho' now a sainted maid:
But all is calm in this eternal sleep;
Here grief forgets to groan, and love to weep,
Ev'n superstition loses ev'ry fear:
For God, not man, absolves our frailties here.
   I come, I come! prepare your roseate bow'rs,
Celestial palms, and ever-blooming flow'rs.
Thither, where sinners may have rest, I go,
Where flames refin'd in breasts seraphic glow.   320
Thou, *Abelard*! the last sad office pay,
And smooth my passage to the realms of day:
See my lips tremble, and my eye-balls roll,
Suck my last breath, and catch my flying soul!
Ah no—in sacred vestments may'st thou stand,
The hallow'd taper trembling in thy hand,
Present the Cross before my lifted eye,
Teach me at once, and learn of me to die.
Ah then, thy once-lov'd *Eloisa* see!
It will be then no crime to gaze on me.   330
See from my cheek the transient roses fly!
See the last sparkle languish in my eye!
Till ev'ry motion, pulse, and breath, be o'er;
And ev'n my *Abelard* be lov'd no more.
O death all-eloquent! you only prove
What dust we doat on, when 'tis man we love.
   Then too, when fate shall thy fair frame destroy,
(That cause of all my guilt, and all my joy)

In trance extatic may thy pangs be drown'd,
Bright clouds descend, and Angels watch thee round,   340
From opening skies may streaming glories shine,
And Saints embrace thee with a love like mine.

     May one kind grave unite each hapless name,
And graft my love immortal on thy fame.
Then, ages hence, when all my woes are o'er,
When this rebellious heart shall beat no more;
If ever chance two wandring lovers brings
To *Paraclete's* white walls, and silver springs,
O'er the pale marble shall they join their heads,
And drink the falling tears each other sheds,   350
Then sadly say, with mutual pity mov'd,
Oh may we never love as these have lov'd!
From the full quire when loud *Hosanna's* rise,
And swell the pomp of dreadful sacrifice,
Amid that scene, if some relenting eye
Glance on the stone where our cold reliques lie,
Devotion's self shall steal a thought from heav'n,
One human tear shall drop, and be forgiv'n.
And sure if fate some future Bard shall join
In sad similitude of griefs to mine,   360
Condemn'd whole years in absence to deplore,
And image charms he must behold no more,
Such if there be, who loves so long, so well;
Let him our sad, our tender story tell;
The well-sung woes will sooth my pensive ghost;
He best can paint 'em, who shall feel 'em most.

ELEGY TO THE MEMORY OF AN
UNFORTUNATE LADY

What beck'ning ghost, along the moonlight shade
Invites my step, and points to yonder glade?
'Tis she!——but why that bleeding bosom gor'd,
Why dimly gleams the visionary sword?
Oh ever beauteous, ever friendly! tell,
Is it, in heav'n, a crime to love too well?
To bear too tender, or too firm a heart,
To act a Lover's or a *Roman's* part?
Is there no bright reversion in the sky,
For those who greatly think, or bravely die?   10

   Why bade ye else, ye Pow'rs! her soul aspire
Above the vulgar flight of low desire?
Ambition first sprung from your blest abodes;
The glorious fault of Angels and of Gods:
Thence to their Images on earth it flows,
And in the breasts of Kings and Heroes glows!
Most souls, 'tis true, but peep out once an age,
Dull sullen pris'ners in the body's cage:
Dim lights of life that burn a length of years,
Useless, unseen, as lamps in sepulchres;   20
Like Eastern Kings a lazy state they keep,
And close confin'd to their own palace sleep.

   From these perhaps (ere nature bade her die)
Fate snatch'd her early to the pitying sky.
As into air the purer spirits flow,
And sep'rate from their kindred dregs below;
So flew the soul to its congenial place,
Nor left one virtue to redeem her Race.

   But thou, false guardian of a charge too good,
Thou, mean deserter of thy brother's blood!   30
See on these ruby lips the trembling breath,
These cheeks, now fading at the blast of death:

Cold is that breast which warm'd the world before,
And those love-darting eyes must roll no more.
Thus, if eternal justice rules the ball,
Thus shall your wives, and thus your children fall:
On all the line a sudden vengeance waits,
And frequent herses shall besiege your gates.
There passengers shall stand, and pointing say,
(While the long fun'rals blacken all the way)   40
Lo these were they, whose souls the Furies steel'd,
And curs'd with hearts unknowing how to yield.
Thus unlamented pass the proud away,
The gaze of fools, and pageant of a day!
So perish all, whose breast ne'er learn'd to glow
For others' good, or melt at others' woe.
    What can atone (oh ever-injur'd shade!)
Thy fate unpity'd, and thy rites unpaid?
No friend's complaint, no kind domestic tear
Pleas'd thy pale ghost, or grac'd thy mournful bier;   50
By foreign hands thy dying eyes were clos'd,
By foreign hands thy decent limbs compos'd,
By foreign hands thy humble grave adorn'd,
By strangers honour'd, and by strangers mourn'd!
What tho' no friends in sable weeds appear,
Grieve for an hour, perhaps, then mourn a year,
And bear about the mockery of woe
To midnight dances, and the publick show?
What tho' no weeping Loves thy ashes grace,
Nor polish'd marble emulate thy face?   60
What tho' no sacred earth allow thee room,
Nor hallow'd dirge be mutter'd o'er thy tomb?
Yet shall thy grave with rising flow'rs be drest,
And the green turf lie lightly on thy breast:
There shall the morn her earliest tears bestow,
There the first roses of the year shall blow;
While Angels with their silver wings o'ershade
The ground, now sacred by thy reliques made.
    So peaceful rests, without a stone, a name,
What once had beauty, titles, wealth, and fame.   70

How lov'd, how honour'd once, avails thee not,
To whom related, or by whom begot;
A heap of dust alone remains of thee;
'Tis all thou art, and all the proud shall be!
    Poets themselves must fall, like those they sung;
Deaf the prais'd ear, and mute the tuneful tongue.
Ev'n he, whose soul now melts in mournful lays,
Shall shortly want the gen'rous tear he pays;
Then from his closing eyes thy form shall part,
And the last pang shall tear thee from his heart,   80
Life's idle business at one gasp be o'er,
The Muse forgot, and thou belov'd no more!

EPISTLE

TO A YOUNG LADY, ON HER LEAVING THE TOWN AFTER THE CORONATION

As some fond virgin, whom her mother's care
Drags from the town to wholsom country air,
Just when she learns to roll a melting eye,
And hear a spark, yet think no danger nigh;
From the dear man unwilling she must sever,
Yet takes one kiss before she parts for ever:
Thus from the world fair *Zephalinda* flew,
Saw others happy, and with sighs withdrew;
Not that their pleasures caus'd her discontent,
She sigh'd not that They stay'd, but that She went.   10
   She went, to plain-work, and to purling brooks,
Old-fashion'd halls, dull aunts, and croaking rooks,
She went from Op'ra, park, assembly, play,
To morning walks, and pray'rs three hours a day;
To pass her time 'twixt reading and Bohea,
To muse, and spill her solitary Tea,
Or o'er cold coffee trifle with the spoon,
Count the slow clock, and dine exact at noon;
Divert her eyes with pictures in the fire,
Hum half a tune, tell stories to the squire;   20
Up to her godly garret after sev'n,
There starve and pray, for that's the way to heav'n.
   Some Squire, perhaps, you take delight to rack;
Whose game is Whisk, whose treat a toast in sack,
Who visits with a gun, presents you birds,
Then gives a smacking buss, and cries—No words!
Or with his hound comes hollowing from the stable,
Makes love with nods, and knees beneath a table;
Whose laughs are hearty, tho' his jests are coarse,
And loves you best of all things—but his horse.   30

In some fair evening, on your elbow laid,
You dream of triumphs in the rural shade;
In pensive thought recall the fancy'd scene,
See Coronations rise on ev'ry green;
Before you pass th'imaginary sights
Of Lords, and Earls, and Dukes, and garter'd Knights;
While the spread Fan o'ershades your closing eyes;
Then give one flirt, and all the vision flies.
Thus vanish sceptres, coronets, and balls,
And leave you in lone woods, or empty walls.   40
  So when your slave, at some dear, idle time,
(Not plagu'd with headachs, or the want of rhime)
Stands in the streets, abstracted from the crew,
And while he seems to study, thinks of you:
Just when his fancy points your sprightly eyes,
Or sees the blush of soft *Parthenia* rise,
Gay pats my shoulder, and you vanish quite;
Streets, chairs, and coxcombs rush upon my sight;
Vext to be still in town, I knit my brow,
Look sow'r, and hum a tune—as you may now.   50

EPISTLES TO SEVERAL PERSONS

Epistle II

TO A LADY: OF THE CHARACTERS OF WOMEN

Nothing so true as what you once let fall,
'Most Women have no Characters at all'.
Matter too soft a lasting mark to bear,
And best distinguish'd by black, brown, or fair.
  How many pictures of one Nymph we view,
All how unlike each other, all how true!
Arcadia's Countess, here, in ermin'd pride,
Is there, Pastora by a fountain side:
Here Fannia, leering on her own good man,
Is there, a naked Leda with a Swan.   10
Let then the Fair one beautifully cry,
In Magdalen's loose hair and lifted eye,
Or drest in smiles of sweet Cecilia shine,
With simp'ring Angels, Palms, and Harps divine;
Whether the Charmer sinner it, or saint it,
If Folly grows romantic, I must paint it.
  Come then, the colours and the ground prepare!
Dip in the Rainbow, trick her off in Air,
Chuse a firm Cloud, before it fall, and in it
Catch, ere she change, the Cynthia of this minute. 20
  Rufa, whose eye quick-glancing o'er the Park,
Attracts each light gay meteor of a Spark,
Agrees as ill with Rufa studying Locke,
As Sappho's diamonds with her dirty smock,
Or Sappho at her toilet's greasy task,
With Sappho fragrant at an ev'ning Mask:
So morning Insects that in muck begun,
Shine, buzz, and fly-blow in the setting-sun.

How soft is Silia! fearful to offend,
The Frail one's advocate, the Weak one's friend: 30
To her, Calista prov'd her conduct nice,
And good Simplicius asks of her advice.
Sudden, she storms! she raves! You tip the wink,
But spare your censure; Silia does not drink.
All eyes may see from what the change arose,
All eyes may see—a Pimple on her nose.

   Papillia, wedded to her doating spark,
Sighs for the shades—'How charming is a Park!'
A Park is purchas'd, but the Fair he sees
All bath'd in tears—'Oh odious, odious Trees!'   40
   Ladies, like variegated Tulips, show,
'Tis to their Changes that their charms they owe;
Their happy Spots the nice admirer take,
Fine by defect, and delicately weak.
'Twas thus Calypso once each heart alarm'd,
Aw'd without Virtue, without Beauty charm'd;
Her Tongue bewitch'd as odly as her Eyes,
Less Wit than Mimic, more a Wit than wise:
Strange graces still, and stranger flights she had,
Was just not ugly, and was just not mad;   50
Yet ne'er so sure our passion to create,
As when she touch'd the brink of all we hate.

   Narcissa's nature, tolerably mild,
To make a wash, would hardly stew a child;
Has ev'n been prov'd to grant a Lover's pray'r,
And paid a Tradesman once to make him stare,
Gave alms at Easter, in a Christian trim,
And made a Widow happy, for a whim.
Why then declare Good-nature is her scorn,
When 'tis by that alone she can be born?   60
Why pique all mortals, yet affect a name?
A fool to Pleasure, and a slave to Fame:
Now deep in Taylor and the Book of Martyrs,
Now drinking citron with his Grace and Chartres.
Now Conscience chills her, and now Passion burns;
And Atheism and Religion take their turns;

A very Heathen in the carnal part,
Yet still a sad, good Christian at her heart.
  See Sin in State, majestically drunk,
Proud as a Peeress, prouder as a Punk;   70
Chaste to her Husband, frank to all beside,
A teeming Mistress, but a barren Bride.
What then? let Blood and Body bear the fault,
Her Head's untouch'd, that noble Seat of Thought:
Such this day's doctrine—in another fit
She sins with Poets thro' pure Love of Wit.
What has not fir'd her bosom or her brain?
Cæsar and Tall-boy, Charles and Charlema'ne.
As Helluo, late Dictator of the Feast,
The Nose of Hautgout, and the Tip of Taste,   80
Critick'd your wine, and analyz'd your meat,
Yet on plain Pudding deign'd at-home to eat;
So Philomedé, lect'ring all mankind
On the soft Passion, and the Taste refin'd,
Th'Address, the Delicacy—stoops at once,
And makes her hearty meal upon a Dunce.
  Flavia's a Wit, has too much sense to Pray,
To Toast our wants and wishes, is her way;
Nor asks of God, but of her Stars to give
The mighty blessing, 'while we live, to live'.   90
Then all for Death, that Opiate of the soul!
Lucretia's dagger, Rosamonda's bowl.
Say, what can cause such impotence of mind?
A Spark too fickle, or a Spouse too kind.
Wise Wretch! with Pleasures too refin'd to please,
With too much Spirit to be e'er at ease,
With too much Quickness ever to be taught,
With too much Thinking to have common Thought:
Who purchase Pain with all that Joy can give,
And die of nothing but a Rage to live.   100
  Turn then from Wits; and look on Simo's Mate,
No Ass so meek, no Ass so obstinate:
Or her, that owns her Faults, but never mends,
Because she's honest, and the best of Friends:

Or her, whose life the Church and Scandal share,
For ever in a Passion, or a Pray'r:
Or her, who laughs at Hell, but (like her Grace)
Cries, 'Ah! how charming if there's no such place!'
Or who in sweet vicissitude appears
Of Mirth and Opium, Ratafie and Tears,   110
The daily Anodyne, and nightly Draught,
To kill those foes to Fair ones, Time and Thought.
Woman and Fool are two hard things to hit,
For true No-meaning puzzles more than Wit.
    But what are these to great Atossa's mind?
Scarce once herself, by turns all Womankind!
Who, with herself, or others, from her birth
Finds all her life one warfare upon earth:
Shines, in exposing Knaves, and painting Fools,
Yet is, whate'er she hates and ridicules.   120
No Thought advances, but her Eddy Brain
Whisks it about, and down it goes again.
Full sixty years the World has been her Trade,
The wisest Fool much Time has ever made.
From loveless youth to unrespected age,
No Passion gratify'd except her Rage.
So much the Fury still out-ran the Wit,
The Pleasure miss'd her, and the Scandal hit.
Who breaks with her, provokes Revenge from Hell,
But he's a bolder man who dares be well: 130
Her ev'ry turn with Violence pursu'd,
Nor more a storm her Hate than Gratitude.
To that each Passion turns, or soon or late;
Love, if it makes her yield, must make her hate:
Superiors? death! and Equals? what a curse!
But an Inferior not dependant? worse.
Offend her, and she knows not to forgive;
Oblige her, and she'll hate you while you live:
But die, and she'll adore you—Then the Bust
And Temple rise—then fall again to dust.   140
Last night, her Lord was all that's good and great,
A Knave this morning, and his Will a Cheat.

Strange! by the Means defeated of the Ends,
By Spirit robb'd of Pow'r, by Warmth of Friends,
By Wealth of Follow'rs! without one distress
Sick of herself thro' very selfishness!
Atossa, curs'd with ev'ry granted pray'r,
Childless with all her Children, wants an Heir.
To Heirs unknown descends th'unguarded store
Or wanders, Heav'n-directed, to the Poor.   150
    Pictures like these, dear Madam, to design,
Asks no firm hand, and no unerring line;
Some wand'ring touch, or some reflected light,
Some flying stroke alone can hit 'em right:
For how should equal Colours do the knack?
Chameleons who can paint in white and black?
    'Yet Cloe sure was form'd without a spot—'
Nature in her then err'd not, but forgot.
'With ev'ry pleasing, ev'ry prudent part,
'Say, what can Cloe want?'—she wants a Heart.   160
She speaks, behaves, and acts just as she ought;
But never, never, reach'd one gen'rous Thought.
Virtue she finds too painful an endeavour,
Content to dwell in Decencies for ever.
So very reasonable, so unmov'd,
As never yet to love, or to be lov'd.
She, while her Lover pants upon her breast,
Can mark the figures on an Indian chest;
And when she sees her Friend in deep despair,
Observes how much a Chintz exceeds Mohair.   170
Forbid it Heav'n, a Favour or a Debt
She e'er should cancel—but she may forget.
Safe is your Secret still in Cloe's ear;
But none of Cloe's shall you ever hear.
Of all her Dears she never slander'd one,
But cares not if a thousand are undone.
Would Cloe know if you're alive or dead?
She bids her Footman put it in her head.
Cloe is prudent—would you too be wise?
Then never break your heart when Cloe dies.   180

82

One certain Portrait may (I grant) be seen,
Which Heav'n has varnish'd out, and made a *Queen*:
The same for ever! and describ'd by all
With Truth and Goodness, as with Crown and Ball:
Poets heap Virtues, Painters Gems at will,
And show their zeal, and hide their want of skill.
'Tis well—but, Artists! who can paint or write,
To draw the Naked is your true delight:
That Robe of Quality so struts and swells,
None see what Parts of Nature it conceals.   190
Th'exactest traits of Body or of Mind,
We owe to models of an humble kind.
If QUEENSBERRY to strip there's no compelling,
'Tis from a Handmaid we must take a Helen.
From Peer or Bishop 'tis no easy thing
To draw the man who loves his God, or King:
Alas! I copy (or my draught would fail)
From honest Mah'met, or plain Parson Hale.
    But grant, in Public Men sometimes are shown,
A Woman's seen in Private life alone: 200
Our bolder Talents in full light display'd,
Your Virtues open fairest in the shade.
Bred to disguise, in Public 'tis you hide;
There, none distinguish 'twixt your Shame or Pride,
Weakness or Delicacy; all so nice,
That each may seem a Virtue, or a Vice.
    In Men, we various Ruling Passions find,
In Women, two almost divide the kind;
Those, only fix'd, they first or last obey,
The Love of Pleasure, and the Love of Sway.   210
    That, Nature gives; and where the lesson taught
Is still to please, can Pleasure seem a fault?
Experience, this; by Man's oppression curst,
They seek the second not to lose the first.
    Men, some to Bus'ness, some to Pleasure take;
But ev'ry Woman is at heart a Rake:
Men, some to Quiet, some to public Strife;
But ev'ry Lady would be Queen for life.

Yet mark the fate of a whole Sex of Queens!
Pow'r all their end, but Beauty all the means.   220
In Youth they conquer, with so wild a rage,
As leaves them scarce a Subject in their Age:
For foreign glory, foreign joy, they roam;
No thought of Peace or Happiness at home.
But Wisdom's Triumph is well-tim'd Retreat,
As hard a science to the Fair as Great!
Beauties, like Tyrants, old and friendless grown,
Yet hate to rest, and dread to be alone,
Worn out in public, weary ev'ry eye,
Nor leave one sigh behind them when they die   230
    Pleasures the sex, as children Birds, pursue,
Still out of reach, yet never out of view,
Sure, if they catch, to spoil the Toy at most,
To covet flying, and regret when lost:
At last, to follies Youth could scarce defend,
'Tis half their Age's prudence to pretend;
Asham'd to own they gave delight before,
Reduc'd to feign it, when they give no more:
As Hags hold Sabbaths, less for joy than spight,
So these their merry, miserable Night;   240
Still round and round the Ghosts of Beauty glide,
And haunt the places where their Honour dy'd.
    See how the World its Veterans rewards!
A Youth of frolicks, an old Age of Cards,
Fair to no purpose, artful to no end,
Young without Lovers, old without a Friend,
A Fop their Passion, but their Prize a Sot,
Alive, ridiculous, and dead, forgot!
    Ah Friend! to dazzle let the Vain design,
To raise the Thought and touch the Heart, be thine!   250
That Charm shall grow, while what fatigues the Ring
Flaunts and goes down, an unregarded thing.
So when the Sun's broad beam has tir'd the sight,
All mild ascends the Moon's more sober light,
Serene in Virgin Modesty she shines,
And unobserv'd the glaring Orb declines.

Oh! blest with Temper, whose unclouded ray
Can make to morrow chearful as to day;
She, who can love a Sister's charms, or hear
Sighs for a Daughter with unwounded ear;   260
She, who ne'er answers till a Husband cools,
Or, if she rules him, never shows she rules;
Charms by accepting, by submitting sways,
Yet has her humour most, when she obeys;
Lets Fops or Fortune fly which way they will;
Disdains all loss of Tickets, or Codille;
Spleen, Vapours, or Small-pox, above them all,
And Mistress of herself, tho' China fall.

And yet, believe me, good as well as ill,
Woman's at best a Contradiction still.   270
Heav'n, when it strives to polish all it can
Its last best work, but forms a softer Man;
Picks from each sex, to make its Fav'rite blest,
Your love of Pleasure, our desire of Rest,
Blends, in exception to all gen'ral rules,
Your Taste of Follies, with our Scorn of Fools,
Reserve with Frankness, Art with Truth ally'd,
Courage with Softness, Modesty with Pride,
Fix'd Principles, with Fancy ever new;
Shakes all together, and produces—You.   280
Be this a Woman's Fame: with this unblest,
Toasts live a scorn, and Queens may die a jest.
This Phœbus promis'd (I forget the year)
When those blue eyes first open'd on the sphere;
Ascendant Phœbus watch'd that hour with care,
Averted half your Parents simple Pray'r,
And gave you Beauty, but deny'd the Pelf
Which buys your sex a Tyrant o'er itself.
The gen'rous God, who Wit and Gold refines,
And ripens Spirits as he ripens Mines,   290
Kept Dross for Duchesses, the world shall know it,
To you gave Sense, Good-humour, and a Poet.

TO ALLEN LORD BATHURST

Who shall decide, when Doctors disagree,
And soundest Casuists doubt, like you and me?
You hold the word, from Jove to Momus giv'n,
That Man was made the standing jest of Heav'n;
And Gold but sent to keep the fools in play,
For some to heap, and some to throw away.
    But I, who think more highly of our kind,
(And surely, Heav'n and I are of a mind)
Opine, that Nature, as in duty bound,
Deep hid the shining mischief under ground: 10
But when by Man's audacious labour won,
Flam'd forth this rival to, its Sire, the Sun,
Then careful Heav'n supply'd two sorts of Men,
To squander these, and those to hide agen.
    Like Doctors thus, when much dispute has past,
We find our tenets just the same at last.
Both fairly owning, Riches in effect
No grace of Heav'n or token of th'Elect;
Giv'n to the Fool, the Mad, the Vain, the Evil,
To Ward, to Waters, Chartres, and the Devil.   20
What Nature wants, commodious Gold bestows,
'Tis thus we eat the bread another sows:
But how unequal it bestows, observe,
'Tis thus we riot, while who sow it, starve,
What Nature wants (a phrase I much distrust)
Extends to Luxury, extends to Lust:
And if we count among the Needs of life
Another's Toil, why not another's Wife?
Useful, I grant, it serves what life requires,
But dreadful too, the dark Assassin hires: 30
Trade it may help, Society extend;
But lures the Pyrate, and corrupts the Friend:

It raises Armies in a Nation's aid,
But bribes a Senate, and the Land's betray'd.
    Oh! that such bulky Bribes as all might see,
Still, as of old, incumber'd Villainy!
In vain may Heroes fight, and Patriots rave;
If secret Gold saps on from knave to knave.
Could France or Rome divert our brave designs,
With all their brandies or with all their wines?   40
What could they more than Knights and Squires confound,
Or water all the Quorum ten miles round?
A Statesman's slumbers how this speech would spoil!
'Sir, Spain has sent a thousand jars of oil;
'Huge bales of British cloth blockade the door;
'A hundred oxen at your levee roar.'
    Poor Avarice one torment more would find;
Nor could Profusion squander all in kind.
Astride his cheese Sir Morgan might we meet,
And Worldly crying coals from street to street,   50
(Whom with a wig so wild, and mien so maz'd,
Pity mistakes for some poor tradesman craz'd).
Had Colepepper's whole wealth been hops and hogs,
Could he himself have sent it to the dogs?
His Grace will game: to White's a Bull be led,
With spurning heels and with a butting head.
To White's be carried, as to ancient games,
Fair Coursers, Vases, and alluring Dames.
Shall then Uxorio, if the stakes he sweep,
Bear home six Whores, and make his Lady weep?   60
Or soft Adonis, so perfum'd and fine,
Drive to St James's a whole herd of swine?
Oh filthy check on all industrious skill,
To spoil the nation's last great trade, Quadrille!
    Once, we confess, beneath the Patriot's cloak,
From the crack'd bag the dropping Guinea spoke,
And gingling down the back-stairs, told the crew,
'Old Cato is as great a Rogue as you.'
Blest paper-credit! last and best supply!
That lends Corruption lighter wings to fly!   70

87

Gold imp'd by thee, can compass hardest things,
Can pocket States, can fetch or carry Kings;
A single leaf shall waft an Army o'er,
Or ship off Senates to a distant Shore;
A leaf, like Sibyl's, scatter to and fro
Our fates and fortunes, as the winds shall blow:
Pregnant with thousands flits the Scrap unseen,
And silent sells a King, or buys a Queen.
   Since then, my Lord, on such a World we fall,
What say you? 'Say? Why take it, Gold and all.'   80
   What Riches give us let us then enquire:
Meat, Fire, and Cloaths. What more? Meat, Cloaths, and Fire.
Is this too little? would you more than live?
Alas! 'tis more than Turner finds they give.
Alas! 'tis more than (all his Visions past)
Unhappy Wharton, waking, found at last!
What can they give? to dying Hopkins Heirs;
To Chartres, Vigour; Japhet, Nose and Ears?
Can they, in gems bid pallid Hippia glow,
In Fulvia's buckle ease the throbs below,   90
Or heal, old Narses, thy obscener ail,
With all th'embroid'ry plaister'd at thy tail?
They might (were Harpax not too wise to spend)
Give Harpax self the blessing of a Friend;
Or find some Doctor that would save the life
Of wretched Shylock, spite of Shylock's Wife:
But thousands die, without or this or that,
Die, and endow a College, or a Cat:
To some, indeed, Heav'n grants the happier fate,
T'enrich a Bastard, or a Son they hate.   100
   Perhaps you think the Poor might have their part?
Bond damns the Poor, and hates them from his heart:
The grave Sir Gilbert holds it for a rule,
That 'every man in want is knave or fool:'
'God cannot love (says Blunt, with tearless eyes)
'The wretch he starves'—and piously denies:
But the good Bishop, with a meeker air,
Admits, and leaves them, Providence's care.

Yet, to be just to these poor men of pelf,
Each does but hate his Neighbour as himself: 110
Damn'd to the Mines, an equal fate betides
The Slave that digs it, and the Slave that hides.
Who suffer thus, mere Charity should own,
Must act on motives pow'rful, tho' unknown:
Some War, some Plague, or Famine they foresee,
Some Revelation hid from you and me.
Why Shylock wants a meal, the cause is found,
He thinks a Loaf will rise to fifty pound.
What made Directors cheat in South-sea year?
To live on Ven'son when it sold so dear.   120
Ask you why Phryne the whole Auction buys?
Phryne foresees a general Excise.
Why she and Sappho raise that monstrous sum?
Alas! they fear a man will cost a plum.
    Wise Peter sees the World's respect for Gold,
And therefore hopes this Nation may be sold:
Glorious Ambition! Peter, swell thy store,
And be what Rome's great Didius was before.
    The Crown of Poland, venal twice an age,
To just three millions stinted modest Gage.   130
But nobler scenes Maria's dreams unfold,
Hereditary Realms, and worlds of Gold.
Congenial souls! whose life one Av'rice joins,
And one fate buries in th'Asturian Mines.
    Much injur'd Blunt! why bears he Britain's hate?
A wizard told him in these words our fate:
'At length Corruption, like a gen'ral flood,
'(So long by watchful Ministers withstood)
'Shall deluge all; and Av'rice creeping on,
'Spread like a low-born mist, and blot the Sun;   140
'Statesman and Patriot ply alike the stocks,
'Peeress and Butler share alike the Box,
'And Judges job, and Bishops bite the town,
'And mighty Dukes pack cards for half a crown.
'See Britain sunk in lucre's sordid charms,
'And France reveng'd of ANNE's and EDWARD's arms!'

No mean Court-badge, great Scriv'ner! fir'd thy brain,
No lordly Luxury, nor City Gain:
No, 'twas thy righteous end, asham'd to see
Senates degen'rate, Patriots disagree,   150
And nobly wishing Party-rage to cease,
To buy both sides, and give thy Country peace.
   'All this is madness,' cries a sober sage:
But who, my friend, has reason in his rage?
   'The ruling Passion, be it what it will,
'The ruling Passion conquers Reason still.'
Less mad the wildest whimsey we can frame,
Than ev'n that Passion, if it has no Aim;
For tho' such motives Folly you may call,
The Folly's greater to have none at all.   160
   Hear then the truth: ' 'Tis Heav'n each Passion sends,
'And diff'rent men directs to diff'rent ends.
'Extremes in Nature equal good produce,
'Extremes in Man concur to gen'ral use.'
Ask we what makes one keep, and one bestow?
That Pow'r who bids the Ocean ebb and flow,
Bids seed-time, harvest, equal course maintain,
Thro' reconcil'd extremes of drought and rain,
Builds Life on Death, on Change Duration founds,
And gives th'eternal wheels to know their rounds.   170
   Riches, like insects, when conceal'd they lie,
Wait but for wings, and in their season, fly.
Who sees pale Mammon pine amidst his store,
Sees but a backward steward for the Poor;
This year a Reservoir, to keep and spare,
The next a Fountain, spouting thro' his Heir,
In lavish streams to quench a Country's thirst,
And men and dogs shall drink him 'till they burst.
   Old Cotta sham'd his fortune and his birth,
Yet was not Cotta void of wit or worth: 180
What tho' (the use of barb'rous spits forgot)
His kitchen vy'd in coolness with his grot?
His court with nettles, moats with cresses stor'd,
With soups unbought and sallads blest his board.

If Cotta liv'd on pulse, it was no more
Than Bramins, Saints, and Sages did before;
To cram the Rich was prodigal expence,
And who would take the Poor from Providence?
Like some lone Chartreux stands the good old Hall,
Silence without, and Fasts within the wall;   190
No rafter'd roofs with dance and tabor sound,
No noontide-bell invites the country round;
Tenants with sighs the smoakless tow'rs survey,
And turn th'unwilling steeds another way:
Benighted wanderers, the forest o'er,
Curse the sav'd candle, and unop'ning door;
While the gaunt mastiff growling at the gate,
Affrights the beggar whom he longs to eat.
    Not so his Son, he mark'd this oversight,
And then mistook reverse of wrong for right.   200
(For what to shun will no great knowledge need,
But what to follow, is a task indeed.)
What slaughter'd hecatombs, what floods of wine,
Fill the capacious Squire, and deep Divine!
Yet no mean motive this profusion draws,
His oxen perish in his country's cause;
'Tis GEORGE and LIBERTY that crowns the cup,
And Zeal for that great House which eats him up.
The woods recede around the naked seat,
The Sylvans groan—no matter—for the Fleet: 210
Next goes his Wool—to clothe our valiant bands,
Last, for his Country's love, he sells his Lands.
To town he comes, completes the nation's hope,
And heads the bold Train-bands, and burns a Pope.
And shall not Britain now reward his toils,
Britain, that pays her Patriots with her Spoils?
In vain at Court the Bankrupt pleads his cause,
His thankless Country leaves him to her Laws.
    The Sense to value Riches, with the Art
T'enjoy them, and the Virtue to impart,
Not meanly, nor ambitiously pursu'd,
Not sunk by sloth, nor rais'd by servitude;

To balance Fortune by a just expence,
Join with Œconomy, Magnificence;
With Splendor, Charity; with Plenty, Health;
Oh teach us, BATHURST! yet unspoil'd by wealth!
That secret rare, between th'extremes to move
Of mad Good-nature, and of mean Self-love.

　　To Worth or Want well-weigh'd, be Bounty giv'n,
And ease, or emulate, the care of Heav'n.　　　　　　　　230
Whose measure full o'erflows on human race,
Mend Fortune's fault, and justify her grace.
Wealth in the gross is death, but life diffus'd,
As Poison heals, in just proportion us'd:
In heaps, like Ambergrise, a stink it lies,
But well-dispers'd, is Incense to the Skies.

　　Who starves by Nobles, or with Nobles eats?
The Wretch that trusts them, and the Rogue that cheats.
Is there a Lord, who knows a cheerful noon
Without a Fiddler, Flatt'rer, or Buffoon?　　　　　　　　240
Whose table, Wit, or modest Merit share,
Un-elbow'd by a Gamester, Pimp, or Play'r?
Who copies Your's, or OXFORD's better part,
To ease th'oppress'd, and raise the sinking heart?
Where-e'er he shines, oh Fortune, gild the scene,
And Angels guard him in the golden Mean!
There, English Bounty yet a-while may stand,
And Honour linger ere it leaves the land.

　　But all our praises why should Lords engross?
Rise, honest Muse! and sing the MAN of ROSS:　　　　　　250
Pleas'd Vaga echoes thro' her winding bounds,
And rapid Severn hoarse applause resounds.
Who hung with woods yon mountain's sultry brow?
From the dry rock who bade the waters flow?
Not to the skies in useless columns tost,
Or in proud falls magnificently lost,
But clear and artless, pouring thro' the plain
Health to the sick, and solace to the swain.
Whose Cause-way parts the vale with shady rows?
Whose Seats the weary Traveller repose?　　　　　　　　260

Who taught that heav'n-directed spire to rise?
The MAN of Ross, each lisping babe replies.
Behold the Market-place with poor o'erspread!
The MAN of Ross divides the weekly bread:
Behold yon Alms-house, neat, but void of state,
Where Age and Want sit smiling at the gate:
Him portion'd maids, apprentic'd orphans blest,
The young who labour, and the old who rest.
Is any sick? the MAN of Ross relieves,
Prescribes, attends, the med'cine makes, and gives.   270
Is there a variance? enter but his door,
Balk'd are the Courts, and contest is no more.
Despairing Quacks with curses fled the place,
And vile Attornies, now an useless race.
     'Thrice happy man! enabled to pursue
'What all so wish, but want the pow'r to do!
'Oh say, what sums that gen'rous hand supply?
'What mines, to swell that boundless charity?'
     Of Debts, and Taxes, Wife and Children clear,
This man possest—five hundred pounds a year.   280
Blush, Grandeur, blush! proud Courts, withdraw your blaze!
Ye little Stars! hide your diminish'd rays.
     'And what? no monument, inscription, stone?
'His race, his form, his name almost unknown?'
Who builds a Church to God, and not to Fame,
Will never mark the marble with his Name:
Go, search it there, where to be born and die,
Of rich and poor makes all the history;
Enough, that Virtue fill'd the space between;
Prov'd, by the ends of being, to have been.   290
When Hopkins dies, a thousand lights attend
The wretch, who living sav'd a candle's end:
Should'ring God's altar a vile image stands,
Belies his features, nay extends his hands;
That live-long wig which Gorgon's self might own,
Eternal buckle takes in Parian stone.
Behold what blessings Wealth to life can lend!
And see, what comfort it affords our end.

In the worst inn's worst room, with mat half-hung,
The floors of plaister, and the walls of dung,   300
On once a flock-bed, but repair'd with straw,
With tape-ty'd curtains, never meant to draw,
The George and Garter dangling from that bed
Where tawdry yellow strove with dirty red,
Great Villiers lies—alas! how chang'd from him,
That life of pleasure, and that soul of whim!
Gallant and gay, in Cliveden's proud alcove,
The bow'r of wanton Shrewsbury and love;
Or just as gay, at Council, in a ring
Of mimick'd Statesmen, and their merry King.   310
No Wit to flatter, left of all his store!
No Fool to laugh at, which he valu'd more.
There, Victor of his health, of fortune, friends,
And fame; this lord of useless thousands ends.

His Grace's fate sage Cutler could foresee,
And well (he thought) advis'd him, 'Live like me.'
As well his Grace reply'd, 'Like you, Sir John?
'That I can do, when all I have is gone.'
Resolve me, Reason, which of these is worse,
Want with a full, or with an empty purse?   320
Thy life more wretched, Cutler, was confess'd,
Arise, and tell me, was thy death more bless'd?
Cutler saw tenants break, and houses fall,
For very want; he could not build a wall.
His only daughter in a stranger's pow'r,
For very want; he could not pay a dow'r.
A few grey hairs, his rev'rend temples crown'd,
'Twas very want that sold them for two pound.
What ev'n deny'd a cordial at his end,
Banish'd the doctor, and expell'd the friend?   330
What but a want, which you perhaps think mad,
Yet numbers feel, the want of what he had.
Cutler and Brutus, dying both exclaim,
'Virtue! and Wealth! what are ye but a name!'

Say, for such worth are other worlds prepar'd?
Or are they both, in this their own reward?

94

A knotty point! to which we now proceed.
But you are tir'd—I'll tell a tale. 'Agreed.'
   Where London's column, pointing at the skies,
Like a tall bully, lifts the head, and lyes;   340
There dwelt a Citizen of sober fame,
A plain good man, and Balaam was his name;
Religious, punctual, frugal, and so forth;
His word would pass for more than he was worth.
One solid dish his week-day meal affords,
An added pudding solemniz'd the Lord's:
Constant at Church, and Change; his gains were sure,
His givings rare, save farthings to the poor.
   The Dev'l was piqu'd such saintship to behold,
And long'd to tempt him like good Job of old: 350
But Satan now is wiser than of yore,
And tempts by making rich, not making poor.
   Rouz'd by the Prince of Air, the whirlwinds sweep
The surge, and plunge his Father in the deep;
Then full against his Cornish lands they roar,
And two rich ship-wrecks bless the lucky shore.
   Sir Balaam now, he lives like other folks,
He takes his chirping pint, and cracks his jokes:
'Live like yourself,' was soon my Lady's word;
And lo! two puddings smoak'd upon the board.   360
   Asleep and naked as an Indian lay,
An honest factor stole a Gem away:
He pledg'd it to the knight; the knight had wit,
So kept the Diamond, and the rogue was bit.
Some scruple rose, but thus he eas'd his thought,
'I'll now give six-pence where I gave a groat,
'Where once I went to church, I'll now go twice—
'And am so clear too of all other vice.'
   The Tempter saw his time; the work he ply'd;
Stocks and Subscriptions pour on ev'ry side,   370
'Till all the Dæmon makes his full descent,
In one abundant show'r of Cent. per Cent.,
Sinks deep within him, and possesses whole,
Then dubs Director, and secures his soul.

Behold Sir Balaam, now a man of spirit,
Ascribes his gettings to his parts and merit,
What late he call'd a Blessing, now was Wit,
And God's good Providence, a lucky Hit.
Things change their titles, as our manners turn:
His Compting-house employ'd the Sunday-morn;   380
Seldom at Church ('twas such a busy life)
But duly sent his family and wife.
There (so the Dev'l ordain'd) one Christmas-tide
My good old Lady catch'd a cold, and dy'd.
  A Nymph of Quality admires our Knight;
He marries, bows at Court, and grows polite:
Leaves the dull Cits, and joins (to please the fair)
The well-bred cuckolds in St James's air:
First, for his Son a gay Commission buys,
Who drinks, whores, fights, and in a duel dies: 390
His daughter flaunts a Viscount's tawdry wife;
She bears a Coronet and P—x for life.
In Britain's Senate he a seat obtains,
And one more Pensioner St Stephen gains.
My Lady falls to play; so bad her chance,
He must repair it; takes a bribe from France;
The House impeach him; Coningsby harangues;
The Court forsake him, and Sir Balaam hangs:
Wife, son, and daughter, Satan, are thy own,
His wealth, yet dearer, forfeit to the Crown: 400
The Devil and the King divide the prize,
And sad Sir Balaam curses God and dies.

EPISTLE IV

TO RICHARD BOYLE, EARL OF BURLINGTON

'Tis strange, the Miser should his Cares employ,
To gain those Riches he can ne'er enjoy:
Is it less strange, the Prodigal should waste
His wealth, to purchase what he ne'er can taste?

Not for himself he sees, or hears, or eats;
Artists must chuse his Pictures, Music, Meats:
He buys for Topham, Drawings and Designs,
For Pembroke Statues, dirty Gods, and Coins;
Rare monkish Manuscripts for Hearne alone,
And Books for Mead, and Butterflies for Sloane.   10
Think we all these are for himself? no more
Than his fine Wife, alas! or finer Whore.
    For what has Virro painted, built, and planted?
Only to show, how many Tastes he wanted.
What brought Sir Visto's ill got wealth to waste?
Some Dæmon whisper'd, 'Visto! have a Taste.'
Heav'n visits with a Taste the wealthy fool,
And needs no Rod but Ripley with a Rule.
See! sportive fate, to punish aukward pride,
Bids Bubo build, and sends him such a Guide: 20
A standing sermon, at each year's expense,
That never Coxcomb reach'd Magnificence!
    You show us, Rome was glorious, not profuse,
And pompous buildings once were things of Use.
Yet shall (my Lord) your just, your noble rules
Fill half the land with Imitating Fools;
Who random drawings from your sheets shall take,
And of one beauty many blunders make;
Load some vain Church with old Theatric state,
Turn Arcs of triumph to a Garden-gate;   30
Reverse your Ornaments, and hang them all
On some patch'd dog-hole ek'd with ends of wall,
Then clap four slices of Pilaster on't,
That, lac'd with bits of rustic, makes a Front.
Or call the winds thro' long Arcades to roar,
Proud to catch cold at a Venetian door;
Conscious they act a true Palladian part,
And if they starve, they starve by rules of art.
    Oft have you hinted to your brother Peer,
A certain truth, which many buy too dear: 40
Something there is more needful than Expence,
And something previous ev'n to Taste—'tis Sense:

Good Sense, which only is the gift of Heav'n,
And tho' no science, fairly worth the sev'n:
A Light, which in yourself you must perceive;
Jones and Le Nôtre have it not to give.

To build, to plant, whatever you intend,
To rear the Column, or the Arch to bend,
To swell the Terras, or to sink the Grot;
In all, let Nature never be forgot. ·   50
But treat the Goddess like a modest fair,
Nor over-dress, nor leave her wholly bare; ·
Let not each beauty ev'ry where be spy'd,
Where half the skill is decently to hide.
He gains all points, who pleasingly confounds,
Surprizes, varies, and conceals the Bounds.

Consult the Genius of the Place in all;
That tells the Waters or to rise, or fall,
Or helps th'ambitious Hill the heav'n to scale,
Or scoops in circling theatres the Vale,   60
Calls in the Country, catches opening glades,
Joins willing woods, and varies shades from shades,
Now breaks, or now directs, th'intending Lines;
Paints as you plant, and, as you work, designs.

Still follow Sense, of ev'ry Art the Soul,
Parts answ'ring parts shall slide into a whole,
Spontaneous beauties all around advance,
Start ev'n from Difficulty, strike from Chance;
Nature shall join you, Time shall make it grow
A Work to wonder at—perhaps a STOW.   70

Without it, proud Versailles! thy glory falls;
And Nero's Terraces desert their walls:
The vast Parterres a thousand hands shall make,
Lo! COBHAM comes, and floats them with a Lake:
Or cut wide views thro' Mountains to the Plain,
You'll wish your hill or shelter'd seat again.
Ev'n in an ornament its place remark,
Nor in an Hermitage set Dr Clarke.

Behold Villario's ten-years toil compleat;
His Quincunx darkens, his Espaliers meet,   80

The Wood supports the Plain, the parts unite,
And strength of Shade contends with strength of Light;
A waving Glow his bloomy beds display,
Blushing in bright diversities of day,
With silver-quiv'ring rills mæander'd o'er—
Enjoy them, you! Villario can no more;
Tir'd of the scene Parterres and Fountains yield,
He finds at last he better likes a Field.

    Thro' his young Woods how pleas'd Sabinus stray'd,
Or sat delighted in the thick'ning shade,   90
With annual joy the red'ning shoots to greet,
Or see the stretching branches long to meet!
His Son's fine Taste an op'ner Vista loves,
Foe to the Dryads of his Father's groves,
One boundless Green, or flourish'd Carpet views,
With all the mournful family of Yews;
The thriving plants ignoble broomsticks made,
Now sweep those Alleys they were born to shade.

    At Timon's Villa let us pass a day,
Where all cry out, 'What sums are thrown away!'   100
So proud, so grand, of that stupendous air,
Soft and Agreeable come never there.
Greatness, with Timon, dwells in such a draught
As brings all Brobdignag before your thought.
To compass this, his building is a Town,
His pond an Ocean, his parterre a Down:
Who but must laugh, the Master when he sees,
A puny insect, shiv'ring at a breeze!
Lo, what huge heaps of littleness around!
The whole, a labour'd Quarry above ground.   110
Two Cupids squirt before: a Lake behind
Improves the keenness of the Northern wind.
His Gardens next your admiration call,
On ev'ry side you look, behold the Wall!
No pleasing Intricacies intervene,
No artful wildness to perplex the scene;
Grove nods at grove, each Alley has a brother,
And half the platform just reflects the other.

The suff'ring eye inverted Nature sees,
Trees cut to Statues, Statues thick as trees,   120
With here a Fountain, never to be play'd,
And there a Summer-house, that knows no shade;
Here Amphitrite sails thro' myrtle bow'rs;
There Gladiators fight, or die, in flow'rs;
Un-water'd see the drooping sea-horse mourn,
And swallows roost in Nilus' dusty Urn.

 My Lord advances with majestic mien,
Smit with the mighty pleasure, to be seen:
But soft—by regular approach—not yet—
First thro' the length of yon hot Terrace sweat,   130
And when up ten steep slopes you've dragg'd your thighs,
Just at his Study-door he'll bless your eyes.
His Study! with what Authors is it stor'd?
In Books, not Authors, curious is my Lord;
To all their dated Backs he turns you round,
These Aldus printed, those Du Suëil has bound.
Lo some are Vellom, and the rest as good
For all his Lordship knows, but they are Wood.
For Locke or Milton 'tis in vain to look,
These shelves admit not any modern book.   140

 And now the Chapel's silver bell you hear,
That summons you to all the Pride of Pray'r:
Light quirks of Musick, broken and uneven,
Make the soul dance upon a Jig to Heaven.
On painted Cielings you devoutly stare,
Where sprawl the Saints of Verrio or Laguerre,
On gilded clouds in fair expansion lie,
And bring all Paradise before your eye.
To rest, the Cushion and soft Dean invite,
Who never mentions Hell to ears polite.   150

 But hark! the chiming Clocks to dinner call;
A hundred footsteps scrape the marble Hall:
The rich Buffet well-colour'd Serpents grace,
And gaping Tritons spew to wash your face.
Is this a dinner? this a Genial room?
No, 'tis a Temple, and a Hecatomb.

A solemn Sacrifice, perform'd in state,
You drink by measure, and to minutes eat.
So quick retires each flying course, you'd swear
Sancho's dread Doctor and his Wand were there.   160
Between each Act the trembling salvers ring,
From soup to sweet-wine, and God bless the King.
In plenty starving, tantaliz'd in state,
And complaisantly help'd to all I hate,
Treated, caress'd, and tir'd, I take my leave,
Sick of his civil Pride from Morn to Eve;
I curse such lavish cost, and little skill,
And swear no Day was ever past so ill.

    Yet hence the Poor are cloath'd, the Hungry fed;
Health to himself, and to his Infants bread   170
The Lab'rer bears: What his hard Heart denies,
His charitable Vanity supplies.

    Another age shall see the golden Ear
Imbrown the Slope, and nod on the Parterre,
Deep Harvests bury all his pride has plann'd,
And laughing Ceres re-assume the land.

    Who then shall grace, or who improve the Soil?
Who plants like BATHURST, or who builds like BOYLE.
'Tis Use alone that sanctifies Expence,
And Splendor borrows all her rays from Sense.   180

    His Father's Acres who enjoys in peace,
Or makes his Neighbours glad, if he encrease;
Whose chearful Tenants bless their yearly toil,
Yet to their Lord owe more than to the soil;
Whose ample Lawns are not asham'd to feed
The milky heifer and deserving steed;
Whose rising Forests, not for pride or show,
But future Buildings, future Navies grow;
Let his plantations stretch from down to down,
First shade a Country, and then raise a Town.   190

    You too proceed! make falling Arts your care,
Erect new wonders, and the old repair,
Jones and Palladio to themselves restore,
And be whate'er Vitruvius was before:

Till Kings call forth th'Idea's of your mind,
Proud to accomplish what such hands design'd,
Bid Harbors open, public Ways extend,
Bid Temples, worthier of the God, ascend;
Bid the broad Arch the dang'rous Flood contain,
The Mole projected break the roaring Main;   200
Back to his bounds their subject Sea command,
And roll obedient Rivers thro' the Land;
These Honours, Peace to happy Britain brings,
These are Imperial Works, and worthy Kings.

IMITATIONS OF HORACE

The First Satire of the Second Book of Horace

TO MR FORTESCUE

P. There are (I scarce can think it, but am told)
There are to whom my Satire seems too bold,
Scarce to wise *Peter* complaisant enough,
And something said of *Chartres* much too rough.
The Lines are weak, another's pleased to say,
Lord *Fanny* spins a thousand such a Day.
Tim'rous by Nature, of the Rich in awe,
I come to Council learned in the Law.
You'll give me, like a Friend both sage and free,
Advice; and (as you use) without a Fee.   10
   F. I'd write no more.
                    P. Not write? but then I *think*,
And for my Soul I cannot sleep a wink.
I nod in Company, I wake at Night,
Fools rush into my Head, and so I write.
   F. You could not do a worse thing for your Life.
Why, if the Nights seem tedious—take a Wife;
Or rather truly, if your Point be Rest,
Lettuce and Cowslip Wine; *Probatum est.*
But talk with *Celsus, Celsus* will advise
Hartshorn, or something that shall close your Eyes.   20
Of if you needs must write, write Cæsar's Praise:
You'll gain at least a *Knighthood*, or the *Bays.*
   P. What? like Sir *Richard*, rumbling, rough and fierce,
With Arms, and George, and Brunswick crowd the Verse?
Rend with tremendous Sound your ears asunder,
With Gun, Drum, Trumpet, Blunderbuss & Thunder?
Or nobly wild, with *Budgell's* Fire and Force,

Paint Angels trembling round his *falling Horse*?

    F. Then all your Muse's softer Art display,
Let *Carolina* smooth the tuneful Lay,   30
Lull with *Amelia's* liquid Name the Nine,
And sweetly flow through all the Royal Line.

    P. Alas! few Verses touch their nicer Ear;
They scarce can bear their *Laureate* twice a Year:
And justly CÆSAR scorns the Poet's Lays,
It is to *History* he trusts for Praise.

    F. Better be *Cibber*, I'll maintain it still,
Than ridicule all *Taste*, blaspheme *Quadrille*,
Abuse the City's best good Men in Metre,
And laugh at Peers that put their trust in *Peter*.   40
Ev'n those you touch not, hate you.

                              P. What should ail 'em?

    F. A hundred smart in *Timon* and in *Balaam*:
The fewer still you name, you wound the more;
Bond is but one, but *Harpax* is a Score.

    P. Each Mortal has his Pleasure: None deny
Scarsdale his Bottle, *Darty* his Ham-Pye;
Ridotta sips and dances, till she see
The doubling Lustres dance as fast as she;
F(ox) loves the *Senate*, *Hockley-Hole* his Brother
Like in all else, as one Egg to another.   50
I love to pour out all myself, as plain
As downright *Shippen*, or as old *Montagne*.
In them, as certain to be lov'd as seen,
The Soul stood forth, nor kept a Thought within;
In me what Spots (for Spots I have) appear,
Will prove at least the Medium must be clear.
In this impartial Glass, my Muse intends
Fair to expose myself, my Foes, my Friends;
Publish the present Age, but where my Text
Is Vice too high, reserve it for the next: 60
My Foes shall wish my Life a longer date,
And ev'ry Friend the less lament my Fate.

    My Head and Heart thus flowing thro' my Quill,
Verse-man or Prose-man, term me which you will,

Papist or Protestant, or both between,
Like good *Erasmus* in an honest Mean,
In Moderation placing all my Glory,
While Tories call me Whig, and Whigs a Tory.
    Satire's my Weapon, but I'm too discreet
To run a Muck, and tilt at all I meet;   70
I only wear it in a Land of Hectors,
Thieves, Supercargoes, Sharpers, and Directors.
Save but our *Army*! and let *Jove* incrust
Swords, Pikes, and Guns with everlasting Rust!
Peace is my dear Delight—not *Fleury's* more:
But touch me, and no Minister so sore.
Who-e'er offends, at some unlucky Time
Slides into Verse, and hitches in a Rhyme,
Sacred to Ridicule! his whole Life long,
And the sad Burthen of some merry Song.   80
    Slander or Poyson, dread from *Delia's* Rage,
Hard Words or Hanging, if your Judge be *Page*.
From furious *Sappho* scarce a milder Fate,
P—x'd by her Love, or libell'd by her Hate:
Its proper Pow'r to hurt, each Creature feels,
Bulls aim their horns, and Asses lift their heels,
'Tis a Bear's Talent not to kick, but hug,
And no man wonders he's not stung by Pug:
So drink with *Waters*, or with *Chartres* eat,
They'll never poison you, they'll only cheat.   90
    Then learned Sir! (to cut the Matter short)
Whate'er my Fate, or well or ill at Court,
Whether old Age, with faint, but chearful Ray,
Attends to gild the Evening of my Day,
Or Death's black Wing already be display'd
To wrap me in the Universal Shade;
Whether the darken'd Room to muse invite,
Or whiten'd Wall provoke the Skew'r to write,
In Durance, Exile, Bedlam, or the Mint,
Like *Lee* or *Budgell*, I will Rhyme and Print.   100
    F. Alas young Man! your Days can ne'er be long,
In Flow'r of Age you perish for a Song!

Plums, and Directors, *Shylock* and his Wife,
Will club their Testers, now, to take your Life!
    P. What? arm'd for *Virtue* when I point the Pen,
Brand the bold Front of shameless, guilty Men,
Dash the proud Gamester in his gilded Car,
Bare the mean Heart that lurks beneath a Star;
Can there be wanting to defend Her Cause,
Lights of the Church, or Guardians of the Laws?   110
Could pension'd *Boileau* lash in honest Strain
Flatt'rers and Bigots ev'n in *Louis*' Reign?
Could Laureate *Dryden* Pimp and Fry'r engage,
Yet neither *Charles* nor *James* be in a Rage?
And I not strip the Gilding off a Knave,
Un-plac'd, un-pension'd, no Man's Heir, or Slave?
I will, or perish in the gen'rous Cause.
Hear this, and tremble! you, who 'scape the Laws.
Yes, while I live, no rich or noble knave
Shall walk the World, in credit, to his grave.   120
To VIRTUE ONLY and HER FRIENDS, A FRIEND,
The World beside may murmur, or commend.
Know, all the distant Din that World can keep
Rolls o'er my *Grotto*, and but sooths my Sleep.
There, my Retreat the best Companions grace,
Chiefs, out of War, and Statesmen, out of Place.
There *St John* mingles with my friendly Bowl,
The Feast of Reason and the Flow of Soul:
And He, whose Lightning pierc'd th'*Iberian* Lines,
Now, forms my Quincunx, and now ranks my Vines,   130
Or tames the Genius of the stubborn Plain,
Almost as quickly as he conquer'd *Spain*.
    Envy must own, I live among the Great,
No Pimp of Pleasure, and no Spy of State,
With Eyes that pry not, Tongue that ne'er repeats,
Fond to spread Friendships, but to cover Heats,
To help who want, to forward who excel;
This, all who know me, know; who love me, tell;
And who unknown defame me, let them be
Scriblers or Peers, alike are *Mob* to me.   140

This is my Plea, on this I rest my Cause—
What saith my Council learned in the Laws?
   F. Your Plea is good. But still I say, beware!
Laws are explain'd by Men—so have a care.
It stands on record, that in *Richard's* Times
A Man was hang'd for very honest Rhymes.
Consult the Statute: *quart.* I think it is,
Edwardi Sext. or *prim. & quint. Eliz:*
See *Libels, Satires*—here you have it—read.
   P. Libels and *Satires!* lawless Things indeed!   150
But grave *Epistles*, bringing Vice to light,
Such as a *King* might read, a *Bishop* write,
Such as Sir *Robert* would approve—
                        F. Indeed?
The Case is alter'd—you may then proceed.
In such a Cause the Plaintiff will be hiss'd,
My Lords the Judges laugh, and you're dismiss'd.

The Second Satire of the Second Book of Horace

TO MR BETHEL

   What, and how great, the Virtue and the Art
To live on little with a chearful heart,
(A Doctrine sage, but truly none of mine)
Lets talk, my friends, but talk before we dine:
Not when a gilt Buffet's reflected pride
Turns you from sound Philosophy aside;
Not when from Plate to Plate your eyeballs roll,
And the brain dances to the mantling bowl.
   Hear Bethel's Sermon, one not vers'd in schools,
But strong in sense, and wise without the rules.   10
   Go work, hunt, exercise! (he thus began)
Then scorn a homely dinner, if you can.
Your wine lock'd up, your Butler stroll'd abroad,
Or fish deny'd, (the River yet un-thaw'd)

If then plain Bread and milk will do the feat,
The pleasure lies in *you*, and not the meat.
Preach as I please, I doubt our curious men
Will chuse a *Pheasant* still before a *Hen*;
Yet Hens of *Guinea* full as good I hold,
Except you eat the feathers, green and gold.   20
Of *Carps* and *Mullets* why prefer the *great*,
(Tho' cut in pieces ere my Lord can eat)
Yet for *small Turbots* such esteem profess?
Because God made these large, the other less.

   Oldfield, with more than Harpy throat endu'd,
Cries, 'Send me, Gods! a whole Hog *barbecu'd!*'
Oh blast it, South-winds! till a stench exhale,
Rank as the ripeness of a Rabbit's tail.
By what *Criterion* do ye eat, d'ye think,
If this is priz'd for *sweetness*, that for *stink*?   30
When the tir'd Glutton labours thro' a Treat,
He finds no relish in the sweetest Meat;
He calls for something bitter, something sour,
And the rich feast concludes extremely poor:
Cheap eggs, and herbs, and olives still we see,
Thus much is left of old Simplicity!

   The *Robin-red-breast* till of late had rest,
And children sacred held a *Martin's* nest,
Till *Becca-ficos* sold so dev'lish dear
To one that was, or would have been a Peer.   40
Let me extol a *Cat* on Oysters fed,
I'll have a Party at the *Bedford Head*,
Or ev'n to crack live *Crawfish* recommend,
I'd never doubt at Court to make a Friend.

   'Tis yet in vain, I own, to keep a pother
About one Vice, and fall into the other:
Between Excess and Famine lies a mean,
Plain, but not sordid, tho' not splendid, clean.
Avidien or his Wife (no matter which,
For him you'll call a dog, and her a bitch)   50
Sell their presented Partridges, and Fruits,
And humbly live on rabbits and on roots:

One half-pint bottle serves them both to dine,
And is at once their vinegar and wine.
But on some lucky day (as when they found
A lost Bank-bill, or heard their Son was drown'd)
At such a feast old vinegar to spare,
Is what two souls so gen'rous cannot bear;
Oyl, tho' it stink, they drop by drop impart,
But sowse the Cabbidge with a bounteous heart. 60

   He knows to live, who keeps the middle state,
And neither leans on this side, nor on that:
Nor stops, for one bad Cork, his Butler's pay,
Swears, like Albutius, a good Cook away;
Nor lets, like Nævius, ev'ry error pass,
The musty wine, foul cloth, or greasy glass.

   Now hear what blessings Temperance can bring:
(Thus said our Friend, and what he said I sing.)
First Health: The stomach (cram'd from ev'ry dish,
A Tomb of boil'd, and roast, and flesh, and fish, 70
Where Bile, and wind, and phlegm, and acid jar,
And all the Man is one intestine war)
Remembers oft the School-boy's simple fare,
The temp'rate sleeps, and spirits light as air!

   How pale, each Worshipful and rev'rend Guest
Rise from a Clergy, or a City, feast!
What life in all that ample Body, say,
What heav'nly Particle inspires the clay?
The Soul subsides; and wickedly inclines
To seem but mortal, ev'n in sound Divines. 80
On morning wings how active springs the Mind,
That leaves the load of yesterday behind?
How easy ev'ry labour it pursues?
How coming to the Poet ev'ry Muse?
Not but we may exceed, some Holy time,
Or tir'd in search of Truth, or search of Rhyme.
Ill Health some just indulgence may engage,
And more, the Sickness of long Life, Old-age:
For fainting Age what cordial drop remains,
If our intemp'rate Youth the Vessel drains? 90

Our Fathers prais'd rank Ven'son. You suppose
Perhaps, young men! our Fathers had no nose?
Not so: a Buck was then a week's repast,
And 'twas their point, I ween, to make it last:
More pleas'd to keep it till their friends could come
Than eat the sweetest by themselves at home.
Why had not I in those good times my birth,
E're Coxcomb-pyes or Coxcombs were on earth?
   Unworthy He, the voice of Fame to hear,
(That sweetest Music to an honest ear;   100
For 'faith Lord Fanny! you are in the wrong,
The World's good word is better than a Song)
Who has not learn'd, fresh Sturgeon and Ham-pye
Are no rewards for Want, and Infamy!
When Luxury has lick'd up all thy pelf,
Curs'd by thy neighbours, thy Trustees, thy self,
To friends, to fortune, to mankind a shame,
Think how Posterity will treat thy name;
And buy a Rope, that future times may tell
Thou hast at least bestow'd one penny well.   110
   'Right, cries his Lordship, for a Rogue in need
'To have a Taste, is Insolence indeed:
'In me 'tis noble, suits my birth and state,
'My wealth unwieldy, and my heap too great.'
Then, like the Sun, let Bounty spread her ray,
And shine that Superfluity away.
Oh Impudence of wealth! with all thy store,
How dar'st thou let one worthy man be poor?
Shall half the new-built Churches round thee fall?
Make Keys, build Bridges, or repair White-hall: 120
Or to thy Country let that heap be lent,
As M(arlbor)o's was, but not at five *per Cent*.
   Who thinks that Fortune cannot change her mind,
Prepares a dreadful Jest for all mankind!
And who stands safest, tell me? is it he
That spreads and swells in puff'd Prosperity,
Or blest with little, whose preventing care
In Peace provides fit arms against a War?

Thus Bethel spoke, who always speaks his thought,
And always thinks the very thing he ought: 130
His equal mind I copy what I can,
And as I love, would imitate the Man.
In *South-sea* days not happier, when surmis'd
The Lord of thousands, than if now *Excis'd*;
In Forest planted by a Father's hand,
Than in five acres now of rented land.
Content with little, I can piddle here
On Broccoli and mutton, round the year;
But ancient friends, (tho' poor, or out of play)
That touch my Bell, I cannot turn away.   140
'Tis true, no Turbots dignify my boards,
But gudgeons, flounders, what my Thames affords.
To Hounslow-heath I point, and Bansted-down,
Thence comes your mutton, and these chicks my own:
From yon old wallnut-tree a show'r shall fall;
And grapes, long-lingring on my only wall,
And figs, from standard and Espalier join:
The dev'l is in you if you cannot dine.
Then chearful healths (your Mistress shall have place)
And, what's more rare, a Poet shall say *Grace*.   150
Fortune not much of humbling me can boast;
Tho' double-tax'd, how little have I lost?
My Life's amusements have been just the same,
Before, and after Standing Armies came.
My lands are sold, my Father's house is gone;
I'll hire another's, is not that my own,
And yours my friends? thro' whose free-opening gate
None comes too early, none departs too late;
(For I, who hold sage Homer's rule the best,
Welcome the coming, speed the going guest.)   160
'Pray heav'n it last! (cries Swift) as you go on;
'I wish to God this house had been your own:
'Pity! to build, without a son or wife:
'Why, you'll enjoy it only all your life.'—
Well, if the Use be mine, can it concern one
Whether the Name belong to Pope or Vernon?

What's *Property?* dear Swift! you see it alter
From you to me, from me to Peter Walter,
Or, in a mortgage, prove a Lawyer's share,
Or, in a jointure, vanish from the Heir,   170
Or in pure Equity (the Case not clear)
The Chanc'ry takes your rents for twenty year:
At best, it falls to some ungracious Son
Who cries, my father's damn'd, and all's my own.
Shades, that to Bacon could retreat afford,
Become the portion of a booby Lord;
And Hemsley once proud Buckingham's delight,
Slides to a Scriv'ner or a City Knight.
Let Lands and Houses have what Lords they will,
Let Us be fix'd, and our own Masters still.   180

AN EPISTLE TO DR ARBUTHNOT

Shut, shut the door, good *John!* fatigu'd I said,
Tye up the knocker, say I'm sick, I'm dead,
The Dog-star rages! nay 'tis past a doubt,
All *Bedlam*, or *Parnassus*, is let out:
Fire in each eye, and Papers in each hand,
They rave, recite, and madden round the land.
    What Walls can guard me, or what Shades can hide?
They pierce my Thickets, thro' my Grot they glide,
By land, by water, they renew the charge,
They stop the Chariot, and they board the Barge.   10
No place is sacred, not the Church is free,
Ev'n *Sunday* shines no *Sabbath-day* to me:
Then from the *Mint* walks forth the Man of Ryme,
Happy! to catch me, just at Dinner-time.
    Is there a Parson, much be-mus'd in Beer,
A maudlin Poetess, a ryming Peer,
A Clerk, foredoom'd his Father's soul to cross,
Who pens a Stanza when he should *engross?*
Is there, who lock'd from Ink and Paper, scrawls
With desp'rate Charcoal round his darken'd walls?   20

All fly to *Twit'nam*, and in humble strain
Apply to me, to keep them mad or vain.
Arthur, whose giddy Son neglects the Laws,
Imputes to me and my damn'd works the cause:
Poor *Cornus* sees his frantic Wife elope,
And curses Wit, and Poetry, and *Pope*.

    Friend to my Life, (which did not you prolong,
The World had wanted many an idle Song)
What *Drop* or *Nostrum* can this Plague remove?
Or which must end me, a Fool's Wrath or Love?   30
A dire Dilemma! either way I'm sped,
If Foes, they write, if Friends, they read me dead.
Seiz'd and ty'd down to judge, how wretched I!
Who can't be silent, and who will not lye;
To laugh, were want of Goodness and of Grace,
And to be grave, exceeds all Pow'r of Face.
I sit with sad Civility, I read
With honest anguish, and an aking head;
And drop at last, but in unwilling ears,
This saving counsel, 'Keep your Piece nine years.'   40

    Nine years! cries he, who high in *Drury-lane*
Lull'd by soft Zephyrs thro' the broken Pane,
Rymes e're he wakes, and prints before *Term* ends,
Oblig'd by hunger and Request of friends:
'The Piece you think is incorrect: why take it,
'I'm all submission, what you'd have it, make it.'

    Three things another's modest wishes bound,
My Friendship, and a Prologue, and ten Pound.

    Pitholeon sends to me: 'You know his Grace,
'I want a Patron; ask him for a Place.'   50
Pitholeon libell'd me—'but here's a Letter
'Informs you Sir, 'twas when he knew no better.
'Dare you refuse him? *Curl* invites to dine,
'He'll write a *Journal*, or he'll turn *Divine*.'

    Bless me! a Packet.—' 'Tis a stranger sues,
'A Virgin Tragedy, an Orphan Muse.'
If I dislike it, 'Furies, death and rage!'
If I approve, 'Commend it to the Stage.'

There (thank my Stars) my whole Commission ends,
The Play'rs and I are, luckily, no friends.   60
Fir'd that the House reject him, ' 'Sdeath I'll print it
'And shame the Fools—your Int'rest, Sir, with *Lintot.*'
Lintot, dull rogue! will think your price too much.
'Not Sir, if you revise it, and retouch.'
All my demurrs but double his attacks,
At last he whispers 'Do, and we go snacks.'
Glad of a quarrel, strait I clap the door,
Sir, let me see your works and you no more.

'Tis sung, when *Midas*' Ears began to spring,
(*Midas*, a sacred Person, and a King)   70
His very Minister who spy'd them first,
(Some say his Queen) was forc'd to speak, or burst.
And is not mine, my Friend, a sorer case,
When ev'ry Coxcomb perks them in my face?
'Good friend forbear! you deal in dang'rous things,
'I'd never name Queens, Ministers, or Kings;
'Keep close to Ears, and those let Asses prick,
''Tis nothing'—Nothing? if they bite and kick?
Out with it, *Dunciad*! let the secret pass,
That Secret to each Fool, that he's an Ass: 80
The truth once told, (and wherefore shou'd we lie?)
The Queen of *Midas* slept, and so may I.

You think this cruel? take it for a rule,
No creature smarts so little as a Fool.
Let Peals of Laughter, *Codrus*! round thee break,
Thou unconcern'd canst hear the mighty Crack.
Pit, Box and Gall'ry in convulsions hurl'd,
Thou stand'st unshook amidst a bursting World.
Who shames a Scribler? break one cobweb thro',
He spins the slight, self-pleasing thread anew;   90
Destroy his Fib, or Sophistry; in vain,
The Creature's at his dirty work again;
Thron'd in the Centre of his thin designs;
Proud of a vast Extent of flimzy lines.
Whom have I hurt? has Poet yet, or Peer,
Lost the arch'd eye-brow, or *Parnassian* sneer?

And has not *Colly* still his Lord, and Whore?
His Butchers *Henley*, his Free-masons *Moor*?
Does not one Table *Bavius* still admit?
Still to one Bishop *Philips* seem a Wit?   100
Still *Sapho*—'Hold! for God-sake—you'll offend:
'No Names—be calm—learn Prudence of a Friend:
'I too could write, and I am twice as tall,
'But Foes like these!'—One Flatt'rer's worse than all;
Of all mad Creatures, if the Learn'd are right,
It is the Slaver kills, and not the Bite.
A Fool quite angry is quite innocent;
Alas! 'tis ten times worse when they *repent*.

One dedicates, in high Heroic prose,
And ridicules beyond a hundred foes;   110
One from all *Grubstreet* will my fame defend,
And, more abusive, calls himself my friend.
This prints my Letters, that expects a Bribe,
And others roar aloud, 'Subscribe, subscribe.'
There are, who to my Person pay their court,
I cough like *Horace*, and tho' lean, am short,
Ammon's great Son one shoulder had too high,
Such *Ovid's* nose, and 'Sir! you have an *Eye*—'
Go on, obliging Creatures, make me see
All that disgrac'd my Betters, met in me: 120
Say for my comfort, languishing in bed,
'Just so immortal *Maro* held his head:'
And when I die, be sure you let me know
Great *Homer* dy'd three thousand years ago.

Why did I write? what sin to me unknown
Dipt me in Ink, my Parents', or my own?
As yet a Child, nor yet a Fool to Fame,
I lisp'd in Numbers, for the Numbers came.
I left no Calling for this idle trade,
No Duty broke, no Father dis-obey'd.   130
The Muse but serv'd to ease some Friend, not Wife,
To help me thro' this long Disease, my Life,

To second, ARBUTHNOT! thy Art and Care,
And teach, the Being you preserv'd, to bear.

But why then publish? *Granville* the polite,
And knowing *Walsh*, would tell me I could write;
Well-natur'd *Garth* inflam'd with early praise,
And *Congreve* lov'd, and *Swift* endur'd my Lays;
The Courtly *Talbot, Somers, Sheffield* read,
Ev'n mitred *Rochester* would nod the head,   140
And *St John's* self (great *Dryden's* friends before)
With open arms receiv'd one Poet more.
Happy my Studies, when by these approv'd!
Happier their Author, when by these belov'd!
From these the world will judge of Men and Books,
Not from the *Burnets, Oldmixons,* and *Cooks.*
   Soft were my Numbers, who could take offence
While pure Description held the place of Sense?
Like gentle *Fanny's* was my flow'ry Theme,
A painted Mistress, or a purling Stream.   150
Yet then did *Gildon* draw his venal quill;
I wish'd the man a dinner, and sate still:
Yet then did *Dennis* rave in furious fret;
I never answer'd, I was not in debt:
If want provok'd, or madness made them print,
I wag'd no war with *Bedlam* or the *Mint.*
   Did some more sober Critic come abroad?
If wrong, I smil'd; if right, I kiss'd the rod.
Pains, reading, study, are their just pretence,
And all they want is spirit, taste, and sense.   160
Comma's and points they set exactly right,
And 'twere a sin to rob them of their Mite.
Yet ne'r one sprig of Laurel grac'd these ribalds,
From slashing *Bentley* down to pidling *Tibalds.*
Each Wight who reads not, and but scans and spells,
Each Word-catcher that lives on syllables,
Ev'n such small Critics some regard may claim,
Preserv'd in *Milton's* or in *Shakespear's* name.

Pretty! in Amber to observe the forms
Of hairs, or straws, or dirt, or grubs, or worms;   170
The things, we know, are neither rich nor rare,
But wonder how the Devil they got there?
    Were others angry? I excus'd them too;
Well might they rage; I gave them but their due.
A man's true merit 'tis not hard to find,
But each man's secret standard in his mind,
That Casting-weight Pride adds to Emptiness,
This, who can gratify? for who can *guess*?
The Bard whom pilfer'd Pastorals renown,
Who turns a *Persian* Tale for half a crown,   180
Just writes to make his barrenness appear,
And strains from hard-bound brains eight lines a-year:
He, who still wanting tho' he lives on theft,
Steals much, spends little, yet has nothing left:
And he, who now to sense, now nonsense leaning,
Means not, but blunders round about a meaning:
And he, whose Fustian's so sublimely bad,
It is not Poetry, but Prose run mad:
All these, my modest Satire bad *translate*,
And own'd, that nine such Poets made a *Tate*.   190
How did they fume, and stamp, and roar, and chafe?
And swear, not *Addison* himself was safe.
    Peace to all such! but were there One whose fires
True Genius kindles, and fair Fame inspires,
Blest with each Talent and each Art to please,
And born to write, converse, and live with ease:
Shou'd such a man, too fond to rule alone,
Bear, like the *Turk*, no brother near the throne,
View him with scornful, yet with jealous eyes,
And hate for Arts that caus'd himself to rise;   200
Damn with faint praise, assent with civil leer,
And without sneering, teach the rest to sneer;
Willing to wound, and yet afraid to strike,
Just hint a fault, and hesitate dislike;
Alike reserv'd to blame, or to commend,
A tim'rous foe, and a suspicious friend,

Dreading ev'n fools, by Flatterers besieg'd,
And so obliging that he ne'er oblig'd;
Like *Cato*, give his little Senate laws,
And sit attentive to his own applause;   210
While Wits and Templers ev'ry sentence raise,
And wonder with a foolish face of praise.
Who but must laugh, if such a man there be?
Who would not weep, if *Atticus* were he!
    What tho' my Name stood rubric on the walls?
Or plaister'd posts, with Claps in capitals?
Or smoaking forth, a hundred Hawkers load,
On Wings of Winds came flying all abroad?
I sought no homage from the Race that write;
I kept, like *Asian* Monarchs, from their sight: 220
Poems I heeded (now be-rym'd so long)
No more than Thou, great GEORGE! a Birth-day Song.
I ne'r with Wits or Witlings past my days,
To spread about the Itch of Verse and Praise;
Nor like a Puppy daggled thro' the Town,
To fetch and carry Sing-song up and down;
Nor at Rehearsals sweat, and mouth'd, and cry'd,
With Handkerchief and Orange at my side:
But sick of Fops, and Poetry, and Prate,
To *Bufo* left the whole *Castalian* State.   230
    Proud, as *Apollo* on his forked hill,
Sate full-blown *Bufo*, puff'd by ev'ry quill;
Fed with soft Dedication all day long,
Horace and he went hand in hand in song.
His Library, (where Busts of Poets dead
And a true *Pindar* stood without a head)
Receiv'd of Wits an undistinguish'd race,
Who first his Judgment ask'd, and then a Place:
Much they extoll'd his Pictures, much his Seat,
And flatter'd ev'ry day, and some days eat: 240
Till grown more frugal in his riper days,
He pay'd some Bards with Port, and some with Praise,
To some a dry Rehearsal was assign'd,
And others (harder still) he pay'd in kind.

Dryden alone (what wonder?) came not nigh,
Dryden alone escap'd this judging eye:
But still the Great have kindness in reserve,
He help'd to bury whom he help'd to starve.
    May some choice Patron bless each gray goose quill!
May ev'ry *Bavius* have his *Bufo* still!   250
So, when a Statesman wants a Day's defence,
Or Envy holds a whole Week's war with Sense,
Or simple Pride for Flatt'ry makes demands;
May Dunce by Dunce be whistled off my hands!
Blest be the *Great*! for those they take away,
And those they left me—for they left me GAY,
Left me to see neglected Genius bloom,
Neglected die! and tell it on his Tomb;
Of all thy blameless Life the sole Return
My Verse, and QUEENSB'RY weeping o'er thy Urn!   260
Oh let me live my own! and die so too!
('To live and die is all I have to do:')
Maintain a Poet's Dignity and Ease,
And see what friends, and read what books I please.
Above a Patron, tho' I condescend
Sometimes to call a Minister my Friend:
I was not born for Courts or great Affairs,
I pay my Debts, believe, and say my Pray'rs,
Can sleep without a Poem in my head,
Nor know, if *Dennis* be alive or dead.   270
    Why am I ask'd, what next shall see the light?
Heav'ns! was I born for nothing but to write?
Has Life no Joys for me? or (to be grave)
Have I no Friend to serve, no Soul to save?
'I found him close with *Swift*'—'Indeed? no doubt'
(Cries prating *Balbus*) 'something will come out.'
'Tis all in vain, deny it as I will.
'No, such a Genius never can lye still,'
And then for mine obligingly mistakes
The first Lampoon Sir *Will.* or *Bubo* makes.   280
Poor guiltless I! and can I chuse but smile,
When ev'ry Coxcomb knows me by my *Style*?

Curst be the Verse, how well soe'er it flow,
That tends to make one worthy Man my foe,
Give Virtue scandal, Innocence a fear,
Or from the soft-ey'd Virgin steal a tear!
But he, who hurts a harmless neighbour's peace,
Insults fal'n Worth, or Beauty in distress,
Who loves a Lye, lame slander helps about,
Who writes a Libel, or who copies out: 290
That Fop whose pride affects a Patron's name,
Yet absent, wounds an Author's honest fame;
Who can your Merit selfishly approve,
And show the Sense of it, without the Love;
Who has the Vanity to call you Friend,
Yet wants the Honour injur'd to defend;
Who tells whate'er you think, whate'er you say,
And, if he lye not, must at least betray:
Who to the *Dean* and *silver Bell* can swear,
And sees at *Cannons* what was never there: 300
Who reads but with a Lust to mis-apply,
Make Satire a Lampoon, and Fiction, Lye.
A Lash like mine no honest man shall dread,
But all such babling blockheads in his stead.
    Let *Sporus* tremble—'What? that Thing of silk,
'*Sporus*, that mere white Curd of Ass's milk?
'Satire or Sense alas! can *Sporus* feel?
'Who breaks a Butterfly upon a Wheel?'
Yet let me flap this Bug with gilded wings,
This painted Child of Dirt that stinks and stings;   310
Whose Buzz the Witty and the Fair annoys,
Yet Wit ne'er tastes, and Beauty ne'er enjoys,
So well-bred Spaniels civilly delight
In mumbling of the Game they dare not bite.
Eternal Smiles his Emptiness betray,
As shallow streams run dimpling all the way.
Whether in florid Impotence he speaks,
And, as the Prompter breathes, the Puppet squeaks;
Or at the Ear of *Eve*, familiar Toad,
Half Froth, half Venom, spits himself abroad,   320

In Puns, or Politicks, or Tales, or Lyes,
Or Spite, or Smut, or Rymes, or Blasphemies.
His Wit all see-saw between *that* and *this*,
Now high, now low, now Master up, now Miss,
And he himself one vile Antithesis.
Amphibious Thing! that acting either Part,
The trifling Head, or the corrupted Heart!
Fop at the Toilet, Flatt'rer at the Board,
Now trips a Lady, and now struts a Lord.
Eve's Tempter thus the Rabbins have exprest,   330
A Cherub's face, a Reptile all the rest;
Beauty that shocks you, Parts that none will trust,
Wit that can creep, and Pride that licks the dust.

   Not Fortune's Worshipper, nor Fashion's Fool,
Not Lucre's Madman, nor Ambition's Tool,
Not proud, nor servile, be one Poet's praise
That, if he pleas'd, he pleas'd by manly ways;
That Flatt'ry, ev'n to Kings, he held a shame,
And thought a Lye in Verse or Prose the same:
That not in Fancy's Maze he wander'd long,   340
But stoop'd to Truth, and moraliz'd his song:
That not for Fame, but Virtue's better end,
He stood the furious Foe, the timid Friend,
The damning Critic, half-approving Wit,
The Coxcomb hit, or fearing to be hit;
Laugh'd at the loss of Friends he never had,
The dull, the proud, the wicked, and the mad;
The distant Threats of Vengeance on his head,
The Blow unfelt, the Tear he never shed;
The Tale reviv'd, the Lye so oft o'erthrown;   350
Th'imputed Trash, and Dulness not his own;
The Morals blacken'd when the Writings scape;
The libel'd Person, and the pictur'd Shape;
Abuse on all he lov'd, or lov'd him, spread,
A Friend in Exile, or a Father, dead;
The Whisper that to Greatness still too near,
Perhaps, yet vibrates on his SOVEREIGN's Ear—
Welcome for thee, fair Virtue! all the past:

For thee, fair Virtue! welcome ev'n the *last*!
  'But why insult the Poor, affront the Great?'   360
A Knave's a Knave, to me, in ev'ry State,
Alike my scorn, if he succeed or fail,
Sporus at Court, or *Japhet* in a Jayl,
A hireling Scribler, or a hireling Peer,
Knight of the Post corrupt, or of the Shire,
If on a Pillory, or near a Throne,
He gain his Prince's Ear, or lose his own.
  Yet soft by Nature, more a Dupe than Wit,
Sapho can tell you how this Man was bit:
This dreaded Sat'rist *Dennis* will confess   370
Foe to his Pride, but Friend to his Distress:
So humble, he has knock'd at *Tibbald's* door,
Has drunk with *Cibber*, nay has rym'd for *Moor*.
Full ten years slander'd, did he once reply?
Three thousand Suns went down on *Welsted's* Lye:
To please a *Mistress*, One aspers'd his life;
He lash'd him not, but let her be his *Wife*:
Let *Budgel* charge low *Grubstreet* on his quill,
And write whate'er he pleas'd, except his *Will*;
Let the *Two Curls* of Town and Court, abuse   380
His Father, Mother, Body, Soul, and Muse.
Yet why? that Father held it for a rule
It was a Sin to call our Neighbour Fool,
That harmless Mother thought no Wife a Whore,—
Hear this! and spare his Family, *James More*!
Unspotted Names! and memorable long,
If there be Force in Virtue, or in Song.
  Of gentle Blood (part shed in Honour's Cause,
While yet in *Britain* Honour had Applause)
Each Parent sprung—'What Fortune, pray?'—Their
    own,   390
And better got than *Bestia's* from the Throne.
Born to no Pride, inheriting no Strife,
Nor marrying Discord in a Noble Wife,
Stranger to Civil and Religious Rage,
The good Man walk'd innoxious thro' his Age.

No Courts he saw, no Suits would ever try,
Nor dar'd an Oath, nor hazarded a Lye:
Un-learn'd, he knew no Schoolman's subtle Art,
No Language, but the Language of the Heart.
By Nature honest, by Experience wise,   400
Healthy by Temp'rance and by Exercise:
His Life, tho' long, to sickness past unknown,
His Death was instant, and without a groan.
Oh grant me thus to live, and thus to die!
Who sprung from Kings shall know less joy than I.
   O Friend! may each Domestick Bliss be thine!
Be no unpleasing Melancholy mine:
Me, let the tender Office long engage
To rock the Cradle of reposing Age,
With lenient Arts extend a Mother's breath,   410
Make Languor smile, and smooth the Bed of Death,
Explore the Thought, explain the asking Eye,
And keep a while one Parent from the Sky!
On Cares like these if Length of days attend,
May Heav'n, to bless those days, preserve my Friend,
Preserve him social, chearful, and serene,
And just as rich as when he serv'd a QUEEN!
Whether that Blessing be deny'd, or giv'n,
Thus far was right, the rest belongs to Heav'n.

THE FIRST EPISTLE OF THE SECOND BOOK OF HORACE

TO AUGUSTUS

  While You, great Patron of Mankind, sustain
The balanc'd World, and open all the Main;
Your Country, chief, in Arms abroad defend,
At home, with Morals, Arts, and Laws amend;
How shall the Muse, from such a Monarch, steal
An hour, and not defraud the Publick Weal?
  Edward and Henry, now the Boast of Fame,
And virtuous Alfred, a more sacred Name,

After a Life of gen'rous Toils endur'd,
The Gaul subdu'd, or Property secur'd,   10
Ambition humbled, mighty Cities storm'd,
Or Laws establish'd, and the World reform'd;
Clos'd their long Glories with a sigh, to find
Th'unwilling Gratitude of base mankind!
All human Virtue to its latest breath
Finds Envy never conquer'd, but by Death.
The great Alcides, ev'ry Labour past,
Had still this Monster to subdue at last.
Sure fate of all, beneath whose rising ray
Each Star of meaner merit fades away;   20
Oppress'd we feel the Beam directly beat,
Those Suns of Glory please not till they set.

To Thee, the World its present homage pays,
The Harvest early, but mature the Praise:
Great Friend of LIBERTY! in *Kings* a Name
Above all Greek, above all Roman Fame:
Whose Word is Truth, as sacred and rever'd,
As Heav'n's own Oracles from Altars heard.
Wonder of Kings! like whom, to mortal eyes
None e'er has risen, and none e'er shall rise.   30

Just in one instance, be it yet confest
Your People, Sir, are partial in the rest.
Foes to all living worth except your own,
And Advocates for Folly dead and gone.
Authors, like Coins, grow dear as they grow old;
It is the rust we value, not the gold.
Chaucer's worst ribaldry is learn'd by rote,
And beastly Skelton Heads of Houses quote:
One likes no language but the Faery Queen;
A Scot will fight for Christ's Kirk o' the Green;   40
And each true Briton is to Ben so civil,
He swears the Muses met him at the Devil.

Tho' justly Greece her eldest sons admires,
Why should not we be wiser than our Sires?
In ev'ry publick Virtue we excell,
We build, we paint, we sing, we dance as well,

And learned Athens to our Art must stoop,
Could she behold us tumbling thro' a hoop.
　If Time improve our Wit as well as Wine,
Say at what age a Poet grows divine?　　　　　　　50
Shall we, or shall we not, account him so,
Who dy'd, perhaps, an hundred years ago?
End all dispute; and fix the year precise
When British bards begin t'Immortalize?
　'Who lasts a Century can have no flaw,
'I hold that Wit a Classick, good in law.'
　Suppose he wants a year, will you compound?
And shall we deem him Ancient, right and sound,
Or damn to all Eternity at once,
At ninety nine, a Modern, and a Dunce?　　　　　60
　'We shall not quarrel for a year or two;
'By Courtesy of England, he may do.'
　Then, by the rule that made the Horse-tail bare,
I pluck out year by year, as hair by hair,
And melt down Ancients like a heap of snow:
While you, to measure merits, look in Stowe,
And estimating Authors by the year,
Bestow a Garland only on a Bier.
　Shakespear, (whom you and ev'ry Play-house bill
Style the divine, the matchless, what you will)　　70
For gain, not glory, wing'd his roving flight,
And grew Immortal in his own despight.
Ben, old and poor, as little seem'd to heed
The Life to come, in ev'ry Poet's Creed.
Who now reads Cowley? if he pleases yet,
His moral pleases, not his pointed wit;
Forgot his Epiic, nay Pindaric Art,
But still I love the language of his Heart.
　'Yet surely, surely, these were famous men!
'What Boy but hears the saying of old Ben?　　　80
'In all debates where Criticks bear a part,
'Not one but nods, and talks of Johnson's Art,
'Of Shakespear's Nature, and of Cowley's Wit;
'How Beaumont's Judgment check'd what Fletcher writ;

'How Shadwell hasty, Wycherly was slow;
'But, for the Passions, Southern sure and Rowe.
'These, only these, support the crouded stage,
'From eldest Heywood down to Cibber's age.'
    All this may be; the People's Voice is odd,
It is, and it is not, the voice of God.   90
To Gammer Gurton if it give the bays,
And yet deny the Careless Husband praise,
Or say our fathers never broke a rule;
Why then I say, the Publick is a fool.
But let them own, that greater faults than we
They had, and greater Virtues, I'll agree.
Spenser himself affects the obsolete,
And Sydney's verse halts ill on Roman feet:
Milton's strong pinion now not Heav'n can bound,
Now serpent-like, in prose he sweeps the ground,   100
In Quibbles, Angel and Archangel join,
And God the Father turns a School-Divine.
Not that I'd lop the Beauties from his book,
Like slashing Bentley with his desp'rate Hook;
Or damn all Shakespear, like th'affected fool
At Court, who hates whate'er he read at School.
    But for the Wits of either Charles's days,
The Mob of Gentlemen who wrote with Ease;
Sprat, Carew, Sedley, and a hundred more,
(Like twinkling Stars the Miscellanies o'er)   110
One Simile, that solitary shines
In the dry Desert of a thousand lines,
Or lengthen'd Thought that gleams thro' many a page,
Has sanctify'd whole Poems for an age.
    I lose my patience, and I own it too,
When works are censur'd, not as bad, but new;
While if our Elders break all Reason's laws,
These fools demand not Pardon, but Applause.
    On Avon's bank, where flow'rs eternal blow,
If I but ask, if any weed can grow?   120
One Tragic sentence if I dare deride
Which Betterton's grave Action dignify'd,

Or well-mouth'd Booth with emphasis proclaims,
(Tho' but, perhaps, a muster-roll of Names)
How will our Fathers rise up in a rage,
And swear, all shame is lost in George's Age!
You'd think no Fools disgrac'd the former Reign,
Did not some grave Examples yet remain,
Who scorn a Lad should teach his Father skill,
And, having once been wrong, will be so still.   130
He, who to seem more deep than you or I,
Extols old Bards, or Merlin's Prophecy,
Mistake him not; he envies, not admires,
And to debase the Sons, exalts the Sires.
Had ancient Times conspir'd to dis-allow
What then was new, what had been ancient now?
Or what remain'd, so worthy to be read
By learned Criticks, of the mighty Dead?

    In Days of Ease, when now the weary Sword
Was sheath'd, and *Luxury* with *Charles* restor'd;   140
In every Taste of foreign Courts improv'd,
'All, by the King's Example, liv'd and lov'd.'
Then Peers grew proud in Horsemanship t'excell,
New-market's Glory rose, as Britain's fell;
The Soldier breath'd the Gallantries of France,
And ev'ry flow'ry Courtier writ Romance.
Then Marble soften'd into life grew warm,
And yielding Metal flow'd to human form:
Lely on animated Canvas stole
The sleepy Eye, that spoke the melting Soul.   150
No wonder then, when all was Love and Sport,
The willing Muses were debauch'd at Court;
On each enervate string they taught the Note
To pant, or tremble thro' an Eunuch's throat.
But Britain, changeful as a Child at play,
Now calls in Princes, and now turns away.
Now Whig, now Tory, what we lov'd we hate;
Now all for Pleasure, now for Church and State;
Now for Prerogative, and now for Laws;
Effects unhappy! from a Noble Cause.   160

Time was, a sober Englishman wou'd knock
His servants up, and rise by five a clock,
Instruct his Family in ev'ry rule,
And send his Wife to Church, his Son to school.
To worship like his Fathers was his care;
To teach their frugal Virtues to his Heir;
To prove, that Luxury could never hold;
And place, on good Security, his Gold.
Now Times are chang'd, and one Poetick Itch
Has seiz'd the Court and City, Poor and Rich:　　170
Sons, Sires, and Grandsires, all will wear the Bays,
Our Wives read Milton, and our Daughters Plays,
To Theatres, and to Rehearsals throng,
And all our Grace at Table is a Song.
I, who so oft renounce the Muses, lye,
Not ——'s self e'er tells more *Fibs* than I;
When, sick of Muse, our follies we deplore,
And promise our best Friends to ryme no more;
We wake next morning in a raging Fit,
And call for Pen and Ink to show our Wit.　　180

He serv'd a'Prenticeship, who sets up shop;
Ward try'd on Puppies, and the Poor, his Drop;
Ev'n Radcliff's Doctors travel first to France,
Nor dare to practise till they've learn'd to dance.
Who builds a Bridge that never drove a pyle?
(Should Ripley venture, all the World would smile)
But those who cannot write, and those who can,
All ryme, and scrawl, and scribble, to a man.

Yet Sir, reflect, the mischief is not great;
These Madmen never hurt the Church or State:　　190
Sometimes the Folly benefits mankind;
And rarely Av'rice taints the tuneful mind.
Allow him but his Play-thing of a Pen,
He ne'er rebels, or plots, like other men:
Flight of Cashiers, or Mobs, he'll never mind;
And knows no losses while the Muse is kind.
To cheat a Friend, or Ward, he leaves to Peter;
The good man heaps up nothing but mere metre,

Enjoys his Garden and his Book in quiet;
And then—a perfect Hermit in his Diet.   200
Of little use the Man you may suppose,
Who says in verse what others say in prose;
Yet let me show, a Poet's of some weight,
And (tho' no soldier) useful to the State.
What will a Child learn sooner than a song?
What better teach a Foreigner the tongue?
What's long or short, each accent where to place,
And speak in publick with some sort of grace.
I scarce can think him such a worthless thing,
Unless he praise some monster of a King,   210
Or Virtue, or Religion turn to sport,
To please a lewd, or un-believing Court.
Unhappy Dryden!—In all Charles's days,
Roscommon only boasts unspotted Bays;
And in our own (excuse some Courtly stains)
No whiter page than Addison remains.
He, from the taste obscene reclaims our Youth,
And sets the Passions on the side of Truth;
Forms the soft bosom with the gentlest art,
And pours each human Virtue in the heart.   220
Let Ireland tell, how Wit upheld her cause,
Her Trade supported, and supply'd her Laws;
And leave on Swift this grateful verse ingrav'd,
The Rights a Court attack'd, a Poet sav'd.
Behold the hand that wrought a Nation's cure,
Stretch'd to relieve the Idiot and the Poor,
Proud Vice to brand, or injur'd Worth adorn,
And stretch the Ray to Ages yet unborn.
Not but there are, who merit other palms;
Hopkins and Sternhold glad the heart with Psalms;   230
The Boys and Girls whom Charity maintains,
Implore your help in these pathetic strains:
How could Devotion touch the country pews,
Unless the Gods bestow'd a proper Muse?
Verse chears their leisure, Verse assists their work,
Verse prays for Peace, or sings down Pope and Turk.

The silent Preacher yields to potent strain,
And feels that grace his pray'r besought in vain,
The blessing thrills thro' all the lab'ring throng,
And Heav'n is won by violence of Song.   240
    Our rural Ancestors, with little blest,
Patient of labour when the end was rest,
Indulg'd the day that hous'd their annual grain,
With feasts, and off'rings, and a thankful strain:
The joy their wives, their sons, and servants share,
Ease of their toil, and part'ners of their care:
The laugh, the jest, attendants on the bowl,
Smooth'd ev'ry brow, and open'd ev'ry soul:
With growing years the pleasing Licence grew,
And Taunts alternate innocently flew.   250
But Times corrupt, and Nature, ill-inclin'd,
Produc'd the point that left a sting behind;
Till friend with friend, and families at strife,
Triumphant Malice rag'd thro' private life.
Who felt the wrong, or fear'd it, took th'alarm,
Appeal'd to Law, and Justice lent her arm.
At length, by wholesom dread of statutes bound,
The Poets learn'd to please, and not to wound:
Most warp'd to Flatt'ry's side; but some, more nice,
Preserv'd the freedom, and forbore the vice.   260
Hence Satire rose, that just the medium hit,
And heals with Morals what it hurts with Wit.
    We conquer'd France, but felt our captive's
      charms;
Her Arts victorious triumph'd o'er our Arms:
Britain to soft refinements less a foe,
Wit grew polite, and Numbers learn'd to flow.
Waller was smooth; but Dryden taught to join⎞
The varying verse, the full resounding line,   ⎬
The long majestic march, and energy divine. ⎠
Tho' still some traces of our rustic vein   270
And splay-foot verse, remain'd, and will remain.
Late, very late, correctness grew our care,
When the tir'd nation breath'd from civil war.

Exact Racine, and Corneille's noble fire
Show'd us that France had something to admire.
Not but the Tragic spirit was our own,
And full in Shakespear, fair in Otway shone:
But Otway fail'd to polish or refine,
And fluent Shakespear scarce effac'd a line.
Ev'n copious Dryden, wanted, or forgot,   280
The last and greatest Art, the Art to blot.

    Some doubt, if equal pains or equal fire
The humbler Muse of Comedy require?
But in known Images of life I guess
The labour greater, as th'Indulgence less.
Observe how seldom ev'n the best succeed:
Tell me if Congreve's Fools are Fools indeed?
What pert low Dialogue has Farqu'ar writ!
How Van wants grace, who never wanted wit!
The stage how loosely does Astræa tread,   290
Who fairly puts all Characters to bed:
And idle Cibber, how he breaks the laws,
To make poor Pinky eat with vast applause!
But fill their purse, our Poet's work is done,
Alike to them, by Pathos or by Pun.

    O you! whom Vanity's light bark conveys
On Fame's mad voyage by the wind of Praise;
With what a shifting gale your course you ply;
For ever sunk too low, or born too high!
Who pants for glory finds but short repose,   300
A breath revives him, or a breath o'erthrows!
Farewel the stage! if just as thrives the Play,
The silly bard grows fat, or falls away.

    There still remains to mortify a Wit,
The many-headed Monster of the Pit:
A sense-less, worth-less, and unhonour'd crowd;
Who to disturb their betters mighty proud,
Clatt'ring their sticks, before ten lines are spoke,
Call for the Farce, the Bear, or the Black-joke.
What dear delight to Britons Farce affords!   310
Ever the taste of Mobs, but now of Lords;

(Taste, that eternal wanderer, which flies
From heads to ears, and now from ears to eyes.)
The Play stands still; damn action and discourse,
Back fly the scenes, and enter foot and horse;
Pageants on pageants, in long order drawn,
Peers, Heralds, Bishops, Ermin, Gold, and Lawn;
The Champion too! and, to complete the jest,
Old Edward's Armour beams on Cibber's breast!
With laughter sure Democritus had dy'd,   320
Had he beheld an Audience gape so wide.
Let Bear or Elephant be e'er so white,
The people, sure, the people are the sight!
Ah luckless Poet! stretch thy lungs and roar,
That Bear or Elephant shall heed thee more;
While all its throats the Gallery extends,
And all the Thunder of the Pit ascends!
Loud as the Wolves on Orcas' stormy steep,
Howl to the roarings of the Northern deep.
Such is the shout, the long-applauding note,   330
At Quin's high plume, or Oldfield's petticoat,
Or when from Court a birth-day suit bestow'd
Sinks the lost Actor in the tawdry load.
Booth enters—hark! the Universal Peal!
'But has he spoken?' Not a syllable.
'What shook the stage, and made the people stare?'
Cato's long Wig, flowr'd gown, and lacquer'd chair.
   Yet lest you think I railly more than teach,
Or praise malignly Arts I cannot reach,
Let me for once presume t'instruct the times,   340
To know the Poet from the Man of Rymes:
'Tis He, who gives my breast a thousand pains,
Can make me feel each Passion that he feigns,
Inrage, compose, with more than magic Art,
With Pity, and with Terror, tear my heart;
And snatch me, o'er the earth, or thro' the air,
To Thebes or Athens, when he will, and where.
   But not this part of the poetic state
Alone, deserves the favour of the Great:

Think of those Authors, Sir, who would rely   350
More on a Reader's sense than Gazer's eye.
Or who shall wander where the Muses sing?
Who climb their Mountain, or who taste their spring?
How shall we fill a Library with Wit,
When Merlin's Cave is half unfurnish'd yet?
　　My Liege! why Writers little claim your thought,
I guess; and, with their leave, will tell the fault:
We Poets are (upon a Poet's word)
Of all mankind, the creatures most absurd:
The season, when to come, and when to go,   360
To sing, or cease to sing, we never know;
And if we will recite nine hours in ten,
You lose your patience, just like other men.
Then too we hurt our selves, when to defend
A single verse, we quarrel with a friend;
Repeat unask'd; lament, the Wit's too fine
For vulgar eyes, and point out ev'ry line.
But most, when straining with too weak a wing,
We needs will write Epistles to the King;
And from the moment we oblige the town,   370
Expect a Place, or Pension from the Crown;
Or dubb'd Historians by express command,
T'enroll your triumphs o'er the seas and land;
Be call'd to Court, to plan some work divine,
As once for Louis, Boileau and Racine.
　　Yet think great Sir! (so many Virtues shown)
Ah think, what Poet best may make them known?
Or chuse at least some Minister of Grace,
Fit to bestow the Laureat's weighty place.
　　Charles, to late times to be transmitted fair,   380
Assign'd his figure to Bernini's care;
And great Nassau to Kneller's hand decreed
To fix him graceful on the bounding Steed:
So well in paint and stone they judg'd of merit:
But Kings in Wit may want discerning spirit.
The Hero William, and the Martyr Charles,
One knighted Blackmore, and one pension'd Quarles;

133

Which made old Ben, and surly Dennis swear,
'No Lord's anointed, but a Russian Bear.'
  Not with such Majesty, such bold relief,   390
The Forms august of King, or conqu'ring Chief,
E'er swell'd on Marble; as in Verse have shin'd
(In polish'd Verse) the Manners and the Mind.
Oh! could I mount on the Mæonian wing,
Your Arms, your Actions, your Repose to sing!
What seas you travers'd! and what fields you fought!
Your Country's Peace, how oft, how dearly bought!
How barb'rous rage subsided at your word,
And Nations wonder'd while they dropp'd the sword!
How, when you nodded, o'er the land and deep,   400
Peace stole her wing, and wrapt the world in sleep;
Till Earth's extremes your mediation own,
And Asia's Tyrants tremble at your Throne—
But Verse alas! your Majesty disdains;
And I'm not us'd to Panegyric strains:
The Zeal of Fools offends at any time,
But most of all, the Zeal of Fools in ryme.
Besides, a fate attends on all I write,
That when I aim at praise, they say I bite.
A vile Encomium doubly ridicules;   410
There's nothing blackens like the ink of fools;
If true, a woful likeness, and if lyes,
'Praise undeserv'd is scandal in disguise:'
Well may he blush, who gives it, or receives;
And when I flatter, let my dirty leaves
(Like Journals, Odes, and such forgotten things
As Eusden, Philips, Settle, writ of Kings)
Cloath spice, line trunks, or flutt'ring in a row,
Befringe the rails of Bedlam and Sohoe.

THE FIRST EPISTLE OF THE FIRST BOOK OF HORACE

TO LORD BOLINGBROKE

  St John, whose love indulg'd my labours past
Matures my present, and shall bound my last!

Why will you break the Sabbath of my days?
Now sick alike of Envy and of Praise.
Publick too long, ah let me hide my Age!
See modest Cibber now has left the Stage:
Our Gen'rals now, retir'd to their Estates,
Hang their old Trophies o'er the Garden gates,
In Life's cool evening satiate of applause,
Nor fond of bleeding, ev'n in BRUNSWICK's cause.   10
    A Voice there is, that whispers in my ear,
('Tis Reason's voice, which sometimes one can hear)
'Friend Pope! be prudent, let your Muse take breath,
'And never gallop Pegasus to death;
'Lest stiff, and stately, void of fire, or force,
'You limp, like Blackmore, on a Lord Mayor's horse.'
    Farewell then Verse, and Love, and ev'ry Toy,
The rhymes and rattles of the Man or Boy:
What right, what true, what fit, we justly call,
Let this be all my care—for this is All: 20
To lay this harvest up, and hoard with haste
What ev'ry day will want, and most, the last.
    But ask not, to what Doctors I apply?
Sworn to no Master, of no Sect am I:
As drives the storm, at any door I knock,
And house with Montagne now, or now with Locke.
Sometimes a Patriot, active in debate,
Mix with the World, and battle for the State,
Free as young Lyttelton, her cause pursue,
Still true to Virtue, and as warm as true: 30
Sometimes, with Aristippus, or St Paul,
Indulge my Candor, and grow all to all;
Back to my native Moderation slide,
And win my way by yielding to the tyde.
    Long, as to him who works for debt, the Day;
Long as the Night to her whose love's away;
Long as the Year's dull circle seems to run,
When the brisk Minor pants for twenty-one;
So slow th'unprofitable Moments roll,
That lock up all the Functions of my soul;   40

That keep me from Myself; and still delay
Life's instant business to a future day:
That task, which as we follow, or despise,
The eldest is a fool, the youngest wise;
Which done, the poorest can no wants endure,
And which not done, the richest must be poor.

    Late as it is, I put my self to school,
And feel some comfort, not to be a fool.
Weak tho' I am of limb, and short of sight,
Far from a Lynx, and not a Giant quite,   50
I'll do what MEAD and CHESELDEN advise,
To keep these limbs, and to preserve these eyes.
Not to go back, is somewhat to advance,
And men must walk at least before they dance.

    Say, does thy blood rebel, thy bosom move
With wretched Av'rice, or as wretched Love?
Know, there are Words, and Spells, which can controll
(Between the Fits) this Fever of the soul:
Know, there are Rhymes, which (fresh and fresh apply'd)
Will cure the arrant'st Puppy of his Pride.   60
Be furious, envious, slothful, mad or drunk,
Slave to a Wife or Vassal to a Punk,
A Switz, a High-dutch, or a Low-dutch Bear—
All that we ask is but a patient Ear.

    'Tis the first Virtue, Vices to abhor;
And the first Wisdom, to be Fool no more.
But to the world, no bugbear is so great,
As want of figure, and a small Estate.
To either India see the Merchant fly,
Scar'd at the spectre of pale Poverty!   70
See him, with pains of body, pangs of soul,
Burn through the Tropic, freeze beneath the Pole!
Wilt thou do nothing for a nobler end,
Nothing, to make Philosophy thy friend?
To stop thy foolish views, thy long desires,
And ease thy heart of all that it admires?

    Here, Wisdom calls: 'Seek Virtue first! be bold!
'As Gold to Silver, Virtue is to Gold.'

There, London's voice: 'Get Mony, Mony still!
'And then let Virtue follow, if she will.'   80
This, this the saving doctrine, preach'd to all,
From low St James's up to high St Paul;
From him whose quills stand quiver'd at his ear,
To him who notches Sticks at Westminster.
    BARNARD in spirit, sense, and truth abounds.
'Pray then what wants he?' fourscore thousand pounds,
A Pension, or such Harness for a slave
As Bug now has, and Dorimant would have.
BARNARD, thou art a *Cit*, with all thy worth;
But wretched Bug, his *Honour*, and so forth.   90
    Yet every child another song will sing,
'Virtue, brave boys! 'tis Virtue makes a King.'
True, conscious Honour is to feel no sin,
He's arm'd without that's innocent within;
Be this thy Screen, and this thy Wall of Brass;
Compar'd to this, a Minister's an Ass.
    And say, to which shall our applause belong,
This new Court jargon, or the good old song?
The modern language of corrupted Peers,
Or what was spoke at CRESSY and POITIERS?   100
    Who counsels best? who whispers, 'Be but Great,
'With Praise or Infamy, leave that to fate;
'Get Place and Wealth, if possible, with Grace;
'If not, by any means get Wealth and Place.'
For what? to have a Box where Eunuchs sing,
And foremost in the Circle eye a King.
Or he, who bids thee face with steddy view
Proud Fortune, and look shallow Greatness thro':
And, while he bids thee, sets th'Example too?
If such a Doctrine, in St James's air,   110
Shou'd chance to make the well-drest Rabble stare;
If honest S(chut)z take scandal at a spark,
That less admires the Palace than the Park;
Faith I shall give the answer Reynard gave;
'I cannot like, Dread Sir! your Royal Cave;
'Because I see by all the Tracks about,

137

'Full many a Beast goes in, but none comes out.'
Adieu to Virtue if you're once a Slave:
Send her to Court, you send her to her Grave.
    Well, if a King's a Lion, at the least   120
The People are a many-headed Beast:
Can they direct what measures to pursue,
Who knows themselves so little what to do?
Alike in nothing but one Lust of Gold,
Just half the land would buy, and half be sold:
Their Country's wealth our mightier Misers drain,
Or cross, to plunder Provinces, the Main:
The rest, some farm the Poor-box, some the Pews;
Some keep Assemblies, and wou'd keep the Stews;
Some with fat Bucks on childless Dotards fawn;   130
Some win rich Widows by their Chine and Brawn;
While with the silent growth of ten per Cent,
In Dirt and darkness hundreds stink content.
    Of all these ways, if each pursues his own,
Satire be kind, and let the wretch alone.
But show me one, who has it in his pow'r
To act consistent with himself an hour.
Sir Job sail'd forth, the evening bright and still,
'No place on earth (he cry'd) like Greenwich hill!'
Up starts a Palace, lo! th'obedient base   140
Slopes at its foot, the woods its sides embrace,
The silver Thames reflects its marble face.
Now let some whimzy, or that Dev'l within
Which guides all those who know not what they mean
But give the Knight (or give his Lady) spleen;
'Away, away! take all your scaffolds down,
'For Snug's the word: My dear! we'll live in Town.'
    At am'rous Flavio is the Stocking thrown?
That very night he longs to lye alone.
The Fool whose Wife elopes some thrice a quarter,   150
For matrimonial Solace dies a martyr.
Did ever Proteus, Merlin, any Witch,
Transform themselves so strangely as the Rich?
'Well, but the Poor'—the Poor have the same itch:

They change their weekly Barber, weekly News,
Prefer a new Japanner to their shoes,
Discharge their Garrets, move their Beds, and run
(They know not whither) in a Chaise and one;
They hire their Sculler, and when once aboard,
Grow sick, and damn the Climate—like a Lord.   160
  You laugh, half Beau half Sloven if I stand,
My Wig all powder, and all snuff my Band;
You laugh, if Coat and Breeches strangely vary,
White Gloves, and Linnen worthy Lady Mary!
But when no Prelate's Lawn with Hair-shirt lin'd,
Is half so incoherent as my Mind,
When (each Opinion with the next at strife,
One ebb and flow of follies all my Life)
I plant, root up, I build, and then confound,
Turn round to square, and square again to round;   170
You never change one muscle of your face,
You think this Madness but a common case,
Nor once to Chanc'ry, nor to Hales apply;
Yet hang your lip, to see a Seam awry!
Careless how ill I with myself agree;
Kind to my dress, my figure, not to Me.
Is this my Guide, Philosopher, and Friend?
This, He who loves me, and who ought to mend?
Who ought to make me (what he can, or none),
That Man divine whom Wisdom calls her own,   180
Great without Title, without Fortune bless'd,
Rich ev'n when plunder'd, honour'd while oppress'd,
Lov'd without youth, and follow'd without power,
At home tho' exil'd, free, tho' in the Tower.
In short, that reas'ning, high, immortal Thing,
Just less than Jove, and much above a King,
Nay half in Heav'n—except (what's mighty odd)
A Fit of Vapours clouds this Demi-god.

EPILOGUE TO THE SATIRES

Dialogue I

Fr. Not twice a twelvemonth you appear in Print,
And when it comes, the Court see nothing in't.
You grow *correct* that once with Rapture writ,
And are, besides, too *Moral* for a Wit.
Decay of Parts, alas! we all must feel—
Why now, this moment, don't I see you steal?
'Tis all from *Horace: Horace* long before ye
Said, 'Tories call'd him Whig, and Whigs a Tory;'
And taught his Romans, in much better metre,
'To laugh at Fools who put their trust in *Peter*.'   10
     But *Horace*, Sir, was delicate, was nice;
Bubo observes, he lash'd no sort of *Vice*:
Horace would say, Sir Billy *serv'd the Crown,*
Blunt *could do Bus'ness,* H(u)ggins *knew the Town,*
In *Sappho* touch the *Failing of the Sex,*
In rev'rend Bishops note some *small Neglects,*
And own, the *Spaniard* did a *waggish thing,*
Who cropt our Ears, and sent them to the King.
His sly, polite, insinuating stile
Could please at Court, and make Augustus smile: 20
An artful Manager, that crept between
His Friend and Shame, and was a kind of *Screen*.
But 'faith your very Friends will soon be sore;
Patriots there are, who wish you'd jest no more—
And where's the Glory? 'twill be only thought
The Great man never offer'd you a Groat.
Go see Sir Robert—

                    P. See Sir Robert!—hum—
And never laugh—for all my life to come?
Seen him I have, but in his happier hour
Of Social Pleasure, ill-exchang'd for Pow'r;   30

Seen him, uncumber'd with the Venal tribe,
Smile without Art, and win without a Bribe.
Would he oblige me? let me only find,
He does not think me what he thinks mankind.
Come, come, at all I laugh He laughs, no doubt,
The only diff'rence is, I dare laugh out.

F. Why yes: with *Scripture* still you may be free;
A Horse-laugh, if you please, at *Honesty*;
A Joke on JEKYL, or some odd *Old Whig*,
Who never chang'd his Principle, or Wig: 40
A Patriot is a Fool in ev'ry age,
Whom all Lord Chamberlains allow the Stage:
These nothing hurts; they keep their Fashion still,
And wear their strange old Virtue as they will.

If any ask you, 'Who's the Man, so near
'His Prince, that writes in Verse, and has his Ear?'
Why answer LYTTELTON, and I'll engage
The worthy Youth shall ne'er be in a rage:
But were his Verses vile, his Whisper base,
You'd quickly find him in Lord *Fanny*'s case.   50
Sejanus, *Wolsey*, hurt not honest FLEURY,
But well may put some Statesmen in a fury.

Laugh then at any, but at Fools or Foes;
These you but anger, and you mend not those:
Laugh at your Friends, and if your Friends are sore,
So much the better, you may laugh the more.
To Vice and Folly to confine the jest,
Sets half the World, God knows, against the rest;
Did not the Sneer of more impartial men
At Sense and Virtue, balance all agen.   60
Judicious Wits spread wide the Ridicule,
And charitably comfort Knave and Fool.

P. Dear Sir, forgive the Prejudice of Youth:
Adieu Distinction, Satire, Warmth, and Truth!

Come harmless *Characters* that no one hit,
Come *Henley*'s Oratory, *Osborn*'s Wit!
The Honey dropping from *Favonio*'s tongue,
The Flow'rs of *Bubo*, and the Flow of *Y(o)ng*!
The gracious Dew of Pulpit Eloquence;
And all the well-whipt Cream of Courtly Sense,   70
That first was *H(er)vy*'s, *F(ox)*'s next, and then
The *S(ena)te*'s, and then *H(er)vy*'s once agen.
O come, that easy *Ciceronian* stile,
So *Latin*, yet so *English* all the while,
As, tho' the Pride of *Middleton* and *Bland*,
All Boys may read, and Girls may understand!
Then might I sing without the least Offence,
And all I sung should be the *Nation*'s *Sense*:
Or teach the melancholy Muse to mourn,
Hang the sad Verse on CAROLINA's Urn,   80
And hail her passage to the Realms of Rest,
All Parts perform'd, and *all* her Children blest!
So—Satire is no more—I feel it die—
No *Gazeteer* more innocent than I!
And let, a God's-name, ev'ry Fool and Knave
Be grac'd thro' Life, and flatter'd in his Grave.

F. Why so? if Satire know its Time and Place,
You still may lash the Greatest—in Disgrace:
For Merit will by turns forsake them all;
Would you know when? exactly when they fall.   90
But let all Satire in all Changes spare
Immortal *S(elkir)k*, and grave *De(lawa)re*!
Silent and soft, as Saints remove to Heav'n,
All Tyes dissolv'd, and ev'ry Sin forgiv'n,
These, may some gentle, ministerial Wing
Receive, and place for ever near a King!
There, where no Passion, Pride, or Shame transport,
Lull'd with the sweet *Nepenthe* of a Court;
There, where no Father's, Brother's, Friend's Disgrace
Once break their Rest, or stir them from their Place;   100
But past the Sense of human Miseries,

All Tears are wip'd for ever from all Eyes;
No Cheek is known to blush, no Heart to throb,
Save when they lose a Question, or a Job.

  P. Good Heav'n forbid, that I shou'd blast their Glory,
Who know how like Whig-Ministers to Tory,
And when three Sov'reigns dy'd, could scarce be vext,
Consid'ring what a Gracious Prince was next.
Have I in silent wonder seen such things
As Pride in Slaves, and Avarice in Kings,   110
And at a Peer, or Peeress shall I fret,
Who starves a Sister, or forswears a Debt?
Virtue, I grant you, is an empty boast;
But shall the Dignity of *Vice* be lost?
Ye Gods! shall *Cibber*'s Son, without rebuke
Swear like a Lord? or *Rich* out-whore a Duke?
A Fav'rite's *Porter* with his Master vie,
Be brib'd as often, and as often lie?
Shall *Ward* draw Contracts with a Statesman's skill?
Or *Japhet* pocket, like his Grace, a Will?   120
Is it for *Bond* or *Peter* (paltry Things!)
To pay their Debts or keep their Faith like Kings?
If *Blount* dispatch'd himself, he play'd the man,
And so may'st Thou, Illustrious *Passeran*!
But shall a *Printer*, weary of his life,
Learn from their Books to hang himself and Wife?
This, this, my friend, I cannot, must not bear;
Vice thus abus'd, demands a Nation's care;
This calls the Church to deprecate our Sin,
And hurls the Thunder of the Laws on *Gin*.   130

  Let modest *Foster*, if he will, excell
Ten Metropolitans in preaching well;
A simple Quaker, or a Quaker's Wife,
Out-do *Landaffe*, in Doctrine—yea, in Life;
Let humble ALLEN, with an aukward Shame,
Do good by stealth, and blush to find it Fame.
Virtue may chuse the high or low Degree,

'Tis just alike to Virtue, and to me;
Dwell in a Monk, or light upon a King,
She's still the same, belov'd, contented thing.   140
Vice is undone, if she forgets her Birth,
And stoops from Angels to the Dregs of Earth:
But 'tis the *Fall* degrades her to a Whore;
Let *Greatness* own her, and she's mean no more:
Her Birth, her Beauty, Crowds and Courts confess,
Chaste Matrons praise her, and grave Bishops bless:
In golden Chains the willing World she draws,
And hers the Gospel is, and hers the Laws:
Mounts the Tribunal, lifts her scarlet head,
And sees pale Virtue carted in her stead!   150
Lo! at the Wheels of her Triumphal Car,
Old *England's* Genius, rough with many a Scar,
Dragg'd in the Dust! his Arms hang idly round,
His Flag inverted trails along the ground!
Our Youth, all liv'ry'd o'er with foreign Gold,
Before her dance; behind her crawl the Old!
See thronging Millions to the Pagod run,
And offer Country, Parent, Wife, or Son!
Hear her black Trumpet thro' the Land proclaim,
That 'Not to be corrupted is the Shame.'   160
In Soldier, Churchman, Patriot, Man in Pow'r,
'Tis Av'rice all, Ambition is no more!
See, all our Nobles begging to be Slaves!
See, all our Fools aspiring to be Knaves!
The Wit of Cheats, the Courage of a Whore,
Are what ten thousand envy and adore.
All, all look up, with reverential Awe,
On Crimes that scape, or triumph o'er the Law:
While Truth, Worth, Wisdom, daily they decry—
'Nothing is Sacred now but Villany.'   170

   Yet may this Verse (if such a Verse remain)
Show there was one who held it in disdain.

Dialogue II

Fr. Tis all a Libel—*Paxton* (Sir) will say.
 P. Not yet, my Friend! to-morrow 'faith it may;
And for that very cause I print to day.
How shou'd I fret, to mangle ev'ry line,
In rev'rence to the Sins of *Thirty-nine*!
Vice with such Giant-strides comes on amain,
Invention strives to be before in vain;
Feign what I will, and paint it e'er so strong,
Some rising Genius sins up to my Song.
 F. Yet none but you by Name the Guilty lash;   10
Ev'n *Guthry* saves half *Newgate* by a Dash.
Spare then the Person, and expose the Vice.
 P. How Sir! not damn the Sharper, but the Dice?
Come on then Satire! gen'ral, unconfin'd,
Spread thy broad wing, and sowze on all the Kind.
Ye Statesmen, Priests, of one Religion all!
Ye Tradesmen vile, in Army, Court, or Hall!
Ye Rev'rend Atheists!—*F.* Scandal! name them, Who?
 P. Why that's the thing you bid me not to do.
Who starv'd a Sister, who forswore a Debt,   20
I never nam'd—the Town's enquiring yet.
The pois'ning Dame—*F.* You mean—*P.* I don't.—*F.* You
  do.
 P. See! now I keep the Secret, and not you.
The bribing Statesman—*F.* Hold! too high you go.
 P. The brib'd Elector—*F.* There you stoop too low.
 P. I fain wou'd please you, if I knew with what:
Tell me, which Knave is lawful Game, which not?
Must great Offenders, once escap'd the Crown,
Like Royal Harts, be never more run down?
Admit your Law to spare the Knight requires;   30
As Beasts of Nature may we hunt the Squires?
Suppose I censure—you know what I mean—
To save a Bishop, may I name a Dean?
 F. A Dean, Sir? no: his Fortune is not made,
You hurt a man that's rising in the Trade.

P. If not the Tradesman who set up to day,
Much less the 'Prentice who to morrow may.
Down, down, proud Satire! tho' a Realm be spoil'd,
Arraign no mightier Thief than wretched *Wild*,
Or if a Court or Country's made a Job,   40
Go drench a Pick-pocket, and join the Mob.
   But Sir, I beg you, for the Love of Vice!
The matter's weighty, pray consider twice:
Have you less Pity for the needy Cheat,
The poor and friendless Villain, than the Great?
Alas! the small Discredit of a Bribe
Scarce hurts the Lawyer, but undoes the Scribe.
Then better sure it Charity becomes
To tax Directors, who (thank God) have Plums;
Still better, Ministers; or if the thing   50
May pinch ev'n there—why lay it on a King.
   F. Stop! stop!
               P. Must Satire, then, nor *rise*, nor *fall*?
Speak out, and bid me blame no Rogues at all.
   F. Yes, strike that *Wild*, I'll justify the blow.
   P. Strike? why the man was hang'd ten years ago:
Who now that obsolete Example fears?
Ev'n *Peter* trembles only for his Ears.
   F. What always *Peter*? *Peter* thinks you mad,
You make men desp'rate if they once are bad:
Else might he take to Virtue some years hence—   60
   P. As *S(elkirk)*, if he lives, will love the PRINCE.
   F. Strange spleen to *S(elkir)k*!
               P. Do I wrong the Man?
God knows, I praise a Courtier where I can.
When I confess, there *is* who feels for Fame,
And melts to Goodness, need I SCARBROW name?
Pleas'd let me own, in *Esher*'s peaceful Grove
(Where *Kent* and Nature vye for PELHAM's Love)
The Scene, the Master, opening to my view,
I sit and dream I see my CRAGS anew!
   Ev'n in a Bishop I can spy Desert;   70
Secker is decent, *Rundel* has a Heart,

Manners with Candour are to *Benson* giv'n,
To *Berkley*, ev'ry Virtue under Heav'n.
    But does the Court a worthy Man remove?
That instant, I declare, he has my Love:
I shun his Zenith, court his mild Decline;
Thus SOMMERS once, and HALIFAX were mine.
Oft in the clear, still Mirrour of Retreat,
I study'd SHREWSBURY, the wise and great:
CARLETON's calm Sense, and STANHOPE's noble Flame,   80
Compar'd, and knew their gen'rous End the same:
How pleasing ATTERBURY's softer hour!
How shin'd the Soul, unconquered in the Tow'r!
How can I PULT'NEY, CHESTERFIELD forget,
While *Roman* Spirit charms, and *Attic* Wit:
ARGYLE, the State's whole Thunder born to wield,
And shake alike the Senate and the Field:
Or WYNDHAM, just to Freedom and the Throne,
The Master of our Passions, and his own.
Names, which I long have lov'd, nor lov'd in vain,   90
Rank'd with their Friends, not number'd with their
     'Train;
And if yet higher the proud List should end,
Still let me say! No Follower, but a Friend.
    Yet think not Friendship only prompts my Lays;
I follow *Virtue*, where she shines, I praise,
Point she to Priest or Elder, Whig or Tory,
Or round a Quaker's Beaver cast a Glory.
I never (to my sorrow I declare)
Din'd with the MAN of ROSS, or my LORD MAY'R.
Some, in their choice of Friends (nay, look not grave)   100
Have still a secret Byass to a Knave:
To find an honest man, I beat about,
And love him, court him, praise him, in or out.
    F. Then why so few commended?

                      P. Not so fierce;
Find you the Virtue, and I'll find the Verse.
But random Praise—the Task can ne'er be done,
Each Mother asks it for her Booby Son,

Each Widow asks it for the Best of Men,
For him she weeps, and him she weds agen.
Praise cannot stoop, like Satire, to the Ground;   110
The Number may be hang'd, but not be crown'd.
Enough for half the Greatest of these days
To 'scape my Censure, not expect my Praise:
Are they not rich? what more can they pretend?
Dare they to hope a Poet for their Friend?
What RICHELIEU wanted, LOUIS scarce could gain,
And what young AMMON wish'd, but wish'd in vain.
No Pow'r the Muse's Friendship can command;
No Pow'r, when Virtue claims it, can withstand:
To *Cato*, *Virgil* pay'd one honest line;   120
O let my Country's Friends illumin mine!
—What are you thinking? F. Faith, the thought's no Sin,
I think your Friends are out, and would be in.
    P. If merely to come in, Sir, they go out,
The way they take is strangely round about.
    F. They too may be corrupted, you'll allow?
    P. I only call those Knaves who are so now.
Is that too little? Come then, I'll comply—
Spirit of *Arnall*! aid me while I lye.
COBHAM's a Coward, POLWARTH is a Slave,   130
And LYTTLETON a dark, designing Knave,
St JOHN has ever been a wealthy Fool—
But let me add, Sir ROBERT's mighty dull,
Has never made a Friend in private life,
And was, besides, a Tyrant to his Wife.
    But pray, when others praise him, do I blame?
Call *Verres*, *Wolsey*, any odious name?
Why rail they then, if but a Wreath of mine
Oh All-accomplish'd St JOHN! deck thy Shrine?
    What? shall each spur-gall'd Hackney of the Day,   140
When *Paxton* gives him double Pots and Pay,
Or each new-pension'd Sycophant, pretend
To break my Windows, if I treat a Friend;
Then wisely plead, to me they meant no hurt,
But 'twas my Guest at whom they threw the dirt?

Sure, if I spare the Minister, no rules
Of Honour bind me, not to maul his Tools;
Sure, if they cannot cut, it may be said
His Saws are toothless, and his Hatchets Lead.
   It anger'd TURENNE, once upon a day,   150
To see a Footman kick'd that took his pay:
But when he heard th'Affront the Fellow gave,
Knew one a Man of Honour, one a Knave;
The prudent Gen'ral turn'd it to a jest,
And begg'd, he'd take the pains to kick the rest.
Which not at present having time to do—
   F. Hold Sir! for God's-sake, where's th'Affront to
      you?
Against your worship when had *S(elkir)k* writ?
Or *P(a)ge* pour'd forth the Torrent of his Wit?
Or grant, the Bard whose Distich all commend,   160
   '*In Pow'r a Servant, out of Pow'r a Friend,*'
To *W(alpo)le* guilty of some venial Sin,
What's that to you, who ne'er was out nor in?
   The Priest whose Flattery be-dropt the Crown,
How hurt he you? he only stain'd the Gown.
And how did, pray, the Florid Youth offend,
Whose Speech you took, and gave it to a Friend?
   P. Faith it imports not much from whom it came⎞
Whoever borrow'd, could not be to blame,   ⎟
Since the whole House did afterwards the same: ⎠ 170
Let Courtly Wits to Wits afford supply,
As Hog to Hog in Huts of *Westphaly*;
If one, thro' Nature's Bounty or his Lord's,
Has what the frugal, dirty soil affords,
From him the next receives it, thick or thin,
As pure a Mess almost as it came in;
The blessed Benefit, not there confin'd,
Drops to the third who nuzzles close behind;
From tail to mouth, they feed, and they carouse;
The last, full fairly gives it to the *House.*   180
   F. This filthy Simile, this beastly Line,
Quite turns my Stomach—*P.* So does Flatt'ry mine;

And all your Courtly Civet-Cats can vent,
Perfume to you, to me is Excrement.
    But hear me further.—*Japhet*, 'tis agreed,
Writ not, and *Chartres* scarce could write or read,
In all the Courts of *Pindus* guiltless quite;
But Pens can forge, my Friend, that cannot write.
And must no Egg in *Japhet*'s Face be thrown,
Because the Deed he forg'd was not my own?   190
Must never Patriot then declaim at Gin,
Unless, good man! he has been fairly in?
No zealous Pastor blame a failing Spouse,
Without a staring Reason on his Brows?
And each Blasphemer quite escape the Rod,
Because the insult's not on Man, but God?
    Ask you what Provocation I have had?
The strong Antipathy of Good to Bad.
When Truth or Virtue an Affront endures,
Th'Affront is mine, my Friend, and should be yours.   200
Mine, as a Foe profess'd to false Pretence,
Who think a Coxcomb's Honour like his Sense;
Mine, as a Friend to ev'ry worthy mind;
And mine as Man, who feel for all mankind.
    F. You're strangely proud.
                      P. So proud, I am no Slave:⎫
So impudent, I own myself no Knave: ⎬
So odd, my Country's Ruin makes me grave.   ⎭
Yes, I am proud; I must be proud to see
Men not afraid of God, afraid of me:
Safe from the Bar, the Pulpit, and the Throne,   210
Yet touch'd and sham'd by *Ridicule* alone.
    O sacred Weapon! left for Truth's defence,
Sole Dread of Folly, Vice, and Insolence!
To all but Heav'n-directed hands deny'd,
The Muse may give thee, but the Gods must guide.
Rev'rent I touch thee! but with honest zeal;
To rowze the Watchmen of the Publick Weal,
To Virtue's Work provoke the tardy Hall,
And goad the Prelate slumb'ring in his Stall.

Ye tinsel Insects! whom a Court maintains, 220
That counts your Beauties only by your Stains,
Spin all your Cobwebs o'er the Eye of Day!
The Muse's wing shall brush you all away:
All his Grace preaches, all his Lordship sings,
All that makes Saints of Queens, and Gods of Kings,
All, all but Truth, drops dead-born from the Press,
Like the last Gazette, or the last Address.
 When black Ambition stains a Publick Cause,
A Monarch's sword when mad Vain-glory draws,
Not *Waller*'s Wreath can hide the Nation's Scar, 230
Nor *Boileau* turn the Feather to a Star.
 Not so, when diadem'd with Rays divine,
Touch'd with the Flame that breaks from Virtue's Shrine,
Her Priestless Muse forbids the Good to dye,
And ope's the Temple of Eternity;
There other *Trophies* deck the truly Brave,
Than such as *Anstis* casts into the Grave;
Far other *Stars* than * and ** wear,
And may descend to *Mordington* from *Stair*:
Such as on HOUGH's unsully'd Mitre shine, 240
Or beam, good DIGBY! from a Heart like thine.
Let Envy howl while Heav'n's whole Chorus sings,
And bark at Honour not confer'd by Kings;
Let Flatt'ry sickening see the Incense rise,
Sweet to the World, and grateful to the Skies:
Truth guards the Poet, sanctifies the line,
And makes Immortal, Verse as mean as mine.
 Yes, the last Pen for Freedom let me draw,
When Truth stands trembling on the edge of Law:
Here, Last of *Britons*! let your Names be read; 250
Are none, none living? let me praise the Dead,
And for that Cause which made your Fathers shine,
Fall, by the Votes of their degen'rate Line!
 F. Alas! alas! pray end what you began,
And write next winter more *Essays on Man*.

THE DUNCIAD

Book IV

Yet, yet a moment, one dim Ray of Light
Indulge, dread Chaos, and eternal Night!
Of darkness visible so much be lent,
As half to shew, half veil the deep Intent.
Ye Pow'rs! whose Mysteries restor'd I sing,
To whom Time bears me on his rapid wing,
Suspend a while your Force inertly strong,
Then take at once the Poet and the Song.

Now flam'd the Dog-star's unpropitious ray,
Smote ev'ry Brain, and wither'd ev'ry Bay;   10
Sick was the Sun, the Owl forsook his bow'r,
The moon-struck Prophet felt the madding hour:
Then rose the Seed of Chaos, and of Night,
To blot out Order, and extinguish Light,
Of dull and venal a new World to mold,
And bring Saturnian days of Lead and Gold.

She mounts the Throne: her head a Cloud conceal'd,
In broad Effulgence all below reveal'd,
('Tis thus aspiring Dulness ever shines)
Soft on her lap her Laureat son reclines.   20

Beneath her foot-stool, *Science* groans in Chains,
And *Wit* dreads Exile, Penalties and Pains.
There foam'd rebellious *Logic*, gagg'd and bound,
There, stript, fair *Rhet'ric* languish'd on the ground;
His blunted Arms by *Sophistry* are born,
And shameless *Billingsgate* her Robes adorn.
Morality, by her false Guardians drawn,
Chicane in Furs, and *Casuistry* in Lawn,
Gasps, as they straiten at each end the cord,
And dies, when Dulness gives her Page the word.   30
Mad *Mathesis* alone was unconfin'd,
Too mad for mere material chains to bind,

152

Now to pure Space lifts her extatic stare,
Now running round the Circle, finds it square.
But held in ten-fold bonds the *Muses* lie,
Watch'd both by Envy's and by Flatt'ry's eye:
There to her heart sad Tragedy addrest
The dagger wont to pierce the Tyrant's breast;
But sober History restrain'd her rage,
And promis'd Vengeance on a barb'rous age.   40
There sunk Thalia, nerveless, cold, and dead,
Had not her Sister Satyr held her head:
Nor cou'd'st thou, CHESTERFIELD! a tear refuse,
Thou wept'st, and with thee wept each gentle Muse.
    When lo! a Harlot form soft sliding by,
With mincing step, small voice, and languid eye;
Foreign her air, her robe's discordant pride
In patch-work flutt'ring, and her head aside:
By singing Peers up-held on either hand,
She tripp'd and laugh'd, too pretty much to stand;   50
Cast on the prostrate Nine a scornful look,
Then thus in quaint Recitativo spoke.
    'O *Cara! Cara!* silence all that train:
Joy to great Chaos! let Division reign:
Chromatic tortures soon shall drive them hence,
Break all their nerves, and fritter all their sense:
One Trill shall harmonize joy, grief, and rage,
Wake the dull Church, and lull the ranting Stage;
To the same notes thy sons shall hum, or snore,
And all thy yawning daughters cry, *encore.*   60
Another Phœbus, thy own Phœbus, reigns,
Joys in my jiggs, and dances in my chains.
But soon, ah soon Rebellion will commence,
If Music meanly borrows aid from Sense:
Strong in new Arms, lo! Giant Handel stands,
Like bold Briareus, with a hundred hands;
To stir, to rouze, to shake the Soul he comes,
And Jove's own Thunders follow Mars's Drums.
Arrest him, Empress; or you sleep no more'——
She heard, and drove him to th'Hibernian shore.   70

153

And now had Fame's posterior Trumpet blown,
And all the Nations summon'd to the Throne.
The young, the old, who feel her inward sway,
One instinct seizes, and transports away.
None need a guide, by sure Attraction led,
And strong impulsive gravity of Head:
None want a place, for all their Centre found,
Hung to the Goddess, and coher'd around.
Not closer, orb in orb, conglob'd are seen
The buzzing Bees about their dusky Queen.   80
   The gath'ring number, as it moves along.
Involves a vast involuntary throng,
Who gently drawn, and struggling less and less,
Roll in her Vortex, and her pow'r confess.
Not those alone who passive own her laws,
But who, weak rebels, more advance her cause.
Whate'er of dunce in College or in Town
Sneers at another, in toupee or gown;
Whate'er of mungril no one class admits,
A wit with dunces, and a dunce with wits.   90
   Nor absent they, no members of her state,
Who pay her homage in her sons, the Great;
Who false to Phœbus, bow the knee to Baal;
Or impious, preach his Word without a call.
Patrons, who sneak from living worth to dead,
With-hold the pension, and set up the head;
Or vest dull Flatt'ry in the sacred Gown;
Or give from fool to fool the Laurel crown.
And (last and worst) with all the cant of wit,
Without the soul, the Muse's Hypocrit.   100
   There march'd the bard and blockhead, side by side,
Who rhym'd for hire, and patroniz'd for pride.
Narcissus, prais'd with all a Parson's pow'r,
Look'd a white lilly sunk beneath a show'r.
There mov'd Montalto with superior air;
His stretch'd-out arm display'd a Volume fair;
Courtiers and Patriots in two ranks divide,
Thro' both he pass'd, and bow'd from side to side:

But as in graceful act, with awful eye
Compos'd he stood, bold Benson thrust him by: 110
On two unequal crutches propt he came,
Milton's on this, on that one Johnston's name.
The decent Knight retir'd with sober rage,
Withdrew his hand, and clos'd the pompous page.
But (happy for him as the times went then)
Appear'd Apollo's May'r and Aldermen,
On whom three hundred gold-capt youths await,
To lug the pond'rous volume off in state.
    When Dulness, smiling—'Thus revive the Wits!
But murder first, and mince them all to bits;   120
As erst Medea (cruel, so to save!)
A new Edition of old Æson gave,
Let standard-Authors, thus, like trophies born,
Appear more glorious as more hack'd and torn,
And you, my Critics! in the chequer'd shade,
Admire new light thro' holes yourselves have made.
    'Leave not a foot of verse, a foot of stone,
A Page, a Grave, that they can call their own;
But spread, my sons, your glory thin or thick,
On passive paper, or on solid brick.   130
So by each Bard an Alderman shall sit,
A heavy Lord shall hang at ev'ry Wit,
And while on Fame's triumphal Car they ride,
Some Slave of mine be pinion'd to their side.'
    Now crowds on crowds around the Goddess press,
Each eager to present the first Address.
Dunce scorning Dunce beholds the next advance,
But Fop shews Fop superior complaisance.
When lo! a Spectre rose, whose index-hand
Held forth the Virtue of the dreadful wand;   140
His beaver'd brow a birchen garland wears,
Dropping with Infant's blood, and Mother's tears.
O'er ev'ry vein a shudd'ring horror runs;
Eton and Winton shake thro' all their Sons.
All Flesh is humbled, Westminster's bold race
Shrink, and confess the Genius of the place:

The pale Boy-Senator yet tingling stands,
And holds his breeches close with both his hands.
   Then thus. 'Since Man from beast by Words is known,
Words are Man's province, Words we teach alone.   150
When Reason doubtful, like the Samian letter,
Points him two ways, the narrower is the better.
Plac'd at the door of Learning, youth to guide,
We never suffer it to stand too wide.
To ask, to guess, to know, as they commence,
As Fancy opens the quick springs of Sense,
We ply the Memory, we load the brain,
Bind rebel Wit, and double chain on chain,
Confine the thought, to exercise the breath;
And keep them in the pale of Words till death.   160
Whate'er the talents, or howe'er design'd,
We hang one jingling padlock on the mind:
A Poet the first day, he dips his quill;
And what the last? a very Poet still.
Pity! the charm works only in our wall,
Lost, lost too soon in yonder House or Hall.
There truant WYNDHAM ev'ry Muse gave o'er,
There TALBOT sunk, and was a Wit no more!
How sweet an Ovid, MURRAY was our boast!
How many Martials were in PULT'NEY lost!   170
Else sure some Bard, to our eternal praise,
In twice ten thousand rhyming nights and days,
Had reach'd the Work, the All that mortal can:
And South beheld that Master-piece of Man.'
   'Oh (cry'd the Goddess) for some pedant Reign!
Some gentle JAMES, to bless the land again:
To stick the Doctor's Chair into the Throne,
Give law to Words, or war with Words alone,
Senates and Courts with Greek and Latin rule,
And turn the Council to a Grammar Sehool!   180
For sure, if Dulness sees a grateful Day,
'Tis in the shade of Arbitrary Sway.
O! if my sons may learn one earthly thing,
Teach but that one, sufficient for a King;

That which my Priests, and mine alone, maintain,
Which as it dies, or lives, we fall, or reign:
May you, may Cam, and Isis preach it long!
"The RIGHT DIVINE of Kings to govern wrong".'
    Prompt at the call, around the Goddess roll
Broad hats, and hoods, and caps, a sable shoal: 190
Thick and more thick the black blockade extends,
A hundred head of Aristotle's friends.
Nor wert thou, Isis! wanting to the day,
(Tho' Christ-church long kept prudishly away.)
Each staunch Polemic, stubborn as a rock,
Each fierce Logician, still expelling Locke,
Came whip and spur, and dash'd thro' thin and thick
On German Crouzaz, and Dutch Burgersdyck.
As many quit the streams that murm'ring fall
To lull the sons of Marg'ret and Clare-hall,   200
Where Bentley late tempestuous wont to sport
In troubled waters, but now sleeps in Port.
Before them march'd that awful Aristarch;
Plow'd was his front with many a deep Remark:
His Hat, which never vail'd to human pride,
Walker with rev'rence took, and lay'd aside.
Low bow'd the rest: He, kingly, did but nod;
So upright Quakers please both Man and God.
'Mistress! dismiss that rabble from your throne:
Avaunt—is Aristarchus yet unknown?   210
Thy mighty Scholiast, whose unweary'd pains
Made Horace dull, and humbled Milton's strains.
Turn what they will to Verse, their toil is vain,
Critics like me shall make it Prose again.
Roman and Greek Grammarians! know your Better:
Author of something yet more great than Letter;
While tow'ring o'er your Alphabet, like Saul,
Stands our Digamma, and o'ertops them all.
'Tis true, on Words is still our whole debate,
Disputes of *Me* or *Te*, of *aut* or *at*,   220
To sound or sink in *cano*, O or A,
Or give up Cicero to C or K.

157

Let Freind affect to speak as Terence spoke,
And Alsop never but like Horace joke:
For me, what Virgil, Pliny may deny,
Manilius or Solinus shall supply:
For Attic Phrase in Plato let them seek,
I poach in Suidas for unlicens'd Greek.
In ancient Sense if any needs will deal,
Be sure I give them Fragments, not a Meal;   230
What Gellius or Stobæus hash'd before,
Or chew'd by blind old Scholiasts o'er and o'er.
The critic Eye, that microscope of Wit,
Sees hairs and pores, examines bit by bit:
How parts relate to parts, or they to whole,
The body's harmony, the beaming soul,
Are things which Kuster, Burman, Wasse shall see,
When Man's whole frame is obvious to a *Flea*.

'Ah, think not, Mistress! more true Dulness lies
In Folly's Cap, than Wisdom's grave disguise.   240
Like buoys, that never sink into the flood,
On Learning's surface we but lie and nod.
Thine is the genuine head of many a house,
And much Divinity without a *Νοῦς*.
Nor could a BARROW work on ev'ry block,
Nor has one ATTERBURY spoil'd the flock.
See! still thy own, the heavy Canon roll,
And Metaphysic smokes involve the Pole.
For thee we dim the eyes, and stuff the head
With all such reading as was never read: 250
For thee explain a thing till all men doubt it,
And write about it, Goddess, and about it:
So spins the silk-worm small its slender store,
And labours till it clouds itself all o'er.

'What tho' we let some better sort of fool
Thrid ev'ry science, run thro' ev'ry school?
Never by tumbler thro' the hoops was shown
Such skill in passing all, and touching none.
He may indeed (if sober all this time)
Plague with Dispute, or persecute with Rhyme.   260

We only furnish what he cannot use,
Or wed to what he must divorce, a Muse:
Full in the midst of Euclid dip at once,
And petrify a Genius to a Dunce:
Or set on Metaphysic ground to prance,
Show all his paces, not a step advance.
With the same Cement, ever sure to bind,
We bring to one dead level ev'ry mind.
Then take him to devellop, if you can,
And hew the Block off, and get out the Man.   270
But wherefore waste I words? I see advance
Whore, Pupil, and lac'd Governor from France.
Walker! our hat'—nor more he deign'd to say,
But, stern as Ajax' spectre, strode away.

In flow'd at once a gay embroider'd race,
And titt'ring push'd the Pedants off the place:
Some would have spoken, but the voice was drown'd
By the French horn, or by the op'ning hound.
The first came forwards, with as easy mien,
As if he saw St James's and the Queen.   280
When thus th'attendant Orator begun.
'Receive, great Empress! thy accomplish'd Son:
Thine from the birth, and sacred from the rod,
A dauntless infant! never scar'd with God.
The Sire saw, one by one, his Virtues wake:
The Mother begg'd the blessing of a Rake.
Thou gav'st that Ripeness, which so soon began,
And ceas'd so soon, he ne'er was Boy, nor Man.
Thro' School and College, thy kind cloud o'ercast,
Safe and unseen the young Æneas past: 290
Thence bursting glorious, all at once let down,
Stunn'd with his giddy Larum half the town.
Intrepid then, o'er seas and lands he flew:
Europe he saw, and Europe saw him too.
There all thy gifts and graces we display,
Thou, only thou, directing all our way!
To where the Seine, obsequious as she runs,
Pours at great Bourbon's feet her silken sons;

Or Tyber, now no longer Roman, rolls,
Vain of Italian Arts, Italian Souls: 300
To happy Convents, bosom'd deep in vines,
Where slumber Abbots, purple as their wines:
To Isles of fragrance, lilly-silver'd vales,
Diffusing languor in the panting gales:
To lands of singing, or of dancing slaves,
Love-whisp'ring woods, and lute-resounding waves.
But chief her shrine where naked Venus keeps,
And Cupids ride the Lyon of the Deeps;
Where, eas'd of Fleets, the Adriatic main
Wafts the smooth Eunuch and enamour'd swain.   310
Led by my hand, he saunter'd Europe round,
And gather'd ev'ry Vice on Christian ground;
Saw ev'ry Court, heard ev'ry King declare
His royal Sense, of Op'ra's or the Fair;
The Stews and Palace equally explor'd,
Intrigu'd with glory, and with spirit whor'd;
Try'd all *hors-d'œuvres*, all *liqueurs* defin'd,
Judicious drank, and greatly-daring din'd;
Dropt the dull lumber of the Latin store,
Spoil'd his own language, and acquir'd no more;   320
All Classic learning lost on Classic ground;
And last turn'd *Air*, the Echo of a Sound!
See now, half-cur'd, and perfectly well-bred,
With nothing but a Solo in his head;
As much Estate, and Principle, and Wit,
As Jansen, Fleetwood, Cibber shall think fit;
Stol'n from a Duel, follow'd by a Nun,
And, if a Borough chuse him, not undone;
See, to my country happy I restore
This glorious Youth, and add one Venus more.   330
Her too receive (for her my soul adores)
So may the sons of sons of sons of whores,
Prop thine, O Empress! like each neighbour Throne,
And make a long Posterity thy own.'
    Pleas'd, she accepts the Hero, and the Dame,
Wraps in her Veil, and frees from sense of Shame.

Then look'd, and saw a lazy, lolling sort,
Unseen at Church, at Senate, or at Court,
Of ever-listless Loit'rers, that attend
No cause, no Trust, no Duty, and no Friend.   340
Thee too, my Paridel! she mark'd thee there,
Stretch'd on the rack of a too easy chair,
And heard thy everlasting yawn confess
The Pains and Penalties of Idleness.
She pity'd! but her Pity only shed
Benigner influence on thy nodding head.

But Annius, crafty Seer, with ebon wand,
And well dissembled em'rald on his hand,
False as his Gems, and canker'd as his Coins,
Came, cramm'd with capon, from where Pollio dines. 350
Soft, as the wily Fox is seen to creep,
Where bask on sunny banks the simple sheep,
Walk round and round, now prying here, now there;
So he; but pious, whisper'd first his pray'r.

'Grant, gracious Goddess! grant me still to cheat,
O may thy cloud still cover the deceit!
Thy choicer mists on this assembly shed,
But pour them thickest on the noble head.
So shall each youth, assisted by our eyes,
See other Cæsars, other Homers rise;   360
Thro' twilight ages hunt th'Athenian fowl,
Which Chalcis Gods, and mortals call an Owl,
Now see an Attys, now a Cecrops clear,
Nay, Mahomet! the Pigeon at thine ear;
Be rich in ancient brass, tho' not in gold,
And keep his Lares, tho' his house be sold;
To headless Phœbe his fair bride postpone,
Honour a Syrian Prince above his own;
Lord of an Otho, if I vouch it true;
Blest in one Niger, till he knows of two.'   370

Mummius o'erheard him: Mummius, Fool-renown'd,
Who like his Cheops stinks above the ground,
Fierce as a startl'd Adder, swel.'d, and said,
Rattling an ancient Sistrum at his head.

'Speak'st thou of Syrian Princes? Traitor base!
Mine, Goddess! mine is all the horned race.
True, he had wit, to make their value rise;
From foolish Greeks to steal them, was as wise;
More glorious yet, from barb'rous hands to keep,
When Sallee Rovers chac'd him on the deep.   380
Then taught by Hermes, and divinely bold,
Down his own throat he risqu'd the Grecian gold;
Receiv'd each Demi-God, with pious care,
Deep in his Entrails—I rever'd them there,
I bought them, shrouded in that living shrine,
And, at their second birth, they issue mine.'

'Witness great Ammon! by whose horns I swore,
(Reply'd soft Annius) this our paunch before
Still bears them, faithful; and that thus I eat,
Is to refund the Medals with the meat.   390
To prove me, Goddess, clear of all design,
Bid me with Pollio sup, as well as dine:
There all the Learn'd shall at the labour stand,
And Douglas lend his soft, obstetric hand.'

The Goddess smiling seem'd to give consent;
So back to Pollio, hand in hand, they went.

Then thick as Locusts black'ning all the ground,
A tribe, with weeds and shells fantastic crown'd,
Each with some wond'rous gift approach'd the Pow'r,
A Nest, a Toad, a Fungus, or a Flow'r.   400
But far the foremost, two, with earnest zeal,
And aspect ardent to the Throne appeal.

The first thus open'd: 'Hear thy suppliant's call,
Great Queen, and common Mother of us all!
Fair from its humble bed I rear'd this Flow'r,
Suckled, and chear'd, with air, and sun, and show'r,
Soft on the paper ruff its leaves I spread,
Bright with the gilded button tipt its head,
Then thron'd in glass, and nam'd it CAROLINE:
Each Maid cry'd, charming! and each Youth, divine! 410
Did Nature's pencil ever blend such rays,
Such vary'd light in one promiscuous blaze?

Now prostrate! dead! behold that Caroline:
No Maid cries, charming! and no Youth, divine!
And lo the wretch! whose vile, whose insect lust
Lay'd this gay daughter of the Spring in dust.
Oh punish him, or to th'Elysian shades
Dismiss my soul, where no Carnation fades.'
    He ceas'd, and wept. With innocence of mien,
Th'Accus'd stood forth, and thus address'd the Queen.   420
'Of all th'enamel'd race, whose silv'ry wing
Waves to the tepid Zephyrs of the spring,
Or swims along the fluid atmosphere,
Once brightest shin'd this child of Heat and Air.
I saw, and started from its vernal bow'r
The rising game, and chac'd from flow'r to flow'r.
It fled, I follow'd; now in hope, now pain;
It stopt, I stopt; it mov'd, I mov'd again.
At last it fix'd, 'twas on what plant it pleas'd,
And where it fix'd, the beauteous bird I seiz'd: 430
Rose or Carnation was below my care;
I meddle, Goddess! only in my sphere.
I tell the naked fact without disguise,
And, to excuse it, need but shew the prize;
Whose spoils this paper offers to your eye,
Fair ev'n in death! this peerless *Butterfly*.'
    'My sons! (she answer'd) both have done your parts:
Live happy both, and long promote our arts.
But hear a Mother, when she recommends
To your fraternal care, our sleeping friends.   440
The common Soul, of Heav'n's more frugal make,
Serves but to keep fools pert, and knaves awake:
A drowzy Watchman, that just gives a knock,
And breaks our rest, to tell us what's a clock.
Yet by some object ev'ry brain is stirr'd;
The dull may waken to a Humming-bird;
The most recluse, discreetly open'd, find
Congenial matter in the Cockle-kind;
The mind, in Metaphysics at a loss,
May wander in a wilderness of Moss: 450

The head that turns at super-lunar things,
Poiz'd with a tail, may steer on Wilkins' wings.
  'O! would the Sons of Men once think their Eyes
And Reason giv'n them but to study *Flies*!
See Nature in some partial narrow shape,
And let the Author of the Whole escape:
Learn but to trifle; or, who most observe,
To wonder at their Maker, not to serve.'
  'Be that my task (replies a gloomy Clerk,
Sworn foe to Myst'ry, yet divinely dark;   460
Whose pious hope aspires to see the day
When Moral Evidence shall quite decay,
And damns implicit faith, and holy lies,
Prompt to impose, and fond to dogmatize:)
Let others creep by timid steps, and slow,
On plain Experience lay foundations low,
By common sense to common knowledge bred,
And last, to Nature's Cause thro' Nature led.
All-seeing in thy mists, we want no guide,
Mother of Arrogance, and Source of Pride!   470
We nobly take the high Priori Road,
And reason downward, till we doubt of God:
Make Nature still incroach upon his plan;
And shove him off as far as e'er we can:
Thrust some Mechanic Cause into his place;
Or bind in Matter, or diffuse in Space.
Or, at one bound o'erleaping all his laws,
Make God Man's Image, Man the final Cause,
Find Virtue local, all Relation scorn,
See all in *Self*, and but for self be born: 480
Of nought so certain as our *Reason* still,
Of nought so doubtful as of *Soul* and *Will*.
Oh hide the God still more! and make us see
Such as Lucretius drew, a God like Thee:
Wrapt up in Self, a God without a Thought,
Regardless of our merit or default.
Or that bright Image to our fancy draw,
Which Theocles in raptur'd vision saw,

164

While thro' Poetic scenes the Genius roves,
Or wanders wild in Academic Groves; 490
That NATURE our Society adores,
Where Tindal dictates, and Silenus snores.'
   Rous'd at his name, up rose the bowzy Sire,
And shook from out his Pipe the seeds of fire;
Then snapt his box, and strok'd his belly down:
Rosy and rev'rend, tho' without a Gown.
Bland and familiar to the throne he came,
Led up the Youth, and call'd the Goddess *Dame*.
Then thus. 'From Priest-craft happily set free,
Lo! ev'ry finish'd Son returns to thee: 500
First slave to Words, then vassal to a Name,
Then dupe to Party; child and man the same;
Bounded by Nature, narrow'd still by Art,
A trifling head, and a contracted heart.
Thus bred, thus taught, how many have I seen,
Smiling on all, and smil'd on by a Queen.
Mark'd out for Honours, honour'd for their Birth,
To thee the most rebellious things on earth:
Now to thy gentle shadow all are shrunk,
All melted down, in Pension, or in Punk! 510
So K(ent) so B(erkeley) sneak'd into the grave,
A Monarch's half, and half a Harlot's slave.
Poor W(arwick) nipt in Folly's broadest bloom,
Who praises now? his Chaplain on his Tomb.
Then take them all, oh take them to thy breast!
Thy *Magus*, Goddess! shall perform the rest.'
   With that, a WIZARD OLD his *Cup* extends;
Which whoso tastes, forgets his former friends,
Sire, Ancestors, Himself. One casts his eyes
Up to a *Star*, and like Endymion dies: 520
A *Feather* shooting from another's head,
Extracts his brain, and Principle is fled,
Lost in his God, his Country, ev'ry thing;
And nothing left but Homage to a King!
The vulgar herd turn off to roll with Hogs,
To run with Horses, or to hunt with Dogs;

But, sad example! never to escape
Their Infamy, still keep the human shape.
　　But she, good Goddess, sent to ev'ry child
Firm Impudence, or Stupefaction mild;　　　　　　　　530
And strait succeeded, leaving shame no room,
Cibberian forehead, or Cimmerian gloom.
　　Kind Self-conceit to some her glass applies,
Which no one looks in with another's eyes:
But as the Flatt'rer or Dependant paint,
Beholds himself a Patriot, Chief, or Saint.
　　On others Int'rest her gay liv'ry flings,
Int'rest, that waves on Party-colour'd wings:
Turn'd to the Sun, she casts a thousand dyes,
And, as she turns, the colours fall or rise.　　　　　　540
Others the Syren Sisters warble round,
And empty heads console with empty sound.
No more, alas! the voice of Fame they hear,
The balm of Dulness trickling in their ear.
Great C(owper), H(arcourt), P(arker), R(aymond), K(ing),
Why all your Toils? your sons have learn'd to sing.
How quick Ambition hastes to ridicule!
The Sire is made a Peer, the Son a Fool.
　　On some, a Priest succinct in amice white
Attends; all flesh is nothing in his sight!　　　　　　550
Beeves, at his touch, at once to jelly turn,
And the huge Boar is shrunk into an Urn:
The board with specious miracles he loads,
Turns Hares to Larks, and Pigeons into Toads.
Another (for in all what one can shine?)
Explains the *Seve* and *Verdeur* of the Vine.
What cannot copious Sacrifice attone?
Thy Treufles, Perigord! thy Hams, Bayonne!
With French Libation, and Italian Strain,
Wash Bladen white, and expiate Hays's stain.　　　　560
Knight lifts the head, for what are crowds undone
To three essential Partriges in one?
Gone ev'ry blush, and silent all reproach,
Contending Princes mount them in their Coach.

Next bidding all draw near on bended knees,
The Queen confers her *Titles* and *Degrees*.
Her children first of more distinguish'd sort,
Who study Shakespeare at the Inns of Court,
Impale a Glow-worm, or Vertù profess,
Shine in the dignity of F.R.S.   570
Some, deep Free-Masons, join the silent race
Worthy to fill Pythagoras's place:
Some Botanists, or Florists at the least,
Or issue Members of an Annual feast.
Nor past the meanest unregarded, one
Rose a Gregorian, one a Gormogon.
The last, not least in honour or applause,
Isis and Cam made Doctors of her Laws.
    Then blessing all, 'Go Children of my care!
To Practice now from Theory repair.   580
All my commands are easy, short, and full:
My Sons! be proud, be selfish, and be dull.
Guard my Prerogative, assert my Throne:
This Nod confirms each Privilege your own.
The Cap and Switch be sacred to his Grace;
With Staff and Pumps the Marquis lead the Race;
From Stage to Stage the licens'd Earl may run,
Pair'd with his Fellow-Charioteer the Sun;
The learned Baron Butterflies design,
Or draw to silk Arachne's subtile line;   590
The Judge to dance his brother Sergeant call;
The Senator at Cricket urge the Ball;
The Bishop stow (Pontific Luxury!)
An hundred Souls of Turkeys in a pye;
The sturdy Squire to Gallic masters stoop,
And drown his Lands and Manors in a Soupe.
Others import yet nobler arts from France,
Teach Kings to fiddle, and make Senates dance.
Perhaps more high some daring son may soar,
Proud to my list to add one Monarch more;   600
And nobly conscious, Princes are but things
Born for First Ministers, as Slaves for Kings,

Tyrant supreme! shall three Estates command,
And MAKE ONE MIGHTY DUNCIAD OF THE LAND!'
　　More she had spoke, but yawn'd—All Nature nods:
What Mortal can resist the Yawn of Gods?
Churches and Chapels instantly it reach'd;
(St James's first, for leaden Gilbert preach'd)
Then catch'd the Schools; the Hall scarce kept awake;
The Convocation gap'd, but could not speak:　　　　610
Lost was the Nation's Sense, nor could be found,
While the long solemn Unison went round:
Wide, and more wide, it spread o'er all the realm;
Ev'n Palinurus nodded at the Helm:
The Vapour mild o'er each Committee crept;
Unfinish'd Treaties in each Office slept;
And Chiefless Armies doz'd out the Campaign;
And Navies yawn'd for Orders on the Main.
　　O Muse! relate (for you can tell alone,
Wits have short Memories, and Dunces none)　　　620
Relate, who first, who last resign'd to rest;
Whose Heads she partly, whose completely blest;
What Charms could Faction, what Ambition lull,
The Venal quiet, and intrance the Dull;
'Till drown'd was Sense, and Shame, and Right, and Wrong—
O sing, and hush the Nations with thy Song!

　　　*　　　*　　　*　　　*　　　*　　　*　　　*

　　In vain, in vain,—the all-composing Hour
Resistless falls: The Muse obeys the Pow'r.
She comes! she comes! the sable Throne behold
Of *Night* Primæval, and of *Chaos* old!　　　　630
Before her, *Fancy's* gilded clouds decay,
And all its varying Rain-bows die away.
Wit shoots in vain its momentary fires,
The meteor drops, and in a flash expires.
As one by one, at dread Medea's strain,
The sick'ning stars fade off th'ethereal plain:
As Argus' eyes by Hermes' wand opprest,
Clos'd one by one to everlasting rest;

Thus at her felt approach, and secret might,
Art after *Art* goes out, and all is Night.   640
See skulking *Truth* to her old Cavern fled,
Mountains of Casuistry heap'd o'er her head!
Philosophy, that lean'd on Heav'n before,
Shrinks to her second cause, and is no more.
Physic of *Metaphysic* begs defence,
And *Metaphysic* calls for aid on *Sense*!
See *Mystery* to *Mathematics* fly!
In vain! they gaze, turn giddy, rave, and die.
Religion blushing veils her sacred fires,
And unawares *Morality* expires.   650
Nor *public* Flame, nor *private*, dares to shine;
Nor *human* Spark is left, nor Glimpse *divine*!
Lo! thy dread Empire, CHAOS! is restor'd;
Light dies before thy uncreating word:
Thy hand, great Anarch! lets the curtain fall;
And Universal Darkness buries All.

NOTES

page 34   *from* AN ESSAY ON CRITICISM

Published May 1711

A few months after the publication of this poem, Addison hailed it in the *Spectator* (No. 253) as 'a Master-Piece in its Kind. The Observations follow one another like those in *Horace*'s *Art of Poetry*, without that methodical Regularity which would have been requisite in a Prose Author. They are some of them uncommon, but such as the Reader must assent to, when he sees them explained with that Elegance and Perspicuity in which they are delivered. As for those which are the most known, and the most received, they are placed in so beautiful a Light, and illustrated with such apt Allusions, that they have in them all the Graces of Novelty, and make the Reader, who was before acquainted with them, still more convinced of their Truth and Solidity.' This comment gives us some idea of what to expect, and what not to expect, of this poem. The 'Kind', the versified Art of Poetry, is virtually a separate one, having affinities to the poetic Epistle and the Essay; Horace's *Ars Poetica* is a pattern, and more recent examples had included verse essays by Mulgrave, Roscommon, Granville and Parnell, and, more important, Boileau's *L'Art Poétique* of 1674. Very early in his career, then, Pope reveals the pervading influence of Horace; he was just 23 when the poem was published, anonymously, and he may have been engaged on it as early as 1706 (see letter No. 1, to Walsh, where he discusses some points that are treated in the poem). The opening is very Horatian, and the general decorum is that of well-bred conversation, witty and familiar but able to rise to an almost sacramental tone as in ll. 57-72 of this selection. The general structure, too, is Horatian, as Addison's remark indicates: there is an easy flow from topic to topic—though Pope does not yet possess the ability to organise his observations into large enough units, so that the poem sometimes reads like a series of detached aphorisms—with the quite methodical framework concealed by an art which gives the *impression* of negligence. Moreover, the *Spectator* quotation warns us not to expect too much 'originality' of thought; Pope is more concerned with convincing us, poetically, of the truth of already 'received' observations.

He is, in fact, presenting a synthesis of the best critical thought of his own and former days. In this he is very like his master, Dryden, whose influence (rather than that of Walsh) is the pervasive 'modern' one here. Pope is at one and the same time discussing the nature of criticism, and the nature of a critic; and it is very apparent that morals enter into the discussion. Pope produces a plea for generosity in the critic, as opposed to the far more common quality of malignity; the critic, as ll. 183-94 show, must be a good man; and in his openness, above all in his humility, the ideal critic is the obverse of Atticus, in *Arbuthnot* ll. 193 ff. Pope is already convinced of the connection between the health of literature and the health of man in society, and the critic, as a guardian of the values of literature, has an important part to play. Many of Pope's dominant themes and images—the praise of Nature (that which instinctively and immediately we recognise as the Truth), the veneration for Art, the contempt for Dulness, the hatred of Pride, the love of Order—all receive their first extended expression here. We find the images of the Sun, of insects, of clouds and mists, which appear so often in Pope's later work; his metaphorical manner of thinking enables him to give liveliness to abstract critical points, and, as Addison says, to bring them forcibly home to the reader.

The discussion is continually given a satirical edge: those who fall short of the ideals of poetry and criticism are treated with scorn, are mocked as fools. Pope here—and in this his tone differs from that of Horace—is a spokesman for a group of enlightened men, rather than an individual voice; there is a certain aloofness in his manner, and it has been observed that the word 'I' does not appear in this poem. With it, Pope took his place among the leading writers of his age; with it, too, he incurred some of his first enmities, notably with the critic John Dennis. But such enmities no longer matter; we are all the better able, now, to appreciate the young poet's dazzling play of wit and felicity of expression, as we watch him announcing some of the themes which were later to receive so much more profound treatment.

(In the notes following, line references are to the text printed in these Selections.)

l. 5. *that*, tiring our patience; *this*, misleading our sense by bad criticism.

l. 7. An indication of the satirical tone of the poem is given by the fact that *Fool* and *Folly* occur 18 times, *Dull*, *Dulness*, etc., 13 times.

ll. 21 ff. The tone becomes loftier as Pope states this dominant theme: compare *Burlington* ll. 50 ff. *et passim*.

l. 22. *still*, always; l. 29 *informing*, animating, giving essential shape and life to.

ll. 33 ff. *Wit*, a key-word of the poem, has multiple meanings; it is associated with Nature (see ll. 99, 109 below) and with Judgment, and perhaps most often means the imaginative faculty, as at l. 33; at l. 34 it seems to mean good sense, or judgment. Elsewhere it may mean simply 'verbal felicity', or it can be a person endowed with wit in any of these meanings. This multiple use of the word occasionally leads to confusion (though usually the context provides a definition), but it is inseparable from Pope's desire to find a synthesis.

l. 41. What exactly is the distinction between the two verbs?

l. 46. *Character*, the essential qualities, those which distinguish him from all others; *Fable*, the plot or series of events in an epic or dramatic poem.

l. 56. *Mantuan*, refers to Virgil, born near Mantua.

l. 62. *consenting*, feeling or thinking together, unanimous; *Pæans*, songs of praise or thanksgiving to Apollo, god of poetry.

l. 70. *must not* suggests a recognition of God's purpose.

l. 76. affords the transition to the second main part of the Essay, the attack on Pride as a barrier to true criticism.

l. 79. *Byass*, the weight on one side of a bowl, in the game of bowls, which gives it its oblique motion—the *weak Head* is no doubt wooden.

l. 82. *Recruits*, fresh supplies.

ll. 87 ff. The pervading Light imagery of the poem; Reason is the Sun, driving away the fogs of Dulness.

l. 92. *Pierian Spring*, a spring sacred to the Muses, near Mt Olympus.

l. 105. *End*, intention.

ll. 109 ff. The first couplet here might suggest that Wit is simply style, something on the surface; but ll. 111-12 go deeper than this. Thus Johnson praises Gray's *Elegy* for its 'images which find a mirror in every mind'; Wit is here, in fact, closely allied to Nature and Truth.

ll. 117 ff. Notice how Pope uses his light imagery here: the perversion of it in *False Eloquence* (*gawdy, glares, without Distinction*), and the true nature of the Sun expressed by *unchanging, clears, improves*. This whole passage is a good example of Pope's ability to present his thought *poetically*.

ll. 130 ff. This is the most celebrated passage in the poem. *Numbers*, metrics generally. Addison, and later Johnson, praised Pope's ability to illustrate his critical points by making them in the form of examples. Thus l. 138 is full of *open Vowels*, l. 139 contains the *Expletive* (a word inserted in order to fill up a line) *do*, l. 140 consists of *ten low Words*, and so on. *Expletives* is stressed on the first syllable.

Exactly *how* does Pope slow down the pace of ll. 150 and 163? Notice that an *Alexandrine* (six-stress line) is not necessarily long in itself; what about l. 166? Notice, too, that Pope is not advocating onomatopœia, strictly speaking; he says the sound must '*seem* an echo to the sense', not necessarily imitate it or serve as a substitute for it; the poet, in fact, uses his technical resources in combination with the 'meaning' of the words in order to dictate how his lines should be read.

ll. 134-6. It was normal eighteenth-century practice to draw attention to triplets—the repetition of a rhyme for three lines—by brackets.

ll. 153-4. *Ease*, a smoothly flowing style, was associated with Edmund *Waller* (1606-87), and *Vigor*, *Strength*, or majesty, with Sir John *Denham* (1615-69).

l. 167. Observe the way in which Pope extends his sun/cloud image.

l. 178. *Sacred Lust* echoes Virgil's *auri sacra fames*, and has here the force of 'accursed'.

(Prose after l. 194.) Pope praises the Earl of *Roscommon* (*c.* 1633-85), whose *Essay on Translated Verse* appeared in 1684-5, and the critic William *Walsh* (1663-1708), a friend of Dryden and one of Pope's earliest literary mentors. Pope had met Walsh about 1705, and, the introduction having been made by the dramatist Wycherley, this formed one of Pope's many links with the writers of the late seventeenth century.

page 41   THE RAPE OF THE LOCK

Published 1714

The rape of the lock was a real incident, which had alienated the two great Catholic families to which Lord Petre (the *Baron*) and Miss Arabella Fermor (*Belinda*) belonged. Pope wrote the first version of his poem in a fortnight in 1711, at the request of his friend John Caryll, Lord Petre's cousin, 'to make a jest of it, and laugh them together again'. This was published, in two cantos, in 1712. During 1713 he set out to improve and expand it, against the advice of Addison to leave well alone, and the final version in five cantos was published in 1714. Pope was justly proud of his additions: it takes a real master to transform a masterpiece, but this is what he achieved.

In setting out to restore a sense of proportion to a situation that had got out of hand, he turned to an ideally suitable poetic 'kind'—the mock heroic. The high style of epic is designed to show huge and important subjects, the fall of Troy, the foundation of Rome, in their true grandeur. If a poet uses a grand style to treat a trivial subject however, every reader is made to feel a disproportion that emphasises the triviality as nothing else could do. There is no better way of showing a little man just how small he is, than putting him into a giant's armour.

> With beating Hearts the dire Event they wait,
> Anxious, and trembling for the Birth of Fate.

This could make vivid to us the forebodings of the Trojans as Hector set out to his death. But what if we apply it to the loss of a lock of hair?

Pope follows Boileau's *Le Lutrin* (1674-83) in scaling down a whole epic rather than inflating a fragment as he was to do in the *Dunciad*, so we get the arming of the hero, an epic voyage, heroic games, feasting, a journey to the underworld and an epic battle, and other-worldly beings involved as the Gods and Goddesses had been in the great Epics. The more we know of these, the more we can enjoy the deftness with which Pope uses their great incidents as lenses to restore a truer perspective, and the more we can appreciate the humour of his adaptations. Yet we must guard against any idea that what mock heroics mock is the heroic. Pope and his contemporaries took epic very seriously, and thought that the epic poet was the greatest of all poets, not because he wrote the biggest poems, but because epic poetry gave scope for the most profound and serious criticism of life. It was precisely a criticism of life, and of his society, that Pope saw implicit in the storm in a teacup from which his poem began. Mock-heroic presented a comic way of bringing that criticism home, but it did so because it is a way of directing satire *through* the style *at* the subject, and to be comic is not necessarily to cease to be serious. When Pope expanded his poem, his important additions—the sylphs and Umbriel, the Toilet, the Cave of Spleen, and Clarissa's speech—all increase the epic reference; but all equally increase the complexity of his satire and the seriousness of its meaning. Even the game of Ombre, so enjoyable in itself, has important things to say, not about heroic games, but about Belinda. The more fully epic he made his poem, the more profoundly revealing it became. Only very occasionally does Pope allow himself a smile in the direction of epic itself, and when he does—in the genealogy of Belinda's bodkin, or the way the sylphs fulfil Milton's ideas about the substance of angels —he is usually mocking epic features that he cannot take seriously. Epic is not to be mocked, in other words, but bad epic is.

What Pope saw in the original incident was disproportion. This is of course a feature of life itself, which mingles the important with the trivial; great Queens do interrupt state business to drink tea, great Statesmen can, almost in a breath, plan vital strategies abroad and affairs with 'Nymphs at home'. Only, sanity consists in keeping one's values straight, and this both the families in life and the characters in the poem have failed to do. And while the results of confused values may be comic, they may become very serious. This is a light-hearted and a funny poem, but it has a sombre core: in several places Pope makes us aware of the long-term implications of what he is saying. The cause of the trouble and the confused values in his poem is very clear— it is the self-centredness of human beings, their Pride, which always involves a turning away from others. It is a terrible inhumanity which makes a man's dinner more important than the lives of other men. It is a dangerous pride that makes young men and women think of their relationship in terms of sex-war rather than of love. And if a young woman's pride in her beauty makes her reject love, what she may have to face may be an unbeautiful old age of loneliness and frustration which can do terrible things to people. Pope's poem is a comic one, and he does not dwell on these things, but they are there and unless we take account of them we shall miss the depth of his meaning. His satire on women and society is a deeply moral one. He attacks human Pride in the cause of humanity, happiness and love.

This does not mean that Pope is not vibrantly aware of the sheer beauty of the feminine world and the glitter of fashionable life. Eighteenth-century high society is exquisitely presented—the visits, the masquerades, the parading in the Park, the box at the theatre, the parties: indeed, it is because the sylphs create so powerfully not only the confusion of coquettish standards and the insubstantiality of Beauty, but also its wonderful delicacy, colourfulness and charm, that the second version of the poem is so much finer than the first. Belinda and her kind *can* make the world seem a brighter place, and for all its satire no poem catches a more poignant sense of this. Yet our perception of beauty deepens the satire rather than modifies it; on the one hand we are convinced that we are seeing a whole truth and not a simplification, on the other the loveliness at the surface deepens our sense of the distortion and the waste beneath. Gay and amusing though the poem is, it has at its heart a touch of the sadness of all Pope's greatest work.

As Pope is using epic models, the diction accordingly possesses, for much of the poem, an appropriate loftiness and dignity which is frequently used to throw Belinda's world into perspective. Thus we have the inversion of syntax, appropriate to an epic proposition, as in the opening lines; words such as *Main, Etherial, Zephyrs, Phœbus* are frequent; the cries of beaux and belles as they fight in Canto V are the cries of epic heroes. Sometimes Pope achieves effects of expansion rather than diminution, which help to remind us that, whatever it may

seem, this is not just a local quarrel: examples of this are the meta-
morphosis of Tortoise and Elephant at I 135-6; *all Arabia*; and such
a line as III 110. Within the predominantly epic framework, though,
Pope allows himself a variety of styles, right down to the slang of
III 17-18, and the speech of Sir Plume at IV 127-30.

I ll. 7-10. When you have read the poem, can you answer these two
questions?

ll. 13-14. This is deliberately exaggerated, but is the first of a
number of touches whereby Pope, while gently mocking, nevertheless
insists on the real beauty of Belinda.

l. 16. There is irony against the conventional idea of sleepless
lovers, and satire on fashionable hours.

ll. 17 ff. When her handbell is not answered she knocks on the
floor. Her watch is a repeater. But she is asleep again by l. 19. Note the
frequency with which *silver* and *gold* occur in this poem. What is their
effect? What, particularly, is the effect of a silver *sound*?

l. 20. Pope borrowed the idea of his spirit world from the five
Rosicrucian discourses known as *Le Comte de Gabalis*. Ariel explains
the nature of Sylphs, Gnomes, Nymphs and Salamanders in ll. 27-114.
Pope only uses the first two categories, as an equivalent for the Gods
and Goddesses who become involved in the classical epics. But they
are far from merely decorative; they help us to see deep into Belinda's
mind, and into the nature and peril of her beauty.

l. 23. Elaborate costumes were worn at the royal birthday celebrations.

l. 32. Silver coins were put, by fairies, into the shoes of industrious
maids. The *circled Green*, the so-called 'fairy ring' on grass.

l. 44. *the Box*, at the theatre; *the Ring*, a drive in Hyde Park.

ll. 45 ff. *Equipage*, a carriage and horses, with attendant footmen:
hence the pun at l. 50. *Chair*, a sedan chair.

ll. 51 ff. Note that these spirits are from the first associated with
the frivolity of fashionable women, their pride, the falseness of moral
language, and their rejection of love.

l. 62. *Tea*, pronounced 'tay' in Pope's time: *Elemental* because
made with water.

ll. 69-70. Milton has this theory about angels in *Paradise Lost*
I 423 ff. Pope is obviously amused by it.

l. 81. *These*, the Gnomes, shown as a corrupting influence (cf.
Umbriel).

ll. 94 ff. *Impertinence*, folly, triviality; *Treat*, an entertainment
given in a lady's honour; *Toyshop*, as toy=a trifle, so a shop stocking, in

Addison's phrase, 'fans, silks, ribbons, laces, gewgaws'; *drive*, i.e. drive out: the excitement of a new coach drives out all thoughts of older ones.

ll. 107 ff. In the Æneid the ghost of Hector appears to the hero to warn him of the sack of Troy.

l. 117. Does report say true? See l. 138.

ll. 121 ff. This is the equivalent of the arming of an epic hero for a noble exploit. What attitude to Belinda is suggested if we compare her making herself up with, say, Hector arming for the defence of Troy? How does Pope suggest the full enormity of her self-love in these 'sacred Rites of Pride'? Cf. *Burlington* ll. 151 ff. What is the point of the confusion on her table at l. 138? Is there more than one possible meaning for words like *Charms, Grace, purer Blush*? How does Belinda achieve *her* kind of transformation? On the other hand, Pope wishes us to be aware that there *is* beauty here. How does he create a vivid sense of this? *nicely*, fastidiously; *curious*, with care and skill; *patches*, small pieces of black cloth stuck on the face as beauty-spots; *awful*, inspiring awe.

II ll. 1 ff. The implied comparison here might be with Æneas sailing up the Tiber.

l. 9. The comparison to the Sun may not be as warm as it looks. What are the implications of *unfix'd* and *on all alike*? Is her *Sweetness void of Pride*? What is the effect of the conditional *might* and *if*?

ll. 19 ff. The locks are nourished for the destruction of Mankind—they are weapons of coquetry, of female power. The Baron's attitude is the masculine equivalent. Is there a possible attitude that would be neither 'having men on a string' on the one hand, nor involve 'Fraud or Force' on the other?

l. 26. *Finny Prey* is not a mere elegant variation for 'fish'. Would 'fish' be right here? *Prey* draws attention to the hunter/hunted metaphor, while *finny* carries the visual suggestion of the fish moving below the surface of the water.

ll. 35 ff. The Baron's idea of Love is partly romantic, partly a deification of his own amorous exploits. The Gods in epic rarely allowed men to have things all their own way.

ll. 55 ff. The sylphs in this passage are a way of saying something imaginatively about the nature of feminine beauty. Cf. ll. 17-20 of *To a Lady*, and contrast Enobarbus' description of Cleopatra's barge in *Antony and Cleopatra*. Lovely colouring and light are deftly transfused with a sense not only of lightness but of insubstantiality and transience.

l. 70. The epic hero was always taller than his followers. Ariel's speech might remind us of those of Satan in *Paradise Lost*. In the elemental activities of spirits Pope is also remembering Ariel's namesake in *The Tempest*.

ll. 91 ff.   What is the effect of these lines after the previous passage? But compare the fusion of beauty and satire with the Toilet scene. *Wash*, a lotion for the complexion; *Furbelo*, like *Flounce*, the pleated border of a petticoat.

l. 103.   *or . . . or*, either . . . or; *Slight*, cunning.

ll. 105 ff.   The comparisons are possible because of the metaphorical richness of such words as *frail, flaw, stain*, etc., but the little word *or* suggests that the things compared are equally 'important'. What point is Pope making? *Diana's Law* is that of virginity. Why does Ariel think it would be a disaster if Belinda lost her heart? For *China* as an emblem of fragile beauty, see also III 159-60, IV 163, and *To a Lady* l. 268. *Drops*, brilliant ear-rings.

ll. 118 ff.   The petticoat is the equivalent of a Homeric shield.

ll. 123 ff.   Notice the appropriateness, the sense of minuteness, and the sensuous particularity of the punishments. *Pomatums*, pomades, ointment for the hair, etc. To *rivel*, to 'contract into wrinkles and corrugations' (Johnson).

III ll. 5-8.   See introduction to this poem. *Three Realms* refers to the recent (1707) union of England and Wales with Scotland.

ll. 11 ff.   *Instructive* is ironical: the talk degenerates into malicious gossip and triviality, marked by a clever lowering of style to l. 18.

ll. 25 ff.   What is the significance of Belinda's excitement, her aggressiveness, and her emotionalism during the game—especially ll. 87-92? *Ombre* was a three-handed card game in which one player (ombre) undertook to make more tricks than either of the other two. Each held nine cards (l. 30), so nine tricks are involved. The card values are peculiar, but, briefly, Belinda holds the three highest cards of all—the *Matadores* (rather like Jokers): *Spadillio*, the Ace of Spades; *Manillio*, here the two of Spades; *Basto*, the Ace of Clubs; and, as she declares trumps (l. 46) another certain trick in the King of Spades. She needs one more to be safe. By l. 54 the third player is out of trumps. Belinda's lead of the King of Clubs is trumped by the Baron's Queen of Spades (l. 67); he then wins three tricks with his high Diamonds (l. 75 ff.). There is only one more trick, which Belinda must win if she is not to be given 'Codille' and have to pay the whole stakes. Her King of Hearts is the highest in the suit—higher than the Ace; but if the Baron can lead any other suit she is lost: fortunately for her, he cannot. *Pam* (l. 61) is the Knave of Clubs, the highest card in the game of Loo, or *Lu*; it is here played by the third player.

Pope uses here the Rouen pack of cards, which, unlike the modern double-headed ones, have feet; his descriptions are accurate.

Notice, at ll. 35-6, the sylph/women equation again; notice also the pun on *Trick* at l. 94. What is the effect of this? *Nice* here is crucial, critical.

ll. 101-4. How seriously do we take this sonorous epic moral?

ll. 105 ff. *Altars of Japan*, lacquered (japanned) tables; *China's Earth*, the coffee-cups—very small, hence *frequent*; *grateful*, causing pleasure, gratifying. Notice *rich Repast* as an ironic comparison to Homeric feasts.

l. 122. *Scylla*, daughter of King *Nisus* of Megara, plucked from her father's head the magic purple hair on which the safety of his kingdom depended. She took it to Minos, who was besieging Megara, but he scorned her, and she was changed into a bird for her impiety.

l. 128. The hero is armed with a pair of scissors: what phrases does Pope use to give it a ludicrous dignity?

ll. 139 ff. What Ariel feared (II 109) has happened: Belinda is secretly in love, presumably with the Baron. Why does this mean the end of Ariel's power?

ll. 150 ff. Again Pope is glancing at Milton's theories about angels.

l. 165. *Atalantis*, a popular scandalous work by Mrs Manley, pub. 1709.

l. 167. Formal visiting in the evenings, attended by servants with lights, played a great part in fashionable life.

ll. 170 ff. What does Pope achieve by comparing the 'rape' of Belinda's hair with the destruction of Monuments, Triumphal Arches, and Troy, which was supposed to have been built by Apollo and Poseidon?

IV ll. 1-8. In each couplet there is a contrast between heroic tragedy and the self-imposed or petty mortifications of proud women, reaching a depth of anti-climax. More important are the first hints of what might happen to Belinda if she prefers pride to love.

ll. 11 ff. The journey to the Underworld is a feature of several epics. We need to remember what Pope had said about gnomes in I 79-82 in order to grasp the significance of the change from Ariel (the light) to Umbriel (the dark). Belinda's first rage is disproportionate, but perhaps natural; the ascendancy of Umbriel, however, marks danger. *Spleen*, or melancholy, in contemporary medical theory, was what we should now call a mental disease, caused by gloomy self-absorption and surrender to bitterness. It made people shun company and cheerfulness (ll. 17-22); and, though it had physical symptoms such as pains in the side (where the spleen is) or migraine headaches (l. 24), the main sickness is in the mind. The denial of love may turn women into twisted old maids pretending virtue as an excuse for running down others (ll. 27-30), or affected ones refusing to acknowledge the loss of youth and beauty, and pretending illness to call attention to themselves —new diseases are imagined in order to show off a new nightdress. Worst of all, it may lead to hallucination and madness; but whether this takes the form of the visions of hermits and virgins, or the pathetic madhouse figures of ll. 47-54, a common source is sexual frustration. The *vapours* was another name for spleen, or nervous depression; hence the puns at ll. 18 and 39, looking forward to l. 59. At ll. 40 ff. Pope also, incidentally, glances satirically at some of the bizarre stage effects of modern pantomime: *rolling Spires* are twisting coils; *Machines*, stage cranes for lowering angels, gods, etc. The allusion at l. 51 is to some self-propelling tripods made by Vulcan (*Iliad* xviii).

l. 56. Æneas carried a golden bough to keep him safe in Hades.

l. 60. Pope ironically cites an old idea that melancholy accompanied creative genius.

l. 69. *Citron-Waters*, brandy with lemon peel. Cf. *To a Lady*, l. 64.

l. 71. An old joke, that a cuckold (one whose wife is unfaithful) grew horns.

ll. 89 ff. After her first outburst (III 155) Belinda is sunk in dejection. As Umbriel opens his bag over her Pope suggests that her first, more natural, reaction has been replaced by self-induced and unnatural emotions, the result of Pride. She has given way to Spleen, and crushed her love.

ll. 105 ff. What ironic meaning is given to *Honour* here? What does it really mean for people like Thalestris? Notice the steadily mounting climax of l. 106. She goes on to talk as if this had been a real rape. How are her values defined at ll. 119-20?

ll. 113 ff. The Baron will make the Lock into a ring.

ll. 117-18. The Ring—the fashionable drive in Hyde Park—was notoriously dusty; and the people of fashion lived in St James's, leaving the City for the middle classes.

ll. 123-30. The 'real' Sir Plume (Sir George Brown) was very angry at this. He is an expert on fashionable externals. His empty-headedness is shown by his speech, which is nothing but a string of meaningless modish swear-words. Note the cleverly broken incoherent speech rhythms.

ll. 133 ff. We might have in mind the great vow of Achilles. The Baron, too, gives the Lock a disproportionate importance—it is a symbol of *his* Pride as well.

ll. 147 ff. What attitude is suggested if we remember Achilles' lament over his dead friend Patroclus? Does the fault lie in the temptations of the Court? Or in Belinda's lack of concealment?

l. 156. *Bohea*, a strong kind of tea.

l. 174. *Sacrilegious*, she still regards her hair as holy.

ll. 175-6. What are the implications of these lines? The indecency is not smutty, but meaningful.

V ll. 5-6. Æneas deserted the love of Dido at the command of the Gods. *Anna* was Dido's sister.

ll. 7 ff. Clarissa's speech appeared first in the 1717 edition. Pope's note reads: 'A new Character introduced . . . to open more clearly the MORAL of the Poem, in a parody of the speech of Sarpedon to Glaucus in Homer' (*Iliad* xii). Against pride in the power of beauty she sets the fact of its transience. Only good sense, virtue, and good humour can keep the love that beauty can gain. Compare the praise of good humour in *To a Lady*, ll. 257 ff. and 292, and in letter 4, p. 19. Lines 25-8 sum up the implications for Belinda's future that we noticed in the Cave of Spleen, setting the Rape of the Lock in its true perspective.

l. 37. *Virago*, 'a female warriour, a woman with the qualities of a man' (Johnson). Thalestris was an Amazon Queen.

ll. 37 ff. The Homeric battle. Lines 45-52 are the most 'heroic' of the poem. What are their effect here? *Dapperwit* (the *Beau*), and *Sir Fopling* (the *Witling*) take their names from characters in comedies by Wycherley and Etherege respectively. Fopling quotes from a recent Italian opera. The battle is decided by Jove (ll. 71-4), as so often in epic. The wits are insubstantial, and the *Hairs* (the women) win.

l. 78. *to die*, an old metaphor for the sexual act. Pope reminds us that this is a sex war, of a rather futile kind.

ll. 88 ff. One of the few places where epic is mocked. In the oldest epics moments of great suspense are interrupted by genealogies of famous weapons.

ll. 109 ff. Ironically, the lock has been completely forgotten.

ll. 113 ff. The *Lunar Sphere*, deriving from Ariosto's *Orlando Furioso*, is here filled with empty, meaningless and insignificant things; but there is an underlying seriousness to some of the hypocrisies mentioned—e.g. *Death-bed Alms*, *Sick Man's Pray'rs*. *Vases* was a near rhyme to *Cases*. For l. 122, compare *Dunciad* IV, 397 ff.

ll. 123 ff. Whereas Romulus himself (l. 125) was reported translated to Heaven, Pope introduces a skilful variation in the translation of the Lock itself. The word 'comet' is derived from a Greek word meaning long-haired; the appropriateness is underlined by l. 128, and *dishevel'd*.

Berenice, Queen of Ptolemy III, dedicated her hair to Venus as a thank-offering, and it became the constellation *Coma Berenices*.

ll. 133 ff. Pope does not wish to leave us with the idea that the Lock is meaningless. The poem has been about Love and its lack; Pope has made the Lock immortal, by giving it a meaning it never had, though he is too tactful to say so directly.

l. 133. the *Mall*, as fashionable a parade as the Ring.

l. 136. *Rosamonda's Lake*, in St James's Park, evidently a resort of lovers.

l. 137. *Partridge*, a quack astrologer and almanack maker, immortalised by Swift's practical joke. Swift pretended to be a rival ('Bickerstaff') and foretold Partridge's 'death'.

l. 147. *fair Suns*, Belinda's eyes: compare I 14, and the sun imagery generally.

page 63   ELOISA TO ABELARD

Published 1717

This poem is based on one of the world's most tragic love stories. Abelard, the great twelfth-century theologian and teacher, fell passionately in love with his seventeen-year-old pupil, whom he could never hope to marry while he remained in holy orders. Their love came to a terrible end when he was emasculated by ruffians hired by her uncle, Fulbert; Eloisa became a nun in the convent of the Paraclete which Abelard founded; and they were reunited only in the grave. A fine modern treatment of the story is found in Helen Waddell's *Peter Abelard* (1933).

Yet if we turn to Pope's poem expecting to be profoundly moved, we are likely to be puzzled and disappointed. There are abundant sighs, tears and exclamations; but the highly wrought rhetorical style is likely to strike us as 'artificial', and the poem seems to thrust its passion at us instead of making us feel it for ourselves. Only, it may help us not to miss the right things by looking for the wrong ones, if we enquire once more into the poetic 'kind' that Pope was writing. The poem is a letter, using the letter-writer's freedom of movement from one thought to another, but it is a letter of a special kind. It is a *heroical* epistle, looking back originally to Ovid's famous series of grand-style letters from famous and forsaken lovers, the *Heroides*. One of these, *Sappho to Phaon*, Pope translated in 1712.

Where the seventeenth century tended to see Ovid as a great wit, the eighteenth generally hailed him as a great poet of 'Nature': what is permanent, fundamental, universal in human feeling, rather than what is uniquely personal and immediate as we might expect love poetry to be. Heroic poetry moreover, especially for Pope, is not mainly interested in the story, which may already be well known, or in emotions for their own sake. The heroic poet seeks above all to delve behind events and feelings in order to illuminate their profoundest moral meaning. This suggests that we ought to try not so much to 'feel with' Eloisa as to detect beneath her words the significance of her conflict. What Pope will be interested in will be something true to universal experience; Eloisa's situation, making it rather larger than life, enables us to see it more clearly. The highly structured and 'artificial' style will have an important and artful purpose: it will be the way that Eloisa is made to present herself to herself for our understanding. The moment we ask not 'Am I being made to feel like Eloisa?' so much as 'Why does Eloisa say this, and what is its significance?' we are on the way to a proper reading, and the poem will begin to come alive.

Eloisa's mind twists and turns in an apparently irreconcilable conflict between Divine Grace and her passion for Abelard. The poem is carefully constructed rather like a piece of music in four movements, each of which reaches a temporary but unsatisfactory resolution, with a coda at the end. In the first movement, the reading of a letter from Abelard to a friend with an account of the tragedy, annihilates in a flash the long years of Eloisa's renunciation. The crucial point is made by the change of tense in ll. 69-72. Her grief wells up, but if we look for the meaning of her tears instead of trying only to feel them we are given a significant index to her state of mind. Her tears change from repentance to self-pity; she begins to indulge and enjoy them; she weeps in rage and shame at the desecration of Abelard; and the tears she remembers shedding at the altar have nothing to do with repentance, they are tears of desolation. Small wonder that she passes so easily from the Cross to an erotic longing for Abelard. Only now does she realise how far she has come, and with a spasm of guilt beg Abelard of all people to make her soul quit him for God.

As we read her words, we should find ourselves making judgments she is unable to make; we can see below the surface as she cannot, and almost every phrase prompts a question which brings up the implicit moral issues. Thus, at ll. 45-8, our 'dialogue' might run:

Tears still are mine—	—or are they God's due?
and those I need not spare	—but what if they are for the wrong object?
Love but demands what else were shed in pray'r	—are the two things equal, then?

No happier task these faded eyes
    pursue   —Happier? Are tears meant for
                               pleasure?

To read . . .   —Read what? Holy Writ—or
                               Abelard's letter?

and weep . . .   —with penitence? or self-pity?
is all they now can do.

The antithesis which jolts us into awareness, the lucidity, may not
be the 'language of the heart', which might have moved us more deeply;
but the style is modelled to show us just what is involved, and that is
its purpose.

The second movement (ll. 129-206) is mainly brilliant psychological
landscape. It hardly matters that much of the scenery derives from
Milton; Pope's object is to use it to reveal the state of Eloisa's mind.
Abelard's letter has not only changed her; in emphasising her loss it has
changed her whole world, for each of us makes his own. Life in the
convent with Abelard was suffused by the reconciling warmth of his
presence. Life in the long years of renunciation was sombre, but retained motion, light, and gayer sounds than just the hollow murmur of
the wind. Now her emotions have brought her to sick depression and
fear. (We remember from *The Rape of the Lock* that Melancholy is a
disease.) Darkness, brownness, blots out all colour, all movement has
gone, the only sounds are gloomy and ominous. She has moved from
life in death to death in life, and over all is a note of horror. In this
state she detests herself, and prays for Grace; but her prayer comes
from despair. She cannot repent, cannot forget, but she is beginning to
realise her situation and the self-pity has gone.

The third movement (ll. 207-302) is both the most 'artificially'
constructed and the most meaningful, a juxtaposition that need no
longer surprise us. It is the crux of the poem, in which Eloisa for the
first time presents the issues squarely to herself and makes a clear choice
between them. The twistings of her mind suddenly formulate themselves into a pattern: there are two carefully managed sets of contrasts,
and two contrasted prayers, one denying the other. In imagining the
soul of a true nun, the 'Eternal sunshine of the spotless mind', Eloisa
measures the possibility of mystical union in holy love against the dreary
melancholy and guilty terror of her own sexual frustration. She then
forces herself to realise for the first time that Abelard is a vestal now,
that he has the same mildness and peace because he is a eunuch. So
bitter is the realisation that a twisted irony breaks in, but as she contrasts her state with his and measures the hypocrisy of her life, it is

with the fear of hell-fire that she is left. In her two contrasted prayers she realises the choices before her—she has been trying in self-deception to have Abelard and heaven, but she cannot; she must either have him and hell, or renounce all thought of him for ever. She prays for this at last, for grace, for hope and faith, and for the rest that comes in death.

The last movement (ll. 303-342) develops her death-wish, but calm and sleep are not in her heart of hearts what Eloisa wants. She wants love. Within seconds 'roseate bowers' and 'refined flames' are mingling in her thoughts with the 'rest' of sinners. At once this brings Abelard back, and her victory over herself is shown to be hollow as she begins to make an erotic experience out of death itself. Try as she may, the conflict appears to be irreconcilable; but if her problem cannot be solved it can be pitied, and in the Coda she makes a human plea. Yet there is no moral relativity, and passion, for Pope, is not all-excusing. Throughout the poem he has placed it in a context of criticism, and if it is right that even in the middle of a Communion with God some relenting eye should drop a tear for her and be forgiven, it is also right that forgiveness should be necessary. When Eloisa longs for a poet who has felt in the hopelessness of her love an image of his own, Pope may well be making a veiled confession about Lady Mary Wortley Montagu, but the purpose of his poem is not emotional or confessional, however much his own feelings may have added warmth to the writing: it is to make us *understand*.

A prose translation, by John Hughes, of the Latin letters, supposedly of Eloisa to Abelard, had appeared in 1713. Pope was at work on this poem by 1716, and it was published in the *Works* next year.

ll. 1-8. The three questions shatter the solemn quietness of the opening and lead to the exclamation of self-discovery.

ll. 9-15. She already thinks not of renunciation, but of disguise. What are the implications of l. 12? Note *lost* in l. 15. *Idea*, the imagined ideal form.

ll. 16 ff. How have her mood, and her attitude to the convent changed? (Note *relentless, voluntary*.) What is the difference between the tears of l. 14, l. 22, l. 28 and ll. 30 ff.? What are the implications of the superbly economical l. 24?

ll. 29 ff. Making Eloisa re-experience the tragedy in reading the letter, allows Pope to remind us of its main points.

ll. 63 ff. *attemp'ring*, moderating, softening their own brilliance; *lambent*, moving about as if touching lightly; *mended*, made still better. Abelard's eloquence was famous; hence *dispute*, to oppose by argument, at l. 282.

ll. 69 ff. A difficult passage: what was in fact sensuous attraction to Abelard had presented itself to her as 'religious' feeling; now she re-experiences the attraction as sexual love, recognising its sensuality.

ll. 92 ff. A defiant parody of the Christian ideas that love fulfils the law, and that in the service of God is perfect freedom and fulfilment.

ll. 99-106. How successful is the rhetoric in conveying emotion? Note however the implications of l. 105.

l. 108. *victims*; a striking word. Their love is being sacrificed. Abelard is present while Eloisa takes the vow.

ll. 119-28. Her conflict is summed up; but both possibilities depend on Abelard. Lines 120, 124 underlie the fact of Abelard's emasculation.

ll. 141 ff. Contrast carefully ll. 141-6, 155-62, 163-70. How exactly does the poetry impress on our *senses* the movement from a dark kind of life to a kind of death?

ll. 201 ff. She sees the need for Grace, and begins to see what was wrong with ll. 125-8.

ll. 207-48. Contrast carefully the two portraits. Line 212 is quoted from Crashaw's *Description of a Religious House*. The *unfading rose* is the mystical emblem of Christ's love. He is the *Spouse* whose wedding ring nuns wear. Note the quiet rhythms of the first picture with its serene dying fall. Contrast the more hectic, then broken rhythms of the second, and again the way the melancholy movement of ll. 241-4 is shattered by nightmare and awakening. *Hymenæals*, marriage songs.

ll. 249 ff. But note that Abelard's calm is *dead, fix'd*, his stillness that of the first day of Creation before life was made. Lines 257-8 are bitter mockery. What are the implications of ll. 261-2?

l. 270. *Bead*, referring to the Rosary.

l. 278. *kind*, reassuring; penitence is the first step to the promise of Grace.

ll. 317-20. She looks forward to the love-bowers of the mystical Rose (cf. l. 217), and the palm of victory over temptation and death. The flaming Seraphim glow in holy love.

l. 324. i.e. with a kiss. Does she mean what she says in l. 336? (note that she wants the dust to be mingled, l. 343); the *Saints* (l. 342) are to embrace Abelard *with a love like mine*. (Abelard, in fact, died first; his remains were carried secretly to the Paraclete. Eloisa was later (1164) buried beside him. The lovers now share a tomb in the cemetery of Père la Chaise in Paris.)

ll. 349-58. Her self-pity returns. Line 350 is sentimental: ll. 355-8 are a more accurate response. See introduction to this poem.

ll. 359 ff. Lady Mary Wortley Montagu was away in Turkey,

where her husband was ambassador. For Pope's relations with her, see note to *Arbuthnot*, p. 214; see also the introduction to this poem for the significance of such biographical material.

ll. 365-6. The closing couplet is hardly worthy of the rest of the poem. Line 365 is sentimental, and quite inadequate as a description of what has gone before; l. 366 seems to drop oddly into the decorum of a familiar letter.

page 73 ELEGY TO THE MEMORY OF AN
UNFORTUNATE LADY

Published 1717

Pope's *Elegy* is often misread in the same way as *Eloisa to Abelara*. If we come to the poem expecting a personal lament, we may be put off by the stagey declamation of the opening, the theatrical exaggeration of Pope's denunciation of the Lady's family, perhaps by the incongruity of comparing her death to a chemical process. What, we may ask, have these to do with real grief? If we do think in this way, however, we are missing one of the finest elegiac poems in our literature.

This Elegy looks back to Ovid, to the Roman elegies of Tibullus and Propertius, and to epic laments like the one for Pompey in Lucan and has many affinities with the heroic epistle. This time the Ovid of Wit is here as well as the Ovid of Nature, for since the poet writes in his own voice *about* a tragedy, it is allowable for him to use the serious wit of the 'Metaphysical' poets to bring out its deepest significance. Once more the important thing is the *interpretation* of the tragedy; we should waste no time wondering about the precise nature of the story, or whether the Lady was a real person or quite imaginary. The poem itself contains all we need to know about her. She is any unfortunate lady, all unfortunate ladies, who are unfortunate in the same universally significant way. What we have to find out is what that way is, and it will not take us long once we realise that Pope's art is not a shoddy substitute for artless grief but a way of focusing our attention on what is really meaningful about his subject.

The hectic rhetoric of the opening points swiftly to the fact that the tragedy is an abomination. While Pope has no wish to dwell on the horror of her suicide, he does want to establish a stark realisation of what the human characteristics he is going to discuss can lead to. The method is rather like the unpleasant exaggeration of a road-safety poster. From it he plunges quickly into the cause of the tragedy . . . the Lady is dead because she has dared to think greatly, love greatly, die greatly;

to aspire to a richer and intenser kind of life. This 'ambition' may be a fault, but it is a glorious one, and Pope soon leads us away from thinking of it as a fault at all. 'Most souls . . . but *peep out* once an age' makes us take up a critical attitude to those who do not aspire, who are like animals, prisoners of their bodies; who are not only dull because the intensity of human life is not for them, but sullenly resentful of their condition, and of those who try to rise above it. Theirs is a dim life-in-death but they have the arrogance to be proud, to convert their laziness and supineness into pomp.

Against this false dignity we are led to see the true dignity of the Lady, and to take up a new attitude towards her terrible death. A chemical reaction is a violent breaking down of a substance; but it is also a liberation and refinement whereby a purer substance frees itself from its dregs. In this it is an exact and serious image of the significance Pope wishes us to see in the Lady's death. He makes us see the point of suffering and death; that they may be necessary in the scheme of things, that perhaps only through them can a human soul be rendered as pure as it wants to be.

We are now well above the rhetoric of the opening, and the dregs of humanity that caused it. It is when we are reconciled to the Lady's death by realising its significance that we can enjoy Pope calling down vengeance on her family. There is a note of comedy in his wit now, a deliberate exaggeration that is the mark of scorn. Yet there is a serious meaning too. For the family *are* deathlike; what the dregs have lost is the ability to feel for others in pity and in love. Here is the explanation of the apparently exaggerated 'Cold is the breast which warm'd the world before'. The Lady has come to stand for the essence of love and pity against the self-centred pride, the anti-humanity, of her family. No love or pity can be due to them, for it is these things that they have renounced and helped to kill in themselves and their world.

True grief, love, and pity are reserved for the Lady. Now the style changes as Pope proceeds to atone for the heartlessness of the world. In a ritualistic lament he brings out the pathos of her death among strangers; but the grief of men is often an empty show, and the note of scorn returns for a moment. Yet it returns with a new purpose, to bring out the nature of true love and grief in contrast to the false. In the most tender lines he ever wrote, Pope contrasts something self-centred, superficial, grudging—and where it pretends to emotion or spirituality, false and dead—with something fresh, true, alive and holy. Against the marble tears of cupids and the muttered dirge we have the freshness of spring flowering, green turf and dew, and the silver wings of the angels of love. Love and pity are holy things. They are also on the side of life and fertility, while pride, self-centredness and hypocrisy are on the side of death.

This would have made a beautiful end to a fine poem; but it is not the end, and because of this the poem that we have is even finer. For Pope proceeds with apparent simplicity to write an epitaph that changes and deepens everything. The Lady was the richness of life and her family its negation, but it is Death which provides the true perspective for all of them. It is Death which triumphs. Dust is all the proud shall be, but it is all the Lady is too; and Pope's Elegy is useless to her. This provides the transition to the ending, for death not only marks a terrible perspective for the aspiration of the Lady, but for the aspiration of poetry and poets too. Pope has loved and honoured poetry, and in his poem he has loved and pitied the quintessence of love and pity, but he is left looking steadily at death and what it involves.

The *Elegy* is a Roman poem in the deepest sense: it is pagan. Where *Eloisa* is not only Christian but Catholic, drawing on Crashaw and Catholic mysticism, the *Elegy* for the most part 'sidesteps' Christianity. It speaks of 'Powers', 'Gods', 'Fate', 'Furies', and where it speaks twice of 'Angels' it is in a daring context not too far from blasphemy. This does not of course mean that Pope was pagan: it is simply that the point of Elegy is to look at Death in itself, as an end to life. To bring in Christianity, which regards death as the gateway to a better life, would be to lose the tragic resonance Pope is after. (The deliberate limitation also avoids complicating the issues with questions of the sin of suicide, and the morality of the Lady, which would involve more realistic detail.) Pope's purpose is to look at human aspiration, the richness of life, and the fact of death, in their own terms, as they relate to this world; here, the grave is peace, and the end of Pope's poem is peace. Yet it is a tragic kind of peace, placing in perspective and bringing out, as nothing else could do, the tragedy of human aspiration in life, in love (and in poetry), that the Unfortunate Lady has come to represent.

ll. 1-4. The ghost comes, as in *Hamlet*, to indicate that something terrible has happened, and to demand that the truth should be revealed.

l. 8. *Roman* ethics permitted suicide. The questions raise, but do not explore, the problem of whether this is forgivable by other standards. The Lady is presumably (l. 6) excluded from *heav'n*; but l. 11 implies that this is unjust.

l. 9. *reversion*, a legalistic term meaning 'the right to future possession'. What are the implications of *in the sky*, taken with the small h of *heav'n*?

ll. 13-14. *Ambition* was the fault of the rebel Angels, and of the Titans who rebelled against Jove. But whereas in the Christian ethos its root cause was Pride (turning away from God), Pope carefully distinguishes it from Pride in the sense of turning away from other people. Her ambition is vital, warm: contrast *glows* (l. 16) with the implications of l. 20. Compare also *Eloisa* ll. 261-2 and l. 320.

l. 17. What is the effect of the deliberately 'low' word *peep* breaking through the heroic language? (cf. *vulgar*, l. 12).

ll. 17-22. How exactly does the poetry create a sense of restricted, barely existing, life-in-death? Contrast the *Kings* of l. 21 with those of l. 16; and note the emphasis, thrown by the rhyme, on *sleep*—hardly a kingly activity.

ll. 29-30. We can infer that her uncle was her guardian, but disowned her, possibly over a love-affair he had forbidden. This is all we need to know.

ll. 31 ff. Contrast the colour and warmth of the Lady with the black funerals flooding in at the gates. Note *glow* again in l. 45.

ll. 61-2. A suicide cannot be given Christian burial in consecrated ground. Pope's tone is critical, and cf. l. 68.

l. 64. *Sit tibi terra levis* (May the earth lie lightly on you) was so common on Roman gravestones that it was often shortened to S.T.T.L.

ll. 65-6. *Roses* again are emblems of love. The *tears* are dew.

l. 71. Note the irony. *Once* covers not only her lifetime, when she wasn't loved and honoured, but now when she has been, in Pope's poem. His Elegy is useless to her.

ll. 80-2. What is the poet's exact tone, and why?

page 76   EPISTLE

TO A YOUNG LADY, ON HER LEAVING THE TOWN AFTER THE CORONATION

Published 1717

This delightful little poem is an example of Pope's mastery of the familiar epistle. In contrast with the heroic epistle, this is an informal, easygoing and conversational letter to a close friend. Teresa Blount, sister of Martha (for whom see notes to *To a Lady*) is the Young Lady, and had known Pope since his days at Binfield.

Verse letters began to go out of fashion in the nineteenth century, when the Romantics insisted that true poetry should be inspired, should deal with man's deepest feelings and his most serious thoughts. The achievement of this poem—its wit and urbanity, its perfect command of tone, its humorous obliquity, might serve as a warning to us not to think of poetry in too restricted a way. The house of poetry has many mansions.

The opening comparison sets the tone of delicious mockery. Teresa leaving Town is compared to an ingenuous maiden unwillingly dragged off by an over-careful Mamma just as she is beginning to taste the pleasures of love. Pope brilliantly imagines the young girls' mind; catches the flavour of girlish speech (the *dear* man); smiles at her desolation (for *ever* . . .); and pokes fun at her for her amorous explosiveness. Perhaps Teresa too feels that she has renounced the whole world, in the excruciating dullness and piety of country life (which Pope lays on with a will), and the coarse vulgarity of her country admirers, so different of course from A. P. and his friends in Town. Perhaps she dreams romantically of Coronations . . . and of *Triumphs* of her own, with great 'catches' for the taking, but alas for the awakening! It is just the opposite for Pope who wants only to be quiet and alone to dream of her. (The humorous exaggeration—your *Slave*— just what a woman expects her admirers to be, carries on the raillery with great tenderness, leaving it amusingly up to her to decide how serious he is being.) But the roar of the City descends on him and there the two of them are, in Town and Country, linked for opposite reasons in humorously sour vexation.

The poem has a further layer of meaning, found in Pope's gentle irony at Teresa's expense: this is the contrast in values implicit in the opposition of town and country. Pope ostensibly sympathises with the Young Lady, dragged away from Town: *wholesom, pray'rs, reading, godly, the way to Heav'n* are words which, used from *her* point of view, are petulant protests; but from the point of view of one who sees the country as a repository of true values, they resume their true meaning. Pope, after all, would hardly regard *reading* as a tedious occupation, however much Teresa might; and his attitude to the Town is expressed by such words as *vext*, the *crew, rush, coxcombs*. If we go outside this poem, we shall find this attitude prevalent throughout Pope's letters; and it is basically the Horatian attitude.

Title. *The Coronation*, that of George I in 1714.
l. 1. *fond*, perhaps with the overtone of 'foolish', as well as affectionate.

l. 4. *spark*, 'a lively, showy, splendid, gay man' (Johnson). The half-concealed metaphor suggests gunpowder, and perhaps the idea of playing with fire, like Belinda.

l. 7. *Zephalinda*, a very romantic-sounding *nom-de-plume* (used by Teresa herself), for one 'flying' from the world.

l. 10. *She went*, notice the repetition of this phrase at l. 11 and l. 13. What is the effect of this?

l. 11. After *plain-work* the conventionally poetic *purling* has ridiculous associations with knitting, and affords a comic tie-up with l. 49. Another device used to shape the poem is the repetition of *hum* (ll. 20, 50).

ll. 13 ff. Contrast the speed of l. 13 with the slowness of the following lines. *Tea* (l. 16) is pronounced 'tay', and *bohea* 'bohay': the repetition of the same rhyme sound in ll. 13-16 helps the effect of monotony. The *solitary* tea contrasts with the parties she would have in town. Note the imitative effect of the sound and rhythm, particularly the k sounds, at ll. 17-18.

ll. 18 ff. A very unfashionable timetable: Belinda was only waking up at noon, and would dine at about 4 (cf. *Rape of the Lock* III 22); the fashionable lady would then be up half the night.

l. 23. Does *rack* indicate anything of Pope's own attitude?

ll. 24 ff. *Whisk*, rustic for whist—a very unfashionable game, not to be compared with ombre or quadrille. Everything about the Squire is unfashionable: do *we* despise him, as compared to the fashionable beaux? For *treat* see *Rape of the Lock* I 96; his consists of slices of toast floating in sherry (or the drinking of the health itself); he *visits* with a gun instead of a clouded cane, and his *presents* are hardly the kind of thing she is used to.

l. 26. Beautifully 'low' decorum: compare *takes one kiss* (l. 6).

l. 32. *triumphs*, ironically, both 'great processions' and 'amorous conquests'. Notice the different diction here.

l. 34. *Coronations*, the plural, with *ev'ry*, conveys her romantic exaggeration.

l. 38. *flirt*, strictly speaking, a flick of the fan; very appropriate here —and ironic, as it brings her back to earth. Her imagination has been working so powerfully that she unconsciously behaves as if she were really there—flirting.

l. 44. *study*, to be lost in thought, 'in a brown study'.

l. 46. *Parthenia*, here probably an allusion to Martha, who used the name Parthenissa in some correspondence.

l. 47. *Gay*, John Gay (1685-1732), poet and friend of Pope. See *Arbuthnot* ll. 256 ff., and letter 8, p. 22.

page 78   EPISTLES TO SEVERAL PERSONS
('MORAL ESSAYS')

In his statement of the 'Design' of the *Essay on Man*, Pope defends the comparative lack of vivacity of what he calls his *general Map* of MAN, on the grounds that he could not sacrifice perspicuity to ornament or break the chain of reasoning. But, he promises, 'these Epistles in their progress . . . will be less dry, and more susceptible of poetical ornament. I am here only opening the *fountains*, and clearing the passage. To deduce the *rivers*, to follow them in their course, and to observe their effects, may be a task more agreeable.'

Part of this promised exploration of the rivers is provided by the four 'Moral Essays', and they are not merely 'less dry' but are amongst the most lively of all Pope's poems. His own title for them was 'Epistles to Several Persons', and this gives a better idea of the decorum of these poems than does the title 'Moral Essays'. They are essays, certainly, in their careful disposition of material, each taking a central theme and developing it; but they have little of the loftiness of tone of the formal essay as represented by the *Essay on Man*, and their manner, with the easy colloquialism admitting a wide variety of tone, is very much that of the Horatian Epistle (see p. 207).

Pope had been planning his grand scheme certainly as early as 1730, and the writing of these epistles went hand in hand with the writing of the *Essay on Man*. Two of them were, indeed, published before that poem: the *Epistle to Burlington* in December 1731, and *To Bathurst* in January 1733. The *Epistle to Cobham* (not in this selection) came out in January 1734, and *To a Lady* in February 1735, just after the *Epistle to Arbuthnot*. Pope first printed them in their present order in 1735; but reading them in the order of publication will give fresh insights into the development of Pope's satirical method.

See the general introduction, p. 6, for the relationship of these poems to the 'Imitations of Horace'.

page 78   TO A LADY: OF THE CHARACTERS
OF WOMEN

Published February 1735

The *Epistle to Cobham*, discussing the impossibility of considering Man in the abstract, goes on to say how inconsistent men are. The only clue, Pope says, is 'Search then the Ruling Passion', and he goes on to develop this idea as it had been explained in the *Essay on Man* II. The

Epistle *To a Lady*, according to the 'Argument', carries this further by considering the characters of women 'only as contra-distinguished from the other sex'; these, we are told, are yet more inconsistent and incomprehensible than those of men. Even those with strongly marked characters—and the Argument goes on to give examples, of the affected (ll. 7-28), the soft-natured (ll. 29-40), the cunning (ll. 45-52), the whimsical (ll. 53-86), the witty (ll. 87-100), the stupid and silly, the shrewish and the heartless—possess inconsistencies. Again one must find the Ruling Passion, best discovered, in women, in their private life: and we conclude with 'the Picture of an esteemable Woman, made up of the best kind of Contrarieties'.

The 'Argument's' account of the poem, however, conveys little of Pope's essential creativity. What we have here is a gradual crescendo, culminating in the portrait of Atossa, of misdirected and destructive energies and passions. In *Windsor Forest* Pope had seen the landscape as a metaphor for Order (see Introduction, p. 9). Atossa is the human equivalent of 'Chaos'. Pope counters this by producing the human equivalent of *harmonious* confusion, who may be 'at best a Contradiction still' but is heaven's 'last best work'; she *blends* the best qualities of both sexes. She has achieved the perfect fusion of 'nature' (what we are born with) and 'good sense' (what we make of it) that all these poems expound.

This 'esteemable woman' is Pope's friend Martha Blount, to whom the Epistle was written: she is present in the poem from the first line, with its quietly intimate conversational tone. As for the less estimable women, many of them are based on actual persons, and no doubt were known to the 'inner circle' of Pope's readers, or those who were interested in literary gossip: but Pope is illustrating a thesis rather than making personal attacks, and it is not worth our while to pursue these identifications. In many cases the names tell us enough—e.g. *Rufa*, a redhead, *Papillia*, a butterfly; similarly, *Arcadia's Countess* (l. 7) is here a type of the frequently-painted great lady (Sir Philip Sidney had addressed his *Arcadia* to the Countess of Pembroke), and this is more relevant than any mere personal allusion. Others, such as *Sappho*, we meet elsewhere (e.g. *Fortescue* ll. 82 ff.).

We are being conducted round a portrait gallery, the metaphor of painting being announced at l. 5, reinforced at ll. 16-20, and maintained by such phrases as 'See', 'look on . . .', or ll. 151-6 and 181-98. The intricate rhythms and range of tone in this poem (compare, e.g. ll. 11-16, 33-40 and 243-8) make it among Pope's finest achievements.

When first published, and in all the texts printed during Pope's life, ll. 69-86, 115-50 and 157-98 were omitted.

ll. 7-16. The use of a single epithet or phrase to convey the effect of the different pictures (all of the same woman, thus making Pope's point about the variability of feminine character) is worth noting: *ermin'd pride, leering* (*Fannia* was a famous Roman adultress), *beautifully cry, loose hair, simp'ring*. What is the effect of the jaunty rhythm and comic rhyme of ll. 15-16?

ll. 25 ff. Compare this passage with the *Rape of the Lock* I ll. 121 ff.: is Belinda's a *greazy task*? What is the difference?

l. 31. *Calista* was the guilty heroine of Rowe's tragedy *The Fair Penitent* (1703): *nice*, fastidious and delicate—which Calista was not.

l. 43. *nice* here is 'discriminating'; the spots on tulips are, in a sense, a defect, a weakness, but they add to the beauty.

ll. 54 ff. a *wash* for the complexion or the hair; the irony of *tolerably mild* is brought out by the comically grim exaggeration of *hardly stew a child*. Narcissa is so whimsical as to be able to alternate between reading Jeremy Taylor's *Holy Living and Holy Dying*, and drinking brandy with lemon-peel with a couple of notorious debauchees (l. 64).

For *Chartres* see *Bathurst* l. 20. *His Grace*, possibly Wharton (see *Bathurst* l. 86).

l. 68. *sad*, solemn.

ll. 69 ff. The tone here, as Pope deals with 'the lewd and vicious', becomes harsher. Notice the successive blows of the balanced half-lines of ll. 69-72, with their series of sharp contrasts and contradictions (e.g. *majestically drunk*; *prouder as a Punk*—i.e. a whore; *chaste/frank; teeming/barren; Mistress/Bride*). The thumping rhyme of 'drunk, Punk' helps the effect.

l. 78. *Tall-boy* is a young booby (in contrast to *Cæsar*) in a seventeenth-century comedy. *Charles* is a typical footman.

l. 79. *Helluo*, a glutton. *Hautgout*—'anything with a strong relish or strong scent, as overkept venison or game' (Johnson).

l. 85. *stoops*, swoops down like a bird of prey. Cf. *Arbuthnot*, l. 341.

ll. 95-100. This summing-up of a character is typical of Pope's method in this poem. Cf. also ll. 113-14, with its effective transition into the following portrait.

l. 110. *Ratafie* a liqueur flavoured with fruit-kernels.

ll. 115 ff. *Atossa*, in history, was the daughter of Cyrus the Great, and sister of the violent Cambyses. Here, she is a devastating example of a whirlpool of inconsistency, involving itself and others in violence. The violence is created by the language (*warfare, Rage, Fury, Revenge, death, curse*), accentuated by *Eddy, Whisks, down it goes, out-ran, pursu'd*. The love is as violent and as unpredictable as the hate. We catch the echo of her own voice at ll. 135-6. Again, the portrait ends in a summary of contradictions. Like Philomedé (l. 72), evidently only her illegitimate children have lived.

l. 150. The mention of a divine providence here is important, and, with the following mention of Martha Blount, reassures us of the theme of the *Essay on Man*, and prepares us for the positive portrait with which the poem ends.

l. 158. 'Did not deliberately break her own rule of making women inconsistent—simply *forgot* to give her a heart.' Note that Martha breaks in in her own person here, making us more aware of her presence —aware also of the good nature and generosity for which she will stand.

l. 181. Pope, because of his political antipathy to the Queen, is being sarcastic: she is never described, he says, except in unvarying terms of exaggerated praise. It is no good trying to get at the real person underneath this conventional *Robe of Quality*, the essentially 'public' figure. *Varnish'd out* suggests the application of a protective coating to preserve this figure for posterity.

ll. 193 ff. The Duchess of Queensberry was one of the most beautiful women of the century; Pope works round to the point that, just as painters have to use humbler models, he has to find humbler models for virtue, being unlikely to find them in high life. *Mah'met* was a Turkish servant of George I; *Hale* was Minister at Teddington.

l. 210. Having given various examples, Pope is now able to generalize about the ruling passion of women. In l. 211 *that* is the Love of Pleasure, *this* (l. 213) the Love of Sway, i.e. power. Lines 219-30 summarise the effects of Power; ll. 231-42, of Pleasure.

l. 231. *the sex*, womankind (here the subject of 'pursue Pleasures').

ll. 234 ff. i.e. to covet *them* (Pleasures, or birds). Notice the way in which the innocent charm of the opening lines here, with the undertone of cruelty (the children would spoil—kill—the bird if they caught it), modulates into the horror of the end. The contrasts expressed in *merry/miserable* (a *Night* is one set aside for receiving visitors) develop into the grim judgment of ll. 243-8, with the antitheses moving inexorably to the contemptuous *Fop* and the rhyme *Sot, forgot*. Cf. similar forecasts for Belinda in the *Rape of the Lock*, but note the darker tone here.

l. 251. *Ring*, the fashionable drive in Hyde Park. *Fatigues*, makes weary by too much glittering, like (l. 253) too much glaring sun.

ll. 257 ff. For Pope's praise of Martha Blount's 'good humour' see letter 4, p. 19. See also Clarissa's speech in the *Rape of the Lock* V ll. 29 ff.; the tone of affectionate mockery in that poem is suggested here by such words as *Codille* (l. 266), from the game of Ombre, the

Spleen, and the reference to China falling. The *Tickets* are lottery tickets. *Small-pox*—which Martha had in 1714—echoes a more sombre note from Clarissa's speech. Is l. 283 a conventional gallant compliment—or does it imply that, for a woman of such qualities, age really does *not* matter?

l. 285. Phœbus refines Gold because the Sun was said to create gold and gems by its rays; he refines Wit because he is the god of poetry, Apollo, and so has given Martha a poet (Pope), but not the worthless gift of gold, or *dross.*

page 86   TO ALLEN LORD BATHURST
('OF THE USE OF RICHES')

Published January 1733

'I never in my life took more care of any poem', wrote Pope to Swift, and he told Caryll that it 'was the work of two years by intervals.' Bearing in mind his remark to Spence that 'the things I have written fastest have always pleased the most', we need not be surprised to find that *Bathurst* suffers somewhat from being over-laboured. It is too much in the shadow of the *Essay on Man,* as in ll. 155-70; the trouble here is that the thesis of those lines, which seems to present itself as the central statement of the poem, is to some extent contradicted by the illustrations. Pope's imaginative realisation undermines his theory.

The poem, then, is not really about this thesis, but about two other, though related, things: the use of riches, and their power to corrupt men. The essence of them both is conveyed by ll. 233-6. The portrait of Buckingham, the 'lord of useless thousands', is set against the positives of Bathurst himself and the Man of Ross. Unfortunately, these positives do not have as much power: the Man of Ross is over-sentimentalised, the creative use of wealth being much better treated in *Burlington.*

This is, in fact, primarily an attacking poem. The treatment of the situation that would arise if bribes were paid in kind, not cash (ll. 35-64), or the mock-lyrical praise of 'blest paper-credit' (ll. 69-78) are exuberantly comic, but as the poison of gold is seen undermining society the poetry becomes grimmer. Avarice 'creeps on', a low-born mist which recalls the baleful fogs of Dulness; the deliberate nastiness of such passages as ll. 88-92, 171-8, 234-5 or 371-4 (with its unpleasant perversion of Jove descending on Danaë in a shower of gold)—all these reveal the basic attitudes of the poem. Corruption is a 'gen'ral flood'; the last word is with Sir Balaam, a corrupted human being who inverts and parodies the progress of Job, and dies cursing God.

For his illustrations, Pope sometimes uses generalised types (to many of which later research has been able to assign a particular identity), sometimes real people, who are named. Of the latter, most were either notorious or dead, so that Pope can operate without fear of a libel action. He wrote lengthy notes about many of them, which may denote a feeling that he had not succeeded in making them sufficiently self-supporting in the poem itself—Swift complained that 'some parts of it are not so obvious to middling Readers'. All we really need to grasp, though, is the general character of this nouveau-riche society, and its attendant corruption.

Once again, the epistle form permits a wide variation of style: in places it is gossipy, in places heroic, even biblical in manner—always a 'witty familiar dialogue' between two men who, despite their difference in birth, held each other in mutual esteem. Allen Bathurst (1685-1775) became Baron Bathurst in 1712, and met Pope around 1718.

ll. 1 ff. This light-hearted discussion of the use of money is hardly sound economics, but enables Pope to introduce his theme of bribery and corruption. The *Doctors* are those of philosophy; *Momus* is the god of Ridicule. For *Sire*, see *To a Lady* l. 289 n.

l. 20. Line 19 defines the characters mentioned: *Ward*, an M.P. expelled from the Commons, and pilloried, for forgery in 1726; Peter *Waters* or Walter (also at l. 125), a notorious moneylender, the original of 'Peter Pounce' in Fielding's *Joseph Andrews*; Francis *Chartres*, an even more notorious gambler and debauchee, who had died in 1731. All three were immensely wealthy.

ll. 41-2. *confound*, confuse the brains of; *water*, intoxicate; the *Quorum*, the Justices of the Peace. With bribery in kind, the effects would be confined to a small area—not a whole nation.

ll. 49 ff. *Sir Morgan* is fictitious. *Worldly*, the avaricious Edward Wortley Montagu, husband of Lady Mary (he is probably *Avidien* in *Bethel* l. 49). Pope complains that certain mine-owners kept prices of coal extravagantly high by a price-ring. Sir William *Colepepper* squandered a fortune by gambling, at such famous gaming-houses as *White's* chocolate-house. Note the appropriateness of the stakes won by *Uxorio* (possibly Hervey's father), and *Adonis* (Hervey himself). *Quadrille* is a fashionable card-game.

ll. 65 ff. Even gold, used for bribery, has its dangers. Pope alleges that this is a true story, of the time of William III. The *Patriot* here is ironically named, for *Cato* had a deserved reputation for honesty. The story leads to a mocking praise of paper-money. To *imp* is to insert a feather into a hawk's damaged wing, to increase its power of flight.

How does Pope convey, in ll. 73-8, the sense of bribery operating in secret? A *Sibyl* is a prophetess of classical legend.

ll. 84 ff. Richard *Turner* (d. 1733), a very wealthy merchant. Pope alleges that, having lost some of his money, Turner stayed in his rooms, thus saving expenses on clothes, etc. The Duke of *Wharton* (d. 1731) Pope describes as 'a nobleman of great qualities' but 'unfortunate in the application of them': he had supported the Old Pretender, was outlawed in 1729, and died in exile. In neither case is the illustration very clear. 'Vulture' *Hopkins*, rich and notoriously mean, left an extremely complicated will, limiting the inheritance to certain heirs; the first heir, however, died before Hopkins himself. *Japhet* Crook, a notorious forger, was pilloried in 1731, his ears cut off and his nose slit. He died in 1734.

ll. 89 ff. Various personalities lie below this passage, but Pope has generalised it. *Narses* is probably the Earl of Cadogan (d. 1726), whom Pope resented for his vindictive attitude to Atterbury, the Bishop of Rochester; he evidently has some such ailment as an anal fistula. *Harpax* means 'robber'; *Shylock* may be Wortley Montagu again. *Bond* (d. 1747), known as 'Damn-the-Poor' Bond, had been expelled from the Commons for a breach of trust; he was a director of the Charitable Corporation, a society ostensibly founded for the relief of the poor, the funds of which were mainly embezzled by the Board. For *Blunt* see l. 135 below.

l. 103. *Sir Gilbert* Heathcote (d. 1733), a founder and governor of the Bank of England: reputed to be the richest commoner in England, worth £700,000, he had a reputation for meanness.

l. 119. In *South-sea year* (1720) the extravagance and luxury pushed up prices. The South-Sea Company was floated in 1711 as a scheme for paying off the National Debt. After much rigging of the market and boosting of shares the 'bubble' burst. Thousands were ruined.

l. 122. The Opposition maintained, wrongly, that Walpole was contemplating a general excise in 1733. *Phryne* (perhaps Maria Skerret, Walpole's mistress and a friend of Lady Mary—*Sappho*) is taking advantage of 'inside information' and investing in antiques, etc. A *plum* is £100,000.

l. 128. The Roman Empire was put up for sale in A.D. 193, and bought by *Didius*, a Roman lawyer.

ll. 129 ff. The Polish throne, to which kings were elected by the venal nobility of Poland, was vacant in 1696, 1707, 1709 and 1733. Joseph *Gage* held an enormous amount of stock in the company formed to develop the Mississippi region, and is said to have offered 3 million pounds for the Polish throne. He later lost his money, but obtained a profitable concession, from the King of Spain, to work all the Spanish gold mines, etc. (l. 134). His second wife, Lady Mary Herbert (*Maria*), had also speculated in the Mississippi; she had determined to marry no one lower than a prince. She met Gage in the mines of Asturia, N.W. Spain.

l. 135. Sir John *Blunt* (d. 1733), an unscrupulous director of the South-Sea Company. Pope declares that Blunt was constantly declaiming, hypocritically, against corruption, luxury, avarice, etc.

ll. 137 ff. This 'prophecy' is seen coming true in the *Dunciad* IV. There is general confusion of rank and order as a result of speculation. *Statesman* and *Patriot* denote Government and Opposition. The *Box* at the theatre would normally only be occupied by the upper class. *Job*, to intrigue for private gain; *bite*, to take in, to cheat.

l. 146. Refers to the victories of Marlborough in the War of the Spanish Succession (1701-14), under Queen *Anne*; and to those of *Edward* III and the Black Prince in the Hundred Years' War.

l. 147. The *great Scriv'ner* (one who lays out money at interest for others) is Blunt. Pope is, of course, ironic. Blunt 'bought both sides' in the sense that members of both parties rushed to buy South-Sea stock.

ll. 153 ff. Having firmly established, by particular examples, the nature of this world of corruption, Pope passes on to theorise about it, and is then able to use more 'general' characters for illustration. His logic is shaky here: he condemns the society, but, instead of being content with saying that Providence is able to bring good out of all this evil, he goes further and maintains that the whole society is, in fact, ordered by Heaven—a fatalistic view. The parallels from Nature (ll. 166-70) are hardly applicable.

ll. 176-8. An unpleasant excess is suggested by *spouting, lavish, dogs* and *burst*; this is hardly a good way to quench one's thirst.

ll. 179 ff. *Cotta* seems to have been based on several people, including Cutler (l. 315), but mere identity is unimportant in this fine portrait of a Miser, the opposite of Chaucer's Franklin. *Pulse* is beans, lentils, etc.; *Chartreux*, a Carthusian monastery—they were noted for austerity.

ll. 203 ff. *hecatomb*, the sacrifice of a hundred oxen. What effect does this exaggeration (and *floods*) produce? In what sense is the Divine *deep*?

l. 208. Notice the biblical allusion ('The zeal of thine house shall eat me up': John ii. 17). What is the effect of this?

l. 214. *Train-bands*, citizen soldiery. The London bands were usually Whig. Swift speaks of a ceremony in which Whigs burned an effigy of the Pope on Queen Elizabeth's birthday.

ll. 229 ff. *Bounty*, liberality, charity. The expression is clumsy: 'those who are bounteous to their fellow men repair the wrongs done by Fortune, and prove themselves deserving of their own wealth'.

l. 235. *Ambergrise*, used as a fixative in many perfumes.

ll. 237 ff. Most nobles, Pope implies, are *not* like Bathurst or Oxford, but surround themselves with sycophants. Edward Harley, second Earl of *Oxford*, son of the great Tory statesman Robert, was a close friend of Pope and Swift from 1722 until his death in 1741.

ll. 250 ff. Pope has a lengthy note explaining that this refers to John Kyrle (d. 1724) of Ross-on-Wye (the river *Vaga*). He admits, in a letter, 'some small exaggeration', but, 'I was determined the ground work at least should be truth'. It seems that Kyrle was indeed an ideal, benevolent country gentleman; but this portrait lacks power. Compare, for example, the poetic expression of ll. 253-61 with the much finer poetry of *Burlington*. The diction (*swain, vale, lisping*) is too idyllic, l. 263 forced, and ll. 273-4 rather absurd in this context (*variance*, a dispute). Line 279 indicates that Kyrle was a bachelor. Note the veiled allusion to Moses at l. 254; what is its effect?

l. 291. *Hopkins* see l. 87 n. The pompous monuments, erected to themselves by such men, *extend their hands* as if in bounty.

ll. 299 ff. Pope goes on to show how the profuse and the covetous both come to the same end. George *Villiers*, Duke of Buckingham (*Zimri* in Dryden's *Absalom and Achitophel*), died in 1687, though not in the circumstances Pope describes. The emotional effect of this starkly realistic scene is what matters. This is, in a sense, a symbolic setting: the *worst* inn's *worst* room. The prodigal is dying in surroundings that both express most pungently his essential materialism (cf. the walls of *dung* with the *stink* of l. 235), and form an appropriate punishment—like the Prodigal Son's 'husks that the swine did eat'. What is conveyed by ll. 303-4? *Flock-bed*, a bed stuffed with wool, much less fine than a feather-bed. Buckingham acquired *Cliveden* House, on the Thames, but had almost certainly ended his liaison with the wanton Countess of *Shrewsbury*, whose husband he killed in a duel, before then. Villiers, as ll. 309-12 show, had mocked the valuable things of life; Death now mocks him.

ll. 315 ff. Sir John *Cutler* (d. 1693), a wealthy London merchant, unjustly notorious for personal meanness; he was, in fact, a generous man. Most of Pope's allegations here are untrue, but the portrait serves its purpose.

ll. 337-8. A very feeble transition to a fine narrative.

l. 339. The Monument to the Great Fire of London originally bore an inscription saying the fire had been started by the 'treachery and malice of the Popish faction'; this was finally erased in 1831.

ll. 342 ff. Sir *Balaam*, whose name indicates his asinine qualities, is partly based, probably, on Thomas Pitt (d. 1726), who bought the great Pitt Diamond while in India, and sold it at an enormous profit. Again, the important thing is what Pope has made out of his material. How does he suggest the connection between a nominal piety and the world of business? What point does he make about the nature of Balaam's 'good fortune'? What is the exact tone and decorum of ll. 357-60? How does Pope plot the curve of Balaam's relationship with God?

l. 387. *Cits*, contemptuous slang for citizens, bourgeoisie; for St James's and the City, see *Rape of the Lock* IV l. 118.

l. 394. *St Stephen*'s Chapel, Westminster, was used as the House of Commons until 1834.

l. 397. The Earl of *Coningsby*, a prominent anti-Catholic Whig who helped impeach Robert Harley in 1715. Pope's epitaph on him (1729) runs:

> Here lies Lord Coningsby: be civil:
> The rest God knows, perhaps the Devil.

ll. 400-1. These audacious lines were not printed until 1735.

l. 402. *sad*, miserable, but looking ironically back to l. 342 with the meaning 'sober'.

page 96
TO BURLINGTON
('OF FALSE TASTE')

Published December 1731

Richard Boyle, third Earl of Burlington (1695-1753), was a distinguished amateur of architecture and of landscape gardening. His admiration for the Italian Renaissance architect, Palladio, had a considerable influence on Georgian architectural taste; and his patronage of (among others) the landscape architect William Kent was also influential. Pope himself was a pioneer of landscape gardening, and the tone of this epistle, or essay, is that of one man of taste speaking to another. The mutual esteem is obvious, as is the warmth of their friendship: we are not made aware of any barrier of rank or birth. Pope had known Burlington since 1716 or earlier, and the friendship continued until Pope's death.

This is not simply a poem about architecture and gardening, nor even simply about false taste. Pope uses landscape gardening as a kind of metaphor for man's correct attitude to Nature. Good sense (l. 41) is the guide, and it is sent from Heaven—a guide to living, as well as to landscaping and architecture. The ideas of Order and Harmony are being invoked: and there is an echo here of the advice—to 'follow Nature'—given twenty years earlier, in the *Essay on Criticism*.

This epistle follows the typical Horatian pattern: a general statement, about the vanity of expense, is made; it is 'fixed' by several identifiable examples, in which names are mentioned (though with little animus); the point is clinched by a full-scale illustration—Timon's Villa; and the whole is rounded off with a statement of the positive which is opposed to all these negatives.

Timon's pretensions and extravagance are undermined on all counts: the architecture, the gardens, his own vanity, his false taste in books, religion, hospitality. His landscape perverts Nature, instead of using it (see Introduction, p. 9). Timon's Chapel is an empty show: his real religion is the 'solemn sacrifice' of the dinner, dedicated to his own 'civil pride'. But Pride must decay, because it is barren and useless; it must and will make way for Nature again, 'and laughing Ceres reassume the land'.

The description of the Villa is one of the finest things Pope ever did, yet he must many times have regretted the writing of it. Almost from the start contemporaries—some innocently, some maliciously—assumed that it was a satire on the Duke of Chandos' seat, Cannons, near Edgware. Chandos, a millionaire Whig, was not the most popular of noblemen, and, as Pope had recently published the *Dunciad*, the opportunity to hit at both men was too good to miss. Gossip circulated, Pope was accused of being a hypocrite, of biting the hand that fed him (for Chandos was a notable patron, and had subscribed generously to Pope's Homer), and he was genuinely distressed. He did not know Chandos well, but they had many friends in common, including Burlington himself, and it is virtually certain that Pope did not intend the Villa to be a picture of Cannons. He cleared the matter up satisfactorily with Chandos, but the gossip continued; and the affair both sharpened Pope's anger against those 'who read but with a Lust to mis-apply' (see *Arbuthnot* l. 301), and helped convince him that his satire must be more particular still—as, from *Bathurst* onwards, it is.

The tone is easy and flexible: it admits slangy words such as *squirt* and *spew*, and the colloquiality of ll. 32-3; echoes of the pastoral style, as in ll. 83-5; the high style of the close; and many gradations in between.

ll. 1 ff.   The opening lines, which mock the vanity of the 'man of

Taste', introduce various more or less distinguished collectors who benefit from this ostentatiousness: Richard *Topham* (d. 1735), who had a valuable collection of drawings, etc.; the Earl of *Pembroke* (d. 1733), whose collection included many Renaissance bogus-antique statues; Thomas *Hearne* (d. 1735), the great antiquary; Richard *Mead* (see *Bolingbroke* l. 51); Sir Hans *Sloane*, First Physician to George II, whose collection formed the nucleus of the British Museum.

l. 18.   *Ripley*, a carpenter-turned-architect, a protégé of Walpole; see also *Augustus* l. 186.

l. 20.   *Bubo*, Dodington. See *Arbuthnot* l. 280.

ll. 23 ff.   These lines refer to Burlington's recent publication of a volume of Palladio's drawings of ancient Rome. The important word, receiving stress from the rhyme, is *Use*: it looks forward to l. 179. What sins against decorum are enumerated at ll. 29 ff?

l. 34.   *rustic*, masonry with a roughened face.

l. 39.   *your brother Peer*, presumably Bubo; in the original edition, ll. 23-38 followed l. 180, and the transition there was more natural.

l. 46.   Inigo *Jones* (1573-1652), pioneer of classic architecture in England; *Le Nôtre* (1613-1700) laid out the gardens at Versailles and Fontainebleau for Louis XIV. Pope did not like his style of gardening, but this line is not a sneer—it stresses that Good Sense is an *inner* light, which cannot be given to you by other men.

ll. 57 ff.   *Genius*, the presiding spirit, or deity; hence, the creative spirit 'within' the landscape itself. Art becomes genuinely creative when it is natural, when it understands and bodies forth the harmonies of life itself. When Art is fused with the natural order, Time encourages its growth—in contrast to the fate of the Villa. Note the active verbs—*tells*, *helps*, etc.—of this passage.

ll. 60 ff.   *theatres*, stressed on first syllable; *intending*, leading the eye forward.

l. 70.   *Stow*, Viscount Cobham's seat in Buckinghamshire, one of the finest examples of eighteenth-century landscape gardening.

l. 71.   The gardens at *Versailles* were too formal for Pope's taste.

l. 73.   *Parterres*, ornamental arrangements of flower beds and turf.

l. 74.   *floats*, inundates. Cobham is, of course, praised for thus land-scaping a too-formal garden.

l. 78.   Dr Samuel *Clarke* (d. 1729), a philosopher, and favourite of Queen Caroline. The *Hermitage* was an ornamental feature of Rich-mond Park; in 1732 a bust of Clarke, together with some others, was placed there. He was of unorthodox religious views, which made him, perhaps, peculiarly unfitted for a 'hermitage'. These lines (77-78) were added in the 1744 edition.

ll. 79 ff. *Villario*, doubtless a compound figure. *Quincunx*, a group of trees, etc., planted like the five on dice. See *Fortescue* l. 130. *Espaliers*, fruit-trees trained on stakes. The point here is that even the best things become burdensome to the man who lacks Good Sense.

l. 95. 'The two extremes in parterres, which are equally faulty; a *boundless Green*, large and naked as a field, or a *flourish'd Carpet*, where the greatness and nobleness of the piece is lessen'd by being divided into too many parts, with scroll'd works and beds . . .' (Pope's note).

ll. 96 ff. Pope disapproves of the replacement of natural forest-trees by clipped evergreens; contrast *thick'ning, red'ning, stretching, thriving*, with the *mournful* yews and the *ignoble* dead broomsticks.

ll. 99 ff. The tone throughout this passage is one of mocking wonder, of ironically exaggerated praise. Notice how the 'magnificence' is continually being undercut, (*a*) by a word deflating a 'heroic' context (Cupids *squirt*; *gaping* Tritons *spew*; footsteps *scrape* the marble hall); (*b*) by contrast (compare the *puny insect* with the *majestic mien*; the *huge* heaps of *littleness*; the *pride* of *prayer*; in *plenty starving*); (*c*) by exaggeration (e.g. ll. 156-7); (*d*) by the undertone of barren dryness (the fountain, never to be played; *unwatered*; *drooping*; *dusty*). Observe examples of the structure of a line suggesting the sense (e.g. the meticulous regularity of ll. 117, 120; the approach up the terrace at ll. 129-31; the *broken and uneven* rhythm of ll. 143-4; the clock-like precision of l. 158). Notice also the exact choice of word (e.g. the effective transfer of *soft* from *Cushion* to *Dean*; the ironic *improves*; the *suffering* eye; *mourn* at l. 125; *quirks*; *devoutly stare*; *sprawl*; *tantaliz'd*; *his civil pride*). Why are these so effective?

l. 104. *Brobdignag* (properly Brobdingnag), the land of the giants in *Gulliver's Travels*. *Draught* is pronounced like *thought*.

l. 120. Horace Walpole also complains of gardens 'stocked . . . with giants, animals, monsters, coats of arms and mottoes, in yew, box and holly'. *Amphitrite*, the sea-goddess.

l. 136. *Aldus*, Aldo Manutio (1450-1515), a famous Venetian printer; *Du Suëil*, a French bookbinder of the early eighteenth century.

l. 146. Antonio *Verrio* (1639-1707) and Louis *Laguerre* (1663-1721), painters in the Baroque style, the excesses of which are nicely suggested by these lines.

l. 150. Pope notes that 'a reverend Dean preaching at Court, threatned the sinner with punishment in "a place which he thought it not decent to name in so polite an assembly"'.

ll. 151-68. Compare the method of these lines with the Toilet scene in the *Rape of the Lock* I ll. 121 ff.

l. 160. In chapter xlvii of *Don Quixote*, Sancho Panza is entertained to a dinner at which the Governor's Physician, who has charge of his diet, continually whisks food away before Sancho has a chance to eat.

ll. 173 ff. Compare this vision of natural plenty with the barrenness of Timon's Villa. Providence, in fact, asserts itself in two ways: (i) by 'using' Timon's extravagance to bring prosperity to more people, (ii) by eventually taking over altogether, and 'reassuming' the land after the Villa's fall. Notice the personification implied in the active verbs, especially *nod, bury* and *re-assume,* and the effect of *deep* and *laughing.* Is *laughing* just a conventional piece of classicised diction, or is a judgment implied?

l. 186. Would *cow* and *horse* do as well here? If not, why not?

l. 194. M. *Vitruvius* Pollio, born *c.* 88 B.C., author of the treatise *De Architectura.*

ll. 197. ff. On the need for great public works at this time, see also *Bethel* ll. 119-20. They are here regarded as a 'duty' of the great landowner; it is no use waiting for the 'Government' to carry them out. l. 204 may glance again at George II.

page 103   IMITATIONS OF HORACE

Pope attributed to Bolingbroke the initial idea of imitating a Satire of Horace (see his remark to Spence: 'When I had a fever . . .', p. 31). The attacks on Pope had for some time been increasing in vehemence, particularly after the publication of the *Dunciad* in 1728-9; and after the appearance of the *Epistle to Burlington* (1731) Pope had been infuriated, as many of his letters show, by malicious misinterpretations of 'Timon'. A reply and a defence were necessary, and, as Pope's 'advertisement' to these poems declares, 'An Answer from *Horace* was both more full, and of more Dignity, than any I cou'd have made in my own person.' He goes on to make a sharp distinction between the satirist and the libeller: it is the position of the satirist that Pope is defending, and these 'imitations' are at one and the same time a reply to personal attacks, the most wide-ranging application—to politics, literature and society—of his beliefs, and what might be called, in more general terms, the Life of a Poet. Horace seemed to present striking parallels between the world of Augustus, and that of Queen Anne and the Georges; and the view of life he expressed, the calm, balanced outlook, the celebration of friendship, the praise of virtue and the detestation of vice, all helped to form an 'image' that, consciously or not, many men of the age tried to live up to. The whole of Pope's later life is itself a kind of 'imitation of Horace'. The parallels are not, of course, exact; no doubt Pope's temperament did not precisely correspond with that of Horace as we infer it; but the correspondences are close enough, and Pope's use of the basic Augustan metaphor gives his satires great vitality and depth. All the time we should be aware—and the need for awareness was insisted on by Pope's printing the Latin text on the opposite page, where applicable—that not only is there a topical discussion of society being carried on, but also that that society is being evaluated by the standards of Augustan Rome.

So much is this so that, as well as imitating Horace's style and structure, as in *Arbuthnot* and the *Epilogue*, Pope is able to use whole poems of Horace as a kind of prism, turning what the Roman had written of his own times to shed a new light on the England of the 'thirties. We might expect in this latter case to find Pope restricted by the need to follow the Latin, but nearly always the result is the reverse: Pope finds Horace both a concentrating and a liberating influence, and has complete freedom of movement.

The word 'satire' originally seems to have implied a hotch-potch or medley, and could therefore admit of a mixture of styles. Horace sometimes refers to his satires as *sermones*, discourses, and they are essentially conversation-poems, for one or more speakers, having the same kind of ease, colloquiality and abrupt transition from the light-hearted to the serious that one finds in good conversation or a good letter. Pope reproduces this Horatian quality with great skill: there is colloquialism, as in the opening of *Arbuthnot*; the snip-snap of rapid dialogue, as in *Epilogue II*, ll. 13-26; the movement from a relaxed middle style to an almost epic level of denunciation, as in ll. 141-70 of *Epilogue I*; the opposite movement from mockingly high to low, as in ll. 394-410 of *Augustus*; contempt, panegyric, indignation, pathos and farce all within a few lines of each other, as one finds in *Arbuthnot*; all these exemplify Pope's perfect command of tone.

These poems seem to bristle with personalities, and the difficulty is always to know how much notice to take of all these figures: does our identifying them matter a great deal? Here it is worth while remembering two remarks Pope made in connection with the *Dunciad*: 'the Poem was not made for these Authors, but these Authors for the Poem', by which Pope implies that his victims simply presented themselves, so to speak, as illustrations for the vices and follies he found rampant; and, in the same Preface, 'I would not have the reader too much troubled or anxious, if he cannot decypher them; since when he shall have found them out, he will probably know no more of the Persons than before'. Johnson's advice to the reader of Shakespeare is pertinent: 'Let him . . . read every play from the first scene to the last, with utter negligence of all his commentators. When his fancy is once on the wing, let it not stoop at correction or explanation. . . . Let him read on through brightness and obscurity, through integrity and corruption; let him preserve his comprehension of the dialogue and his interest in the fable.' This, with the necessary changes made, is good advice for the reader of Pope. It is a problem which hardly arises with Horace, as it is often impossible to tell whether his satiric victims are individuals or types; what matters is the poetry, and so it is with Pope. The persons named are generally defined by their context, and all that it is necessary for us to know is that these were real people, picked out by Pope partly because they offended him, but also because they represented the things he was attacking. The justice or injustice of it all hardly concerns us any longer: the creatures have been preserved for us like flies in amber—

> The things, we know, are neither rich nor rare,
> But wonder how the devil they got there.

page 103

TO MR FORTESCUE

(Horace, Satires: Book II No. i)

Published February 1733

William Fortescue (1687-1749), whom Pope had known since 1713, was successively Attorney-General to the Prince of Wales, a Justice of the Common Pleas, and Master of the Rolls. Horace's satire is also addressed to a lawyer, Trebatius, and Fortescue gives Pope the same kind of advice as Trebatius gives Horace: to stop writing, or, if he must write, to confine himself to panegyric. This leads into Pope's first full-scale defence of his satiric position. The core of this poem is the distinction between 'Grave Epistles, bringing Vice to light', and merely malicious and personal attack. This is discussed partly in the context of the 'noise and calumny' (in Pope's words) attendant on the recent publication of *Burlington* and *Bathurst*.

ll. 1 ff. Note the ironic exaggeration of *scarce, wise, much too rough*.

ll. 3 ff. The references are to *Bathurst*: for *Peter* and *Chartres* see note to l. 20 of that poem.

l. 6. Lord *Fanny* is Hervey: see *Arbuthnot*. What image is suggested by *spins*? (Cf. *Arbuthnot* ll. 89-94).

ll. 11-14. Notice the change in style, with Pope's startled comic indignation at his friend's laconic advice.

l. 18. *probatum est*. Fortescue is given the lawyer's habit of using Latin catch-phrases. *Lettuce* was supposed to be a soporific.

l. 19. *Celsus* was the chief Roman writer on medicine.

ll. 23 ff. Pope is here following the precepts of *An Essay on Criticism*, ll. 158 ff. *Sir Richard* Blackmore's *Prince Arthur* (1695) is a ponderous epic: see also *Bolingbroke* l. 16. For Eustace *Budgell* (1686-1737), a miscellaneous writer, see *Arbuthnot* l. 378; he wrote a ridiculous poem in praise of George II, in which the death of George's horse in battle is lamented. Note the clogged consonants of l. 24, the thumping of l. 26, and the way in which the deliberately insipid style of ll. 29-32 conveys Pope's scorn both for the flattering court-poets, and for the objects of that flattery, such as Queen *Carolina* and her daughter *Amelia*.

ll. 34-6. The *Laureate* is Colley Cibber (see the *Dunciad*), who had to write two official Odes a year; they were one of the great jokes of the time among men of discrimination. George II's contempt for 'boetry and bainting' was notorious—hence the ironic strategy of *Augustus*.

ll. 38 ff. Fortescue returns again to the effects of *Burlington* and *Bathurst* (see, e.g. *Bathurst* l. 64, and ll. 101 ff.).

ll. 42 ff. Fortescue suggests that, far from being harmless, generalised satire hurts many people. Pope's reply insists on his inability to be other than honest and straightforward. For *Timon* see *Burlington* ll. 99 ff; *Balaam*, *Bond*, and *Harpax* are in *Bathurst*: see ll. 93, 102 and 339 ff.

ll. 46 ff. Charles *Dartineuf* (1664-1737) and the Earl of *Scarsdale* (1682-1736), celebrated bon viveurs. *Ridotta* (from *ridotto*, an evening party with dancing, etc.), a Society type. *Lustres*, candlesticks ornamented with pendants of cut glass. The brothers Henry and Stephen *Fox*, Whig peers, are pilloried here as friends of Hervey and supporters of Walpole: *Hockley-Hole* was a London bear-garden. *Shippen* (1673-1743), the Jacobite leader in the Commons, whose integrity was a by-word, and the essayist *Montagne*, supply the 'positives' here.

ll. 59-62. This is partly a statement of his reticence, partly an acknowledgment of the laws of libel about which his friend has warned him: attacking *Vice too high* might be dangerous.

l. 67. *Moderation* is the essence of the Horatian position.

ll. 71-2. *Hectors*, bullies; *Supercargoes*, the supervisors of cargo, etc., on merchant ships—proverbially wealthy, presumably because of corruption. Notice the juxtaposition of words in l. 72: the unequivocal *thieves* and *sharpers* dictates our attitude to the *supercargoes* and *directors*.

l. 73. Ironic. The Tories continually complained about the size of the standing army maintained by Walpole.

l. 75. *Fleury*, Cardinal, and chief adviser to Louis XV.

ll. 81 ff. Various *creatures* are introduced here, each with a 'proper Pow'r to hurt'. Pope expects the 'animals' he has shown up in his satire to retaliate in their natural (and often beastly) fashion. His own *proper Pow'r* is with the pen (ll. 69, 105), and he implies that this is natural and necessary to him.

Delia, the Countess of Delorain, one of George II's mistresses, an ally of Hervey and Lady Mary Wortley Montagu; gossip alleged that she had poisoned a rival; *Sappho*, as always, is Lady Mary—see notes to *Arbuthnot*.

l. 81. Sir Francis *Page* (1661-1741) a notorious 'hanging judge'.

ll. 91-100. What is the effect of the changes of style here?

l. 99. The *Mint* was a sanctuary for insolvent debtors. See *Arbuthnot* l. 13.

l. 100. Nathaniel *Lee* (d. 1692), a tragic dramatist; he is here as an example of the man who goes on scribbling even in the madhouse (he was said to have written a twenty-five act tragedy while in Bedlam). Pope works himself up here into a comic 'enthusiasm'.

l. 101. This enthusiasm is suitably rebuffed by Fortescue's *Alas young Man*, and *Flow'r of Age*. Pope was nearly 45, his friend a year older.

l. 103. *Plum*, £100,000; here, the possessors of that sum.

l. 103. *Shylock*, an unspecific figure, referring back to *Bathurst* ll. 96, 117; probably the Wortley Montagus again.

l. 104. *Testers*, sixpences, thus carrying on the suggestion of avarice in Shylock.

l. 105. Notice the force given to this passage by the vivid imagery, and vigour of the verbs (*point, brand, dash, bare*). The *Star* is that of an Order such as the Garter. Pope covers here the vices he detested most.

l. 111. *Boileau* (1636-1711); his *Le Lutrin* was a model for the *Rape of the Lock*.

l. 113. Refers to Dryden's *Spanish Friar* (1680), which satirised the morals of the Catholic clergy. James II banned it.

l. 116. Pope's translation of Homer had made him financially independent; he was the first English non-dramatic poet to free himself from the necessity of patronage.

l. 121. Pope translates Horace direct here, but transfers to himself Horace's praise of the satirist Lucilius. The change hardly indicates conceit on Pope's part: the burning sincerity of these lines justifies the statement of his 'public' function—after which he is able to modulate into the comparatively private and personal at ll. 123-32.

l. 130. *Quincunx*, a group of trees, etc., planted like the five on dice.

ll. 127 ff. For *St John*, Viscount Bolingbroke, see the Epistle to him. *He* (129) is the Earl of Peterborough (1658-1735), who as an army general had conducted a brilliant campaign in Spain in 1705-6.

l. 143. Note the skill with which Pope manages the dialogue here, bringing in the lawyer's jargon (these acts all concern libel) while maintaining a firm metrical pattern.

page 107   TO MR BETHEL

(Horace, Satires: Book II No. ii)

Published July 1734

Pope describes this as a 'paraphrase' rather than an 'imitation', and certainly stays very close to Horace's original, though he misses here something of Horace's loftiness of tone. The Latin is put into the mouth of Ofellus, a 'rustic sage . . . a man of home-spun wit'. Pope may originally have had Swift in mind for Ofellus, and the end of the poem shows him as present at this before-dinner praise of moderation; but his final choice, Hugh Bethel (d. 1748) was appropriate enough. Bethel was one of Pope's oldest friends, and apparently accustomed to praising the simple life. Like Horace, Pope moves round to a condemnation of luxury and excess, as well as of the opposite vice of avarice. Luxury brings disgrace and ruin; great possessions are no use to us when we are dead; better to spend wisely, and be masters of ourselves. This poem contains some of Pope's most charming autobiographical writing, and is a reminder that satire may do many other things besides attack. There are few personalities: *Oldfield* (l. 25) was a notorious glutton who was said to spend £1500 a year on eating; *Avidien* and his wife (l. 49) were taken to be a not undeserved picture of the Wortley Montagus; the great Duke of Marlborough (l. 122), here as elsewhere attacked on political grounds, is held up as an example of meanness—he was reckoned to be enormously wealthy; *Peter Walter* (see *Bathurst* l. 20) appears again here; *Vernon* refers to Pope's grasping landlord, and his widow.

ll. 1 ff. The poem begins with pleasant irony, partly at Bethel's expense (l. 3, and the pun on *sermon*, as preaching or conversation piece, at l. 9), partly at that of Pope and his friends, the implication of ll. 4-8 being that they may be in no mood or condition to listen *after* dinner.

l. 8. *mantling*, sparkling.

l. 10. *wise without the rules*, a philosopher of no particular 'school'.

ll. 19 ff. The glutton, it is implied, is deceived by appearances: are pheasants *really* so much nicer than guinea-fowl? After all, one doesn't eat the feathers, attractive though they are. The gourmet's other preferences are illogical, too: what is the point of insisting on the biggest carp and mullet if they're going to be cut up anyway? And why should one demand only small turbots? The same snobbery of taste extends (ll. 27-30) to the inconsistency of prizing some meat for its 'gamey' quality, other meat because it is fresh. Gluttony, in fact, destroys one's taste, and, ironically, the jaded palate prefers some of the simplest foods.

l. 17. *curious*, professing great discrimination of taste.

l. 25. *Harpy*, a rapacious monster.

l. 39. *Becca-ficos*, small birds eaten as a delicacy. The preceding lines imply that robins and martins are eaten instead.

ll. 40-44. Pope associates this kind of foolish luxury with the court, and with social climbing generally. The *Bedford Head* was a famous eating-house near Covent Garden.

l. 49. Horace's Avidienus is nicknamed 'Canis', dog.

l. 51. *presented*, given as presents.

ll. 69-71. The structure of these lines echoes the sense—a cramming together of all the different things in the overloaded stomach. An *intestine war* is a civil war, but here, of course, used punningly.

l. 76. *Clergy* and *City* are Pope's satirical additions to Horace.

ll. 91 ff. As ll. 28-30 have implied that there is little logic in the glutton's preferences, it is necessary now to defend the time-honoured practice of eating venison; the defence is that the good-natured man would make the meat last so that friends arriving later could still enjoy it—a practice the reverse of gluttony, in fact. Here again, as in *Fortescue* l. 101, Pope delights in attributing to his friend the tone of an elderly man putting much younger people to rights.

l. 98. 'cocks-combs' are included in some very elaborate recipes of the time; the other meaning is 'a fool, or fop'.

l. 102. This evidently refers to some cynicism of Lord Hervey.

ll. 119-20. Some suggestions are made here for the useful expenditure of wealth on public works in London. Many of the new churches built earlier in the century were already collapsing; there was a need for more embankments (*keys*) along the Thames; London Bridge was still the only bridge over the river; and the greater part of Whitehall Palace, destroyed by fire forty years before, was still lying in ruins.

ll. 133 ff. For the *South-Sea* Company see *Bathurst* ll. 119 ff. Pope had speculated a certain amount, but described himself as 'among the few who have the good fortune to remain, with half of what they imagined they had'.

l. 134. In 1733 Walpole planned a new Excise scheme (see *Bathurst* l. 122); it caused so much public alarm and misunderstanding that he withdrew it. He had not intended a *general* excise.

ll. 135-6. Pope's father had owned twenty acres in Windsor Forest; Pope now rented five at Twickenham.

l. 137. *piddle*, to trifle, or potter around; here, perhaps, to toy with one's food.

l. 152. As a reprisal for the Jacobite rising of 1715, extra land taxes were laid on the Catholics. A bill for further taxes was passed in 1723. These were not, however, always enforced.

l. 154. *Standing Armies*, see *Fortescue* l. 73.

l. 166. *Vernon* himself died in 1726, but his widow continued to be owner of the land.

l. 172. Delays in the Court of Chancery were notorious.

ll. 173 ff. Pope quotes two examples of how great houses have come into the hands of unworthy descendants. The last days of Buckingham ('Great Villiers') are described in *Bathurst* ll. 299-306. The *City Knight* is Sir Charles Duncombe, who bought Buckingham's estates for £90,000—'the greatest purchase ever made by any subject in England'.

page 112   AN EPISTLE TO DR ARBUTHNOT

Published January 1735

This is in some ways Pope's most complex poem; it is surely the one most often misunderstood. The reasons for this are not hard to find: it springs from such very different causes, develops so many different themes, is constructed with such freedom and fluency (as if Pope were setting down his thoughts simply as they came into his mind, as one so often does in letters), that it seems difficult to see the poem as a whole. Yet it *is* a whole, different from, and more important than, any of its parts.

Is it a poem of anger and revenge? Pope's 'Advertisement' describes it as 'a Sort of Bill of Complaint', and it certainly took shape partly as a retaliation to the abuse of Lord Hervey and Lady Mary Wortley Montagu in their *Verses to the Imitator of Horace* and an *Epistle to a Doctor of Divinity from a Nobleman at Hampton Court*—coarse and scurrilous attacks in which, Pope says, 'not only my Writings (of which being publick the Publick judge) but my *Person, Morals*, and *Family*' were abused. Yet Pope had been used to a lifetime of living in boiling water, and had allowed most attacks to go unanswered. Obviously there is bitterness at the back of this, but the causes of the quarrel are obscure: Lady Mary was a fascinating and witty woman, and Pope's letters to her of 1716-18, romantic in tone, reveal what might be called an infatuation; by 1722 the friendship was cooling; by 1728 it had turned to hostility. But the point to be stressed here is that, however much she may have helped to trigger off the poem, she is hardly present *in* it; similarly, the lines preceding the Sporus portrait show clearly that the attack on Hervey arises primarily because he is one of the malicious distorters of Pope's poetic aims, particularly over the Timon's Villa passage in *Burlington*, and only secondarily because he had abused Pope personally.

It is equally true that the poem derives from his friendship with Arbuthnot, contains moving tributes to several other friends, and ends with a record of Pope's love for his parents. The dedication of this poem to Arbuthnot crowns a lifetime of affection: yet this is no more a poem *about* friendship than about enmity. As letter 11 (p. 25) shows, Arbuthnot had written to Pope, encouraging him to continue as a satirist, but begging him to be more careful; this advice, coming from an old friend who might well be dying, obviously moved Pope deeply: but what it moved him to write was not a poem about Arbuthnot, but a poem about satire, his main *Apologia pro Vita Sua*.

As soon, then, as we think about these different motivations we see that they lead in the same direction, towards not personality but poetry. The poem is many things, but the head at which all its streams meet is the defence of Pope's conception of poetry, from those who malign, or misuse, or misdirect, or misconceive it. Once we grasp this, we can follow the thread of a developing meaning through the apparent fluidity, and find that even though it contains passages that had been written long before (e.g. the Atticus lines), it does weld all its themes and concerns into a powerful whole. We may realise that the 'sources' of a poem are infinitely less important than what is made of them; that we should ask not *why* Pope feels as he does, but what he has made of his feelings. Considerations of personality will fall into their proper perspective, in which the 'truth' about Addison, Dodington and Halifax, and Hervey (whatever the 'truth' may be) is less interesting as well as less meaningful than what Atticus, Bufo and Sporus come to stand for, as the poetry creates them.

The early part of the poem swarms with characters, but they are linked by a fundamental quality that Pope has been hitting at since the *Essay on Criticism* and *The Rape of the Lock*. What the mad scribblers of the opening, the utterly complacent Codrus, the shameless spider-poet spinning his 'slight, self-pleasing thread', and all the rest have in common is self-love, selfishness, Pride. Sanity in the mind, and true value in poetry, have always depended, for Pope, on the proper harmony of good sense, good humour and morality. It is because these things are so important to him that he is driven to pillory the fools who, in their petty self-regard, pervert them. His scorn is exuberant and comically inventive, but there is behind it a note of seriousness: poetry *matters*.

As the crescendo of fools gives way to the sober assessment of Atticus, this note deepens, for we are moving into a sphere where pride can do real damage. Atticus is anything but a fool—he is a great man of letters. But instead of using his position to encourage and stimulate the state of poetry, he hates and thwarts any writer good enough to represent a threat to his own pre-eminence. Pope's use of antithesis is not a mere matter of style, it is deeply structural. It is precisely because Atticus is so richly endowed that his pride and envy are so destructive, and if he is in a moral sense ridiculous ('Who but must laugh?'), the waste is also tragic ('Who would not weep?'). Bufo, on the other hand, is an undiscriminating blockhead, and here a rich comic scorn returns; but his money gives him the same power to affect the state of poetry that the talents of Atticus gave. The only excuse for patronage is the encouragement of the gifted, but Bufo encourages only those who flatter his enormous swollen conceit, and sends the really deserving away. Pride, we are beginning to see, is a destructive force.

Why does poetry matter so much? Because Pope sees, as so many of the greatest writers have seen, the close relationship between literature and morality, between the health of poetry and the moral health of the whole of social and political life; this view is also at the heart of the *Epistle to Augustus*. Poetry, and particularly here that branch of it called Satire, stands in the cause of Virtue against her enemies: it is not personal and subjective, but objective and public. So, when the malicious and mean-minded try to turn poetry into malice and meanness, they are doing something much worse than thwarting or hurting other poets such as Pope himself: they are perverting the very nature of Poetry, making it serve not virtue but vice. At their head is the figure of Sporus, Pope's imaginative creation of the central enemy of poetry, the loathsome antithesis and antagonist of all he cares about most deeply. Sporus is infinitely more than Hervey, more even than a summation of Pope's feelings about the distortion of his deeply meaningful portrait of Timon. We shall not understand what Pope is doing if we persist in seeing Sporus as merely a personal attack, when it is precisely *against* malicious personality, and the perversion of poetry into the service of slander, that Pope is writing with his greatest power.

Sporus at first seems insignificant, with a certain flimsy beauty, as the Friend's interjection suggests; is he really worth bothering about? But what the pretty exterior conceals is dirt, and the power to damage. In the man as such, this power may seem negligible; but when it is allied to a great position—Hervey was the Queen's vice-chamberlain— it is dangerous. Sporus can be like Satan tempting Eve, pouring poison into the ear of the woman who has power over all mankind, because he has the ear of the Queen and is the tool of her Prime Minister. The loathing darkens, because Sporus can spread his perverting influence not only over poetry, but more directly over politics and the whole of society. He is far worse than Atticus or Bufo because his is the deepest Pride which not only prefers its own evil to virtue, but tries to convert goodness to its own corrupt nature; Sporus is an active agent of evil, the antagonist of virtue, the essence of the abnormal and corrupt, spitting itself abroad. In his way he is the Father of Lies, of malice, of pride; an agent of Satan, the enemy not only of poetry but of mankind.

But Pope never allows any piece of destructive satire to stand without reinforcing the positive values from which it springs. After Atticus comes the portrait of the poet who refuses to take part in literary politics and gossip; after Bufo we are given a moving tribute to the kind of poet, such as Gay, that is neglected by these patrons, and an account of the poet—Pope himself—who is above patronage; both before and after Sporus we have a clear and forceful picture of what the true poet, and true poetry, should be like—active in the cause of virtue and goodness against their enemies. That Pope is presenting a somewhat idealised portrait of himself is not a matter of conceit: Pope is speaking not just as himself, but as The Poet, the spokesman and representative of Poetry—see also *Fortescue* l. 121n. His larger purpose in this poem is to liberate true poetry, in our minds, from its enemies and distorters; and he does this finally by emphasising that Poetry is on the side of Nature, of human feeling for others. The tributes to Arbuthnot, and Pope's parents, which end the poem are a last clarification of the difference between the destructive progeny of Pride—envy, malice, hatred, perversion—and the creative harmony of true poetry with virtue, humanity, friendship and love.

To discuss the poem in this way may seem to be making something too systematic out of what Pope described as a piece 'drawn up by snatches'; but what we have here is a great poet, at the height of his powers, writing about the things to which he had devoted his life; the whole stream of his mind is flowing in a particular direction, his insights and intuitions are working away below the surface, and it is this which gives the poem its radical unity. The decorum of a poetical epistle, as of a prose letter, admits, as we have seen, a variety of styles, dictated by the subject-matter and by the nature of the recipient. It is a very flexible form and, as this poem again demonstrates, has much of the nature of a dialogue—implied questions put by the friend are answered, and the friend breaks in at times with direct speech.

Pope is not here 'imitating' any specific poem of Horace, but, except perhaps for the more outspoken attacks, this is very much in the Horatian manner, and has a vivacity and energy of style which help to make it one of his finest achievements.

Pope's attitude to Arbuthnot is obvious from the poem. His friend had been physician to Queen Anne, and the two men had met, through Swift, in 1713. All three friends had collaborated in the 'Scriblerus Club' satires of 1713-14—satires pillorying literary incompetence, pedantry, false taste, etc. Arbuthnot died two months after the publication of this Epistle.

ll. 1 ff. The opening passage, to l. 124, builds up a serio-comic picture of the famous poet besieged by an insect-like swarm of vain scribblers wanting, though never from high motives, his help. The lunatic and the pretender to poetry are equated here (*Bedlam or Parnassus*), and Pope produces, with humorous exaggeration, an almost nightmarish impression of the seething energy of these creatures in the maddening 'Dog-days' of late summer. (Line 3 refers also to the Roman custom of public poetry-readings in August.) The impression is partly given by the choice of such verbs as *rages, rave, madden, pierce, glide, scrawls, fly, curses*; partly by the epithets *be-mus'd* (with the pun on Muse), *maudlin, desp'rate, darken'd, giddy, frantic*; partly by the steadily mounting rhythmic impetus building up from the first 'despairing' cry to his servant, *John*. What else contributes to the general effect?

The *Mint* (l. 13) was a district in Southwark, a sanctuary for insolvent debtors, who could not be arrested on a Sunday. Of the figures appearing in these opening lines, some are named, some are identifiable by allusion, some are simply types: their identity does not matter.

l. 18. *engross*, to write in legal form.

l. 40. The advice is that given by Horace in the *Ars Poetica*.

ll. 41 ff. *Drury-lane* was a very disreputable part of London. The publishers' seasons corresponded with the legal terms. A typical 'apology' offered by poets was that 'friends had pressed them to publish'. What is the reason for the diction of l. 42?

ll. 53, 62. Edmund *Curll* was a disreputable bookseller (see Introduction to Letters, p. 14), *Lintot* a reputable one.

ll. 69 ff. The Midas story is introduced rather abruptly here. Midas judged a musical contest between Apollo and Pan, and, having rashly awarded Pan the honours, was given ass's ears by Apollo as a punishment. He hid the ears under his cap, but they were seen by his barber who, unable to conceal the information, whispered it into a hole. Pope, too, has seen the marks of folly on his Dunces, and cannot keep quiet. The mention of the Queen introduces, as the Friend recognises at l. 76, a political slant which is taken up in the Sporus passage.

ll. 85 ff. Note the implications of *World*. *Pit*, *Box* and *Gall'ry* are a sort of Hell, Earth and Heaven, the bursting of which in laughter leaves the complacency of *Codrus* quite unshaken. Pope parodies here a bathetic passage in Addison's version of Horace's *Odes*.

ll. 89 ff. Note the brilliant extension of this image, by which the identification of spider with scribbler is made complete.

ll. 96 ff. The *eye-brow* is the Peer's, the *sneer* that of the Poet. Colley Cibber, the egregious Poet Laureate, is being glanced at here. See *Fortescue* ll. 34-6n.

ll. 97 ff. The Dunces still prosper by their flattery. *Henley*, an eccentric preacher, delivered a sermon in praise of Butchers at Newport Market; for *Moor* see note to ll. 370 ff; *Bavius* was a minor poet pilloried by Virgil; *Philips*, alluded to again at ll. 179 ff., is Ambrose 'Namby-Pamby' Philips, whose Pastorals were published in the same volume as Pope's and were satirically discussed by him in the *Guardian* No. 40 (1713). In 1724 Philips became secretary to the Bishop of Armagh.

ll. 115 ff. These lines, a fine combination of wry humour and bitter contempt, form the transition to the autobiographical passage following. *Ammon's great Son* is Alexander the Great (see *Dial* II l. 117); *Horace* describes himself as 'short in stature' (Pope was only 4 ft. 6 in.); *Ovid's* family name was Naso, 'large-nosed'; *Maro* is Virgil.

l. 128. *Numbers*, metre, rhythm: he wrote because it came naturally —the contrast here being with the conceit of the scribblers. The line paraphrases a passage in Ovid.

ll. 135 ff. This passage in praise of the friends who had encouraged him in his early days is made the more effective by contrast with the contemptuous l. 146. Hazlitt records how Charles Lamb recited this passage, 'with a slight hectic on his cheek and his eye glistening'; after l. 146, 'his voice totally failed him, and throwing down the book, he said "Do you think I would not wish to have been friends with such a man as this?"'

ll. 147 ff. Pope oversimplifies the difference between his earlier and later poetry. He is referring to such things as the *Pastorals* and *Windsor Forest*, and *The Rape of the Lock* (l. 150). He is correct in saying that he had been attacked, by such critics as the able but irascible John *Dennis*, even at this stage of his career; he is also correct in asserting that he did very little in the way of replying to these attacks for a long time.

ll. 163-4. The double rhyme is usually associated with a contemptuous 'lowering' of tone to give an effect of burlesque. Bentley is *slashing* because of his cavalier treatment of Milton in his edition of *Paradise Lost* (see *Augustus* l. 104). Theobald, or *Tibbald*, edited Shakespeare in 1733, after incurring Pope's enmity for his sarcastic comments on Pope's 1725 edition. *Piddling*, petty, trifling. Mention of these two, and other minutely scholarly 'verbal' critics (*Wight* suggests a dry-as-dust antiquarianism), leads to the image of ll. 169-72. Notice the rhythmic effect of l. 170. Bentley was, in fact, a great classical scholar, but that is here beside the point.

ll. 173 ff. Pope's statement of his honest attitude to his fellow-writers is preparing the ground for the Atticus portrait. Note how, at the beginning of this summarising crescendo of fools, Pope emphasises, at l. 177, the most important thing about them. He mocks the hack-translators (l. 189), although translation would be better than their original—or plagiarised—poems. *Tate*, with Brady, had produced a well-known but very uninspired version of the Psalms in 1714.

ll. 193 ff. These lines were originally written about, and sent to, Joseph Addison, who died in 1719. They got into print somehow—probably without Pope's permission—in 1722, and had been reprinted at least three times. Pope admitted their authorship by publishing them in his joint volume (with Swift) of *Miscellanies* in 1727. It is not entirely clear why they quarrelled—not that the friendship was ever warm. Pope seems to have resented Addison's whole attitude of condescension, and believed, with some justice, that Addison tried to prejudice the success of Pope's Homer by encouraging a rival translation. Pope had also been told, by Addison's stepson, that Addison had commissioned a scurrilous booklet against Pope; although this was untrue, he had at the time no reason to doubt the information. A reconciliation of sorts was, however, effected before Addison's death.

In any case, we should not persist in regarding this as an attack on Addison, true though it may be. *Atticus* is here as the great man of letters who misuses his critical gifts for unworthy motives. The strategy of the passage, as it moves in one long sentence through a series of hypothetical propositions, with the genuine concessions to real greatness being gradually obliterated by the man's pettiness, to the combination of scorn and regret at ll. 213-14, is masterly. The tone of these lines should be compared with that of the Sporus portrait at ll. 305-33.

l. 197. i.e. 'too fond of ruling alone'.

l. 208. 'obleege' was the normal pronunciation.

l. 211. *Templers*, members of the Inns of Court. They applaud (*raise*) every maxim or aphorism (*sentence*).

ll. 215 ff. Famous though Pope is (*rubric*, in red letters on the book-advertisements; his name in *capitals* on *Claps*, or posters clapped on to the wall), he is contemptuous of this homage. What images convey this contempt? In this, he differs from such patrons as *Bufo*, who gorge themselves on praise.

ll. 231 ff. *Bufo* contains elements of Bubb Dodington (*Bubo* at l. 280), and the Earl of Halifax (1661-1715), both famously vain patrons; but, as with the other portraits, the character created by Pope is the important thing. *Bufo* means 'a toad', and *full-blown*, with *puff'd*, carries a suggestion of Æsop's frog who, trying to be big, blew himself up until he burst. *Full-blown* carries also the connotation of 'bloated, over-fed', as Bufo is by the *soft Dedication*, with its unpleasant suggestion of some revolting mush. The *forked hill* is Parnassus. Does *sate* have different associations from *sat*? What is the comic point of l. 236?

ll. 247-8. It is implied here that Halifax did nothing to relieve Dryden's wants in his lifetime (though he subscribed to the translation of Virgil), but helped pay for his funeral.

ll. 249 ff. But there are advantages in the system: the patrons help to take the poetasters and dunces off Pope's hands, and leave him the men of genuine merit, such as John *Gay*. Gay lived with the Duke and Duchess of Queensberry from 1717 until his death in 1732, but he was far from *neglected*: despite losses in the South-Sea Bubble, he left about £6000. Pope's purpose is, however, to *use* Gay to point the contrast with the flatterers Bufo patronises; and Gay, whose *Beggar's Opera* was a great success, did not *depend* on patronage.

ll. 261 ff. Mention of Gay leads Pope to a statement of his own simple, innocent life, expressed in appropriately simple language. Line 262 quotes a poem by Denham. His poetry, equally, is sincere and honest, calculated never to harm virtue and innocence; but—for Pope is now working round to the Sporus portrait—the liars and slanderers, the reverse of all he stands for, must be attacked: and he proceeds to attack a supreme example of them.

l. 280. *Sir Will* Yonge (see Dialogue I, l. 13); *Bubo*, Bubb Dodington (1691-1762), a notable patron, formerly a supporter of Walpole, tasteless and affected.

ll. 291-2. Notice how the preparation for Sporus assimilates both Bufo and Atticus.

ll. 299-300. Refer to the misrepresentation of the 'Timon' passage in *Burlington*.

l. 302. What exactly is Pope's crucial distinction between *Satire* and *Lampoon*, on the evidence of this whole passage? What is the difference between *Fiction* and a *Lye*?

ll. 305 ff. To say, with Sir Leslie Stephen, that 'Pope seems to be actually screaming with malignant fury' in this passage, is to misread it completely. Certainly there are no holds barred here, and the hatred is evident; but the control is perfect. The tactics of the Friend's interruption contribute largely to this: Pope has allowed his voice to work up through the preceding lines to the contemptuous *babling blockheads*, and with the words *Let Sporus tremble* it *does* become overstrained; but this is deliberate. The Friend's question, with its casual, dismissive tone, gives Pope time to recollect himself, as it were, and when he begins again at l. 309 there is almost a note of weariness present. How, and why, does the tone change from *Thing of silk, mere white Curd of Ass's milk*, and *Butterfly*, to the gilded *Bug* (what does this mean in the word 'bugbear'?), and *painted Child*, with their undertone of *stinks, stings, Dirt, annoys*? Notice how explosive consonants, p and b, and hissing sounds, dominate the verse here. What is the exact effect of the spaniel image, and the shallow stream? How does the tone begin to darken in l. 317? (the *Prompter* is Walpole, and the political reference begins to develop). Line 319 refers to *Paradise Lost* iv. 800—Satan in his least dignified form, toad-like at the ear of Eve (here Queen Caroline). Lines 321-2 are notable for the use of juxtaposition: the apparently harmless—*Puns, Rymes*—and the despicable—*Lyes, Spite, Smut, Blasphemies*—are all associated, as *Froth* and *Venom*, with the *Politicks*; he *stings* as well as *stinks*. What is the effect of the triplet at ll. 323-5?

Sporus was a castrated favourite boy of Nero; the sexual ambiguity of Hervey is suggested or stated all the way, even in seemingly innocent references (*Impotence, now Master up, now Miss, Antithesis, Amphibious Thing*, l. 329). Pope intends us to feel a moral revulsion. The Duchess of Marlborough described Hervey as 'the most wretched, profligate man that ever was born, besides ridiculous; a painted face, and not a tooth in his head'. The loathsome beauty of the figure reaches its darkest tone in the last four lines; why?

ll. 334 ff. The attack unwinds, so to speak, by Pope's presentation of himself as the opposite of Hervey—*manly* as opposed to effeminate. At ll. 340-1 Pope again makes the over-simplification of l. 148, *stoop'd*

being the action of a falcon descending on its prey. The allusions of
ll. 348 ff. are true enough: Pope was often threatened:

> "In black and white whilst satire you pursue,
> Take heed the answer is not black and blue."

A pamphlet of 1728 had maliciously alleged that Pope had been beaten
up and had shed tears; the *pictur'd Shape* refers to such things as the
caricatures of him as a hunchbacked ape.

l. 356. The *Whisper* is that of Hervey into the ear of the Queen.

ll. 360 ff. The question, and Pope's answer, are important. Corruption must be attacked wherever it is found. Note the way *hireling*
equates *Scribler* and *Peer*; and the use of *Ear* (some criminals, e.g.
Japhet Crook, were sentenced to loss of ears as well as to the pillory)
to equate *Pillory* and *near a Throne*. A *Knight of the Post* was a pro-
fessional hired witness, willing to perjure himself.

l. 369. *bit*, taken in, deceived.

ll. 370 ff. The poet is forgiving and forbearing. Pope had tried to
help *Dennis* in that critic's old age; it was a good ten years, after the
attacks on him began, before Pope published the *Dunciad*; the poetaster
Welsted had abused Pope on many occasions; so Pope goes on, citing
various instances. Eustace *Budgell* had accused Pope of writing for the
Grub-Street Journal (l. 378), which attacked the Dunces; Budgell
himself was accused, probably justly, of forging a will (*let* here is
'allowed': Pope would permit Budgell to do anything except forge *his*,
Pope's, will). The *Two Curls* are Edmund, the bookseller, and Hervey.
James Moore Smythe, 'Arthur's giddy son' of l. 23, had libelled Pope's
family in a scurrilous pamphlet. He was now dead.

ll. 388 ff. This leads into Pope's defence of his family. That he
overstates the gentility of their descent hardly matters; he may well
have believed it. He was devoted to his parents; his father had died in
1717, his mother in 1733. Pope had written a version of ll. 406-19 in
1731, and doubtless included them now as a tribute to his mother:
they give an air of quiet dignity and tenderness to the end of the poem.
Note the moving paradoxical image of l. 409—the child rocking the
mother.

TO AUGUSTUS

(Horace, Epistles: Book II No. i)

Published May 1737

'Praise undeserv'd is scandal in disguise.' This is Pope's masterpiece
of sustained irony, built on the qualities and policies of Augustus, and
those of George Augustus II. The shortcomings of the King were
widely recognised: Hervey remarks that there was no 'similitude
between the two princes beside their names. George Augustus neither
loved learning nor encouraged men of letters.' He had personal courage,
but the pacific policy of Walpole, which Pope and his friends regarded
as ignoble, prevented him from showing it, and to them his reign and
court seemed to have fostered nothing but corruption. By bringing to
bear on such a monarch Horace's praise of Augustus, moreover, Pope
is able to imply a whole world of standards: the original Augustan age
provides a central image of harmony—civic, martial, political, intellectual, moral—against which the satire on the perversion of all these
things in contemporary England can play. This is primarily a poem
about literature, as Horace's had been, and an attack via the philistine
King on all those who fail to appreciate, or actively decry, the dignity
and vital importance of letters. Yet it keeps broadening out into politics,
morality and religion, for to Pope all these things are inseparably
connected: the state of health of each is immediately affected by the
state of health of the others.

We can see the complexity and depth of the irony in what Pope has
to say about the Restoration (ll. 139 ff.). In Charles II's time English
taste was 'improved' by French, as the Roman had been by the Greek,
and the King himself had taken the lead. So when Pope quotes Granville's line 'All, by the King's Example, liv'd and lov'd' he is tracing
the ironic discrepancy between Augustus, Charles and George. But the
irony immediately complicates itself, for King Charles was an immoral
rake, and the Restoration, though it was a flowering of art in some
senses, was also a flowering of corruption, in which the art was involved.
This is to point up a similarity as well as a difference, for George too
has been instrumental in 'fostering' immorality, with the difference
that he could not be said to have fostered any art but the music of
Handel. Then, with the Court taking the lead in the debauchment of
the Muses, Pope charts the decay of all standards—moral, literary and
political—in utter relativity. The picture ends in chaos, with giddy
opinion bringing in and throwing out princes, moralities and laws for

no reason but childish fickleness—a perversion of both the nobility and responsibility of adult freedom and adult standards. This is the typical movement of the poem: its real villain is not George himself so much as the deterioration of standards of all kinds in the flux of insecurely based opinion. Pope sets out to castigate vulgarity, the chaos of the mob as an intellectual and moral phenomenon, through its apex on the throne.

Yet the irony is still more subtle, and we are involved in it, because Pope is not by any means always speaking in his own voice—he is *using* the voice of Horace. A typical passage begins a discussion of the merits of the moderns as against the ancients:

> Tho' justly Greece her eldest sons admires,
> Why should not we be wiser than our Sires?
> In ev'ry publick Virtue we excell,
> We build, we paint, we sing, we dance as well,
> And learned Athens to our Art must stoop,
> Could she behold us tumbling thro' a hoop.   (43-48)

Pope seems at first simply to be pleading against conservatism, for the merits of the new, just as Horace had done. There *is* no reason why we should not be wiser than our sires. But are we? Irony enters openly in the third line, for Pope does not believe this for a moment; yet it is still complex—in the next line, modern painting and building are at least worthy of comparison with the Greek; but *singing? dancing?* With mock solemnity, Pope is being absurd, and he is revealing through his borrowed voice a lack of discrimination in which values become obscured. The final grotesque assertion of modern superiority, in that Greece had not managed to invent the pantomime, thrusts the point home. Pope begins by tempting us to consider him as a modernist, but before we know where we are he has trapped us, in the service of true discrimination, into a perception of nonsense and vulgarity. If he is not on the side of the modernists, nor is he on the side of the ancients: he is against all ways of thinking that do not discriminate by true standards —against believing on the one hand that Shakespeare could do no wrong, and sanctifying on the other hand a modern poem because it has one good simile in a thousand lines. Horace's voice allows Pope to satirise both the present from the past and the past from the present, holding both against the true values symbolised by the world of Augustus and Horace.

The achievement of the poem lies not only in its meaning, but in the way *we* are made to work—to prove the unmasking of the false, by our own experience as we read. As Pope's irony twists and complicates itself, turning suddenly serious, then trapping us again, it teases and stimulates, making us stretch the full resources of our minds. By making us catch ourselves looking askew, it forces us to look straight, seeing through the shoddy, the confused, the vulgar, the crooked, to the true clarity and depth of Pope's own values. It is not an easy poem to read, but it is very rewarding—not least in its richly varied changes of mood, tone, and style.

ll. 1-6. The irony is announced with full orchestra. Augustus *was* a *great Patron*, George was not. Walpole's policy seemed to prevent England from fulfilling her proper task of 'sustaining' *the balanc'd World*, and the *Main* was so much *open* that Spanish ships were able to attack English merchantmen without reprisal. The *pax Romana* was maintained by vigorous patrolling of the frontiers, whereas George's visits *abroad*, which were all too frequent, were to the *Arms* of his mistress, Mme Walmoden. This sort of thing, and the Court where such behaviour could take place, was singularly unfitted to *amend* the Country with *Morals, Arts, and Laws*, and the Muse had no hope of even *an hour*—though Mme Walmoden had just had several months.

ll. 7-30. The genuine praise of *Alfred* the Great, *Edward* III, *Henry* V and Hercules (*Alcides*) makes the praise of George in ll. 23-30 deeply ironic—as is the fulsome gratitude and homage, which is set against the general rule that Envy prevents the honouring of great men until they are safely dead. The Sun image occurs throughout Pope's work as a symbol of splendour, goodness and truth, clearing away the mists of error; Pope's pose, then, as one of those who are *oppress'd* by the sun's beam is a further key to his satiric position. The grotesque inflation of ll. 23-30 carries its own condemnation; how is it punctured?

l. 35. Pope admired Chaucer and Spenser, but the point of the attack is on antiquity for antiquity's sake, reading Chaucer for the wrong reasons, and liking no language but the archaic style of the *Faery Queen*. Pope did, however, dislike Skelton, as he told Spence, for the very reasons the *Heads* of Oxford and Cambridge Colleges are shown as liking him; but Skelton is many things besides *beastly*. Line 40 refers to a humorous Scots ballad, probably sixteenth century; *the Devil* was a London tavern frequented by Ben Jonson.

ll. 49-106. Pope, still in his role of modernist, now leads supporters of the ancients into a *reductio ad absurdum* argument. *Courtesy of England* is a legal term for the custom of allowing a widower to retain property inherited by his wife, even though he has no 'right' to it. The argument is a good one directed against an absurdity, but it only begins to achieve real resonance when it modulates from debating technique into discrimination. We should set against the popular clichés of ll. 79-88 the discriminating judgments of ll. 75-8 and ll. 89-102. Here we can be sure that we have Pope's own voice.

l. 75. Pope told Spence that he considered *Cowley* (1618-67) 'a fine poet, in spite of all his faults'. The praise of 'the language of his heart' is characteristic of Pope's insistence on the importance of natural feeling in poetry.

l. 92. Pope's only friendly allusion to Cibber, whose *Careless Husband* (1704) had been a great success.

ll. 95 ff. 'It must be own'd that with all these great excellencies, he has almost as great defects' (Preface to Pope's edition of Shakespeare). Ben Jonson had complained that 'Spenser, in affecting the Ancients, writ no language' (cf. l. 39). *Sidney*, like many of his contemporaries, had experimented with classical metres in English verse. Satan and Belial, as they stand scoffing in book VI of *Paradise Lost*, indulge in puns, and God does sound rather like a *School-Divine* in book III (e.g. ll. 80-104).

l. 104. But Pope is anxious to distinguish true discrimination from the conceit of *Bentley*, who thought he could improve Milton, and from the empty foppery of fashionable courtiers. Bentley gets further treatment in *Arbuthnot* ll. 164 ff. A kind of maniac zeal is suggested by *lop*, *slashing* and *desp'rate*, while *Hook* probably puns on the square brackets ('hooks') which Bentley put round passages he thought 'spurious'.

ll. 107-18. Now the irony returns as Pope's 'modernist' voice gets angry, but, in doing so, betrays itself again. *Mob* is meant to indicate how *many* Wits there were, but what is its effect? Are there two implications of *Ease*? The image of multiple brightness is enthusiastic, and leads to the exultant *one Simile*, but the irony is betrayed in the rest of this line and the next: what is the ironical meaning of l. 113, and how does the movement of the line itself enforce it?

ll. 119 ff. He works back 'indignantly' to the idea that the root cause of the depreciation of moderns is envy. But has Pope hinted at other, and better, reasons for depreciating those that do deserve it?

ll. 122-3. *Betterton* (d. 1710) and *Booth* (d. 1733), two famous tragic actors. *Grave* and *well-mouth'd* have sarcastic overtones.

l. 126. All shame *is* lost, of course: though not for the reasons given here.

ll. 139-60. See introduction to this poem. Line 142 is quoted from George Granville, Baron Lansdowne (1667-1735), poet, statesman and a friend of Pope from 1706 onwards. Pope dedicated *Windsor Forest* to him. See also *Arbuthnot* l. 135. How does Pope suggest ironically the corruption of the Court, and how does he suggest that the art it fostered shared in this?

l. 160. *Noble Cause*, liberty.

ll. 161-88. Against a deliberately idealised picture of the 'good old days' Pope sets a hectic portrait of a society of compulsive scribblers (cf. the opening of *Arbuthnot*). The irony is quite open now, though the voice has a nice note of self-satisfaction in l. 175, and we suddenly become aware of deeper implications than we expect at l. 174. Note the brisk methodical rhythm of ll. 161-2, and contrast ll. 169-74. What is the effect of *Itch, raging Fit*? The allusion at l. 176 is not known: there were plenty of candidates. *Ward* (l. 182) was a famous quack, patronised by the King; *Radcliffe* a famous physician. For *Ripley*, see *Burlington* l. 18.

ll. 189 ff. The irony is multiple again: Pope is satirising George from the point of view of Poetry, and scribblers from the point of view of George. Poets are a harmless kind of madmen, poetry keeps them away from politics and plots, and on a pretty spare diet, too—but the irony is also against George's exaggerated fear of plots and suspicion of writers. Line 195 refers to the absconding of the Cashier of the South-Sea Company in 1722. *Peter* (l. 197) is Peter Walter (see *Bathurst* l. 20). Line 202 is an unconscious anticipation of George II's complaint: 'Who is this Pope that I hear so much about? I cannot discover what is his merit. Why will not my subjects write in prose?' Only a utilitarian blockhead could be impressed by the arguments of ll. 201-8 —this, in fact, is just what they suggest the King is! But playful irony turns into deadly earnest in ll. 209-11, the rejection of the ways in which poetry could be of service to George. Note the courage of these lines, in the year of the Stage Licensing Act. The Queen was believed to be a freethinker; for *lewd* see note on the poem's opening.

ll. 215 ff. In contrast, the portraits of *Addison* and *Swift* enforce the true nobility of poetry founded on human feeling, virtue and benevolence. *Dryden* is *unhappy* because of the immorality of some of his writings, which he himself admitted. *Roscommon* (1633-85) wrote an *Essay on Translated Verse*; he is highly praised in *An Essay on Criticism*. The praise of Addison as a writer balances the portrait of the jealous critic in *Arbuthnot* ll. 193 ff. *supply'd* (l. 222), made up for the deficiencies of. Swift wrote a *Proposal for the Universal Use of Irish Manufacture*, and championed the cause of Ireland in the *Drapier's Letters*. When he died in 1745, he left over £10,000 for the relief of 'the Idiot and the Poor'.

ll. 229-40. Now the ironic voice is heard again, guying the popular perversion of what Pope has just said. It is not morality or feeling *alone* that make a poem good—witness the pious mawkishness, the rank bad poetry served up as devotion by *Hopkins and Sternhold*, who made 'metrical versions' of the Psalms in 1549-62. In the crescendo of ll. 235-240 an emotional orgy of singing takes the place of true religion, preaching, and prayer. Pope plays on his own name in Hopkins' 'From Pope and Turk defend us, Lord'—noting also, of course, the prejudice against his religion.

l. 241 ff. The irony vanishes. This conjectural history of satire illustrates Pope's distinction between satire and malice. *Nice*, discriminating.

ll. 263 ff. *France* is here the equivalent of Horace's Greece. Pope gives the accepted account of the 'Augustanization' of English literature in the late seventeenth century. *Join* (l. 267) is pronounced 'jine', and this triplet (very rare in Pope) is a good example of a tribute by imitation—ll. 267-9 have a very Dryden flavour to them, the rhythm of l. 269 'echoes' the sense and is, in fact, lengthened to an alexandrine. The epithet *splay-foot* and the rhythmic awkwardness of l. 271 provide the right contrast. The complaint that Shakespeare was too fluent, and therefore careless, had been made by Ben Jonson.

ll. 289 ff. Pope follows Horace in the point that good comedy is difficult to write, for all its apparent ease. His survey covers Congreve, Farquhar, Vanbrugh and Mrs Aphra Behn (*Astræa*) (1640-89) of the Restoration dramatists, Cibber from more recent times. Aphra Behn wrote several indecent plays—hence *loosely*, and l. 291 (*fairly* because Astræa was goddess of justice). *Pinky* is the comic actor William Penkethman; in one of Cibber's plays he is said to have eaten two chickens in three seconds. The *laws* are those of dramatic construction.

ll. 304 ff. Having, with Horace, shown his distaste for the dramatist's dependence on the philistine applause of the 'many-headed' mob, Pope gives a caustic account of the state of theatrical taste in his day— the popularity of farce and spectacular effect, summed up by l. 313, which Warburton paraphrases 'From *Plays* to *Operas*, and from *Operas* to *Pantomimes*'. The *Black-joke* was a popular song, probably indecent. Observe the imitative quality of ll. 314-17.

l. 319. At the time of George II's coronation, a spectacular production of Shakespeare's *Henry VIII* was put on at Drury Lane: the coronation scene alone cost £1000, and the armour of one of the Kings of England was borrowed from the Tower.

l. 328. *Orcas*, the northernmost promontory of Scotland, opposite the Orkneys. Pope here indulges in some bogus 'sublimity'.

ll. 330 ff. The emphasis on elaborate costume had already been attacked in the *Spectator*. A *birth-day suit* is the magnificent dress worn by courtiers at royal birthday celebrations; as in Elizabethan times, these were often given to the theatrical companies.

l. 338. *railly*, rally, banter.

ll. 338-47. Pope adds, to the portraits of Addison and Swift, his idea of true dramatic poetry.

ll. 352 ff. At this point Horace appeals to Augustus, then building the Palatine Library, to patronise the true poet. Pope presents for contrast *Merlin's Cave*, a little house built for the Queen in Richmond Park, where, Pope says, 'is a small, but choice, Collection of Books'; we may be fairly sure it did not include anything by Pope.

ll. 369 ff. Pope's association of himself (*we*) with this kind of flattering poet is, of course, ironical; and the ironic attack on George II, and from him to Walpole (who had bestowed the Laureateship on Cibber in 1730) is resumed at ll. 376-9.

ll. 382 ff. *Nassau*, William III. Line 387 is unjust in that Blackmore was knighted not for poetry, but because he was Court Physician.

ll. 387-9. The reference to Quarles and Ben Jonson is still obscure.

ll. 390 ff. The first four lines are mainly serious, but even here the irony begins again. What is the effect of *swell'd, polish'd?*; of *the Manners and the Mind?* The diction and tone begin to inflate themselves, while the ironical placing of individual words is impeccable—e.g. *Repose, dearly, nodded* (with its double meaning of giving a command and going to sleep), the ignoble suggestion of *stole*, the sarcastic *subsided*, the rich ironic suggestiveness of *mediated* in this context, and the ludicrously pompous *tremble*. Once again the balloon is burst by a sudden drop at l. 404. The *Mæonian wing* refers to Homer, said to have been born in Mæonia, Asia Minor.

ll. 404 ff. Sadly Pope falls back on his own voice, but with no loss of irony. Lines 410 and 413 are precisely what he *has* done. The contempt of the final lines, with the ultimate worth of the flattering Dunces seen in their penny pamphlets hanging for sale on (appropriately) the railings of Bethlehem Hospital, and Wardour Street, is exactly conveyed by the diction—*dirty, forgotten, flutt'ring*, and *befringe*.

page 134   TO LORD BOLINGBROKE

(Horace, Epistles: Book I No. i)

Published March 1738

Horace's Epistle to his patron Mæcenas, beginning with excuses for having given up lyric poetry in favour of the study of philosophy, works round to a discussion of wisdom and virtue, moderation, and the Stoic ideal of the perfect man. Pope follows this as far as the difference in manners between Roman times and his own will admit.

It is not one of his most powerful poems, but it is a by no means unsuccessful blend of the noble tone of the *Essay on Man* and the livelier satire of the Epistles and Imitations. To address such a poem to Bolingbroke at all was in itself a political gesture, calculated to arouse the anger of Walpole's supporters. Bolingbroke, now nearly sixty, had retired to France in 1735 after his failure to secure the overthrow of Walpole, but was still one of the main hopes of the Opposition. Pope's feelings towards Bolingbroke are evident: he told Spence, 'Lord Bolingbroke is something superior to any thing I have seen in human nature.'

The decorum of Pope's poem, then, is that of a serious letter to a greatly loved and admired friend; the flow is more even than in most of the satires, the language predominantly simple and quiet; there is an atmosphere of moderation, with a certain underlying melancholy. On the whole, the satire consists in a reasoned exposure of folly and weakness, rather than a fierce attack on wickedness, though the magnificently downright vigour of such passages as ll. 128-33 is worth noting. Particularly where Pope is dealing with human inconstancy his tone echoes that of the *Moral Essays*. There are comparatively few personalities here, or topical references.

l. 3. *Sabbath*; Pope was, in 1737, forty-nine, which (being seven times seven) is called the Sabbath year.

l. 10. *Brunswick*, whence came the Hanoverian dynasty; there is thus a sneer here, that the generals had fought in a foreign cause.

l. 16. Compare the hit at *Blackmore* in *Fortescue* l. 23. Pope here imitates another aspect of Blackmore's ponderous verse: the Lord Mayor's horse—usually a 'sober and slow-paced animal'—is a suitable Pegasus for one who was very popular in the City of London.

l. 29. George *Lyttleton* (1709-73), an opposition Whig, was one of the leading younger opponents of Walpole; the opposition referred to themselves as 'Patriots' (l. 27).

l. 31. According to Horace, *Aristippus* sought 'to subject things to myself, not myself to things'. *St Paul* (I Cor. ix. 22) wrote 'I am made all things to all men.' *Candor* is impartiality, sincerity.

l. 45. i.e. 'can want nothing'.

ll. 47-51. *Mead* and *Cheselden* were respectively the most famous physican and surgeon of the day, both friends of Pope. The humorous pathos of ll. 49-50 is typical of Pope's attitude to his 'crazy carcass' throughout his life.

ll. 55 ff. *Thy* is difficult here. It can hardly be Pope himself (cf. *we* at l. 64), or Bolingbroke, for whom l. 74 would be singularly inappropriate. We should probably take this passage as addressed to the reader.

l. 63. Proverbially boorish types (no doubt with a glance at the German king). The point made here is that nobody is beyond the possibility of being civilised, if only he will listen to the voice of culture.

l. 82. *low* and *high* refer to the two parties in the Church; at the time St Paul's had a High Church Dean, St James's a Low-Church Rector. St James's, moreover, was regarded as the 'Court' church, and *low* therefore has overtones of meanness and contempt.

l. 84. Accounts at the Exchequer were kept partly by means of notched sticks, or *:allies*; these were cut into two parts, each marked with notches denoting the debt, and debtor and creditor kept a part each. This system was abolished in 1783. The point here is that some posts at the Exchequer carried huge stipends, and were regarded as political 'prizes'.

l. 85 ff. Sir John *Barnard*, M.P. for the City of London, and a prominent member of the Opposition. Pope strains the sense here in trying to follow Horace: in Rome, the possession of 40,000 sesterces gained admission to the aristocratic ranks of the *equites*; it was not lack of money that kept Barnard from honour at court, but his citizen birth. *Bug* was the nickname of the Duke of Kent, because he was 'strong in nothing but money and smell, the latter to a high degree', according to a contemporary. His *Harness* is the Order of the Garter. *Dorimant* is a fashionable fop in Etherege's *Man of Mode*; possibly Dodington (see *Arbuthnot* l. 280) is meant.

l. 95. *Screen* was a metaphor applied to Walpole's policy of covering up corruption by opposing all Parliamentary enquiries; *Brass* implies Walpole's impudence and effrontery.

l. 98. The *good old song* is that of l. 92.

l. 106. The King's taste for opera, in which many notable *castrati* sang, is regarded with contempt.

l. 111. *Rabble* is a good example of Pope's choice of the surprising word.

l. 112. *Schutz*, whom Horace Walpole called 'a pious pimp . . . a mean, Hanover tool' was keeper of the King's Privy Purse. A *spark* is a gay, sprightly person, in contrast to the sober Schutz.

ll. 115 ff. Not a very good illustration. The implication is rather that people are *made into* beasts by the Court life.

l. 127. Probably a hit at Marlborough.

l. 128. An allusion to the swindling officers of the Charitable Corporation (see *Bathurst*, note to ll. 89 ff.), and to corrupt clergy.

l. 129. *Assemblies*, such as that at Bath, ruled over by Beau Nash. *Stews*, a brothel.

ll. 130-1. General enough, but perhaps referring to Lord Sidney Beauclerck, a notorious fortune-hunter.

ll. 138 ff. Why does Pope write two triplets in a row? What is the function of the rhythm in the first? How does he emphasise that Greenwich Hill is 'subjected' to these whims? What is the effect of the juxtaposition of *silver* and *marble*?

l. 148. 'An old custom according to which on the wedding night the bride's stocking was thrown among the guests; it was supposed that the person hit by it would be the first of the company to be married.' (O.E.D.)

ll. 154 ff. Pope follows Horace here in the satirical attack on the pretentious poor who ape the rich. Japanning was a new method of polishing, recently introduced.

ll. 161 ff. *You* is now Bolingbroke. The complaint here is that people are quick enough to notice external inconsistencies and breaches of decorum, but pass over the far more important internal ones—the correction of which is the duty of one's 'Guide, Philosopher, and Friend' (a quotation from *Essay on Man* IV 390).

l. 164. *Lady Mary* Wortley Montagu was a notorious sloven. Cf. *To a Lady* ll. 24 ff.

l. 173. Richard *Hale* had been physician at Bedlam; Pope seems to be unaware that Hale had died in 1728. The Court of *Chancery* dealt, amongst other things, with the administration of the estates of those deemed 'incapable'.

ll. 179 ff. The syntax of these lines is somewhat obscure: 'that Man divine etc.' is in apposition to 'make me', and so the last nine lines should be a portrait (as in Horace) of the Stoic ideal man, superior to Fortune; this is what Pope wishes to be made, and what only Bolingbroke can make him. At the same time, the portrait itself is very like that of Bolingbroke, who had been dismissed from office in 1714, deprived of his title, *plunder'd* by the forfeiture of his Estates, still *lov'd* in his middle and later years, still *follow'd* though deprived of his seat in Parliament, and exiled. He had not been in the Tower, as he fled without waiting to stand trial. The simplest explanation is that Pope is doing both things at once: Bolingbroke *is* the ideal man, and Pope would wish to be like him. A *fit of vapours*, nervous disorder, corresponds to 'a cold in the head' in Horace—a final joke at the expense of the 'perfect man'.

page 140   EPILOGUE TO THE SATIRES

Dialogue I

Published May 1738

The two Dialogues are amongst the triumphs of Pope's satiric art. The first was subtitled 'A Dialogue Something like Horace', but they are not particularly Horatian in manner, being for the most part much more forthright. They do, however, sum up all the themes and attitudes of Pope's Horatian Imitations: the great picture of Vice at the end of Dialogue I is balanced by the praise of Truth in Dialogue II.

The decorum of language here is simply that of an animated dialogue between equals, and it can range from the easy colloquialism of the openings, through the high-speed cross-talk of II ll. 18-25 and the suavity of I ll. 93-8, to the apocalyptic eloquence of the close of I or the loftiness of II ll. 197-215. Pope secures a further flexibility of diction by having two widely contrasted speakers: the 'Friend' here— good-natured but timidly prudent and rather stupid—is used as a foil to set off the character of the outspoken satirist, and Pope attains a considerable dramatic tension in the clash between the two. Although, in the text, 'P.' of course stands for 'Pope', it also stands for 'Poet': these Dialogues, Pope's final defence of his satire, his 'protest' against the 'insuperable corruption and depravity of manners' of his age, are not in any sense narrowly autobiographical. This is an impersonal voice speaking out for the values of western civilization.

It is arguable that Pope's insistence on fastening on the particular example leads these Dialogues to be, as Swift complained, clogged in places with too many insignificant names. The comic mood of the *Dunciad* often allows Pope to put the names of his Dunces to poetic use, forming as they do a kind of parody of the great names of epic; but here we feel such a passage as II ll. 237-41 to be something of a descent from the preceding heights. Certainly, the poems bristle with person-alities, many of whom the reader of the poems which come before will already have met: they are mainly, as ever, corrupt politicians and courtiers, swindlers, charlatans, dishonest merchants and embezzling directors; and, again as always, their effect is offset by the eloquent praise of the good men of the age.

It should be observed that, despite appearances, Pope's politics are not narrowly partisan. He had stressed his middle position in *Fortescue* l. 68, a line repeated in Dialogue I l. 8; certainly most of the examples of corruption he gives are Whig politicians, followers of Walpole; but the Whigs had been in power for over twenty years, and provided all the evidence. Lines 105-6 of Dialogue I suggest that the Tories as such would not necessarily have been much better: Pope's main concern is with picking out, from either party, the men who embody his own higher conception of public morality as something essentially above party.

ll. 13-22. Pope makes his satiric points by allowing the Friend to make outrageous understatements as alleged examples of the way the *nice* (delicately discriminating) Horace would deal with things. *Sir Billy* is Yonge (also l. 68), a notoriously corrupt and contemptible Whig politician; *Blunt* a Director of the South-Sea Company; *Huggins* the corrupt Warden of the Fleet Prison, whose acquittal on a murder charge in 1729 was partly achieved by the number of gentlemanly character-witnesses he procured. Line 18 refers to the affair of Jenkins' Ear: he was a sea-captain whose ear, he alleged, was cut off by a Spaniard who bid him 'carry it to the King'; this case helped to bring on the war with Spain.

l. 26. *The Great man* was a common appellation of Walpole. Although Pope's tongue is probably in his cheek at ll. 31-2, this private, as opposed to public, assessment of Walpole is not without warmth.

ll. 37 ff. Again the Friend's proposals for satire are solemnly outrageous. The attitudes of ll. 37-44 are very much those of Walpole himself, who notoriously scoffed at religion, honesty, and the principles of such upright men as *Jekyl*—as old-fashioned in his keeping to the full-bottomed wig as in keeping to his moral beliefs. His incorrupt-ibility leads Pope to call him an *old Whig*, as opposed to the new, Walpole, variety.

ll. 45 ff. *Lyttelton* (see *Bolingbroke* l. 29) was Secretary to the Prince of Wales. The Prince had been at loggerheads with his father for some time, and thus became a figurehead of the Opposition. *Fleury* was Louis XV's minister; *Sejanus* and *Wolsey* are presented as types of wicked ministers. The Friend is innocently elaborating his point that nothing can hurt the 'foolish' virtuous people, whereas it is bad taste to attack the powerful wicked.

l. 54. *these*, the Foes; *those*, the Fools.

ll. 63 ff. *Distinction*, the picking out of individuals; *Warmth*, righteous anger. Pope's reply is a parody of the Friend's attitude. How do the imagery and rhythms of ll. 66-82 contribute to the effect?

The figures attacked here include the eccentric preacher *Henley* and the Government journalist James Pitt, whose pseudonym was *Osborne*; both are among the Dunces, and the *Oratory* and *Wit*, like all the qualities named in this paragraph, are ironical. The floridity of Hervey's speech is mentioned in *Arbuthnot* l. 317; Pope suggests that the same speech passed from Hervey to James Fox and back again. *Middleton*, a theologian who wrote a Life of Cicero, was famous for his eloquent style, and was a friend of Hervey; *Bland*, now Provost of Eton, had been at school with Walpole. Pope is referring here to Hervey's Latin epitaph on the Queen, who had died in 1737; he hints that Middleton and Bland wrote it for him.

l. 78. *Nation's Sense*: political jargon for 'public opinion'.

l. 82. Rumour had it that the Queen died without being reconciled to the Prince of Wales, and without taking the last sacrament.

ll. 84 ff. *Gazeteer*, a government journalist. After this, Pope drops the mask and lets his impatience break through; notice the change in style here.

ll. 87 ff. The Friend produces more cynical arguments for satire. *Immortal* and *grave* are, of course, ironic from Pope's point of view—both were Peers who enjoyed the favour of the King. The unction of the Friend's voice here is admirably reproduced in the verse; the religious phraseology, especially the echo of Isaiah in l. 102, is, as so often with Pope, a means of suggesting the perversion of values in those he attacks. *Nepenthe* was a drug supposed to lull sorrow; to *lose a Question* is to have a proposal rejected by Parliament; a *job* is a piece of intrigue, or wire-pulling.

ll. 105 ff. The style of Pope's reply is in sharp contrast. Note the irony of *Gracious Prince*. As Pope takes up the paradoxical position of one who must defend the 'dignity of vice' allusions crowd in: l. 112 probably attacks Lady Mary; *Cibber's Son* Theophilus, and John *Rich*, both actors, take their place in the *Dunciad*; John *Ward* and *Japhet* Crook were forgers; *his Grace* is Archbishop Wake, who was alleged to have had a hand in the suppression of George I's will; for *Bond* and *Peter* Walter see notes to *Bathurst*; *Blount* was a Deist who killed himself, supposedly for love, in 1693; *Passeran* is Alberto Radicati, Count of Passerano, a notorious free-thinker, who held that natural impulses, including the urge to commit suicide, should be obeyed. A London *Printer* had, in fact, recently hanged himself, 'justifying his actions by the reasonings of some of these authors'.

l. 130. The Gin Act of 1736 was an attempt to decrease the terrible amount of drunkenness among the common people; see, for example, Hogarth's 'Gin Lane'.

ll. 131 ff. The tone changes, almost to tenderness, as Pope praises examples of virtue. *Foster* was a popular Dissenting preacher; the *Quaker's Wife* Mary Drummond, a simple and pious woman much to be preferred to the foolish Bishop of *Llandaff*; Ralph *Allen* was a philanthropist of Bath, the model for Squire Allworthy in Fielding's *Tom Jones*, and a warm friend of Pope from 1736 onwards. These references would hardly have been known to the majority of Pope's readers, but they are made as clear as necessary by the context and tone of the passage.

ll. 141 ff. Pope returns to the paradoxical position of l. 114, but this time the humour drops away and the style mounts in intensity. The word *Whore*, *scarlet* at l. 149, and the imagery generally, suggest that Pope was thinking of St John's vision of the Whore of Babylon in Revelation xvii. This, in fact, gives us the key to the meaning of this whole passage: it is a kind of parody of the Last Judgment (compare the mood of the closing lines of the *Dunciad*), with the Whore enthroned instead of Christ. Note *chaste*, *grave Bishops bless*, the inversion of religious values emphasised by the stress on *hers* at l. 148, the *Pagod* (a temple to a—false—idol), the *black* Trumpet, *reverential awe*, *Sacred*.

The poetry of this magnificent passage is worth close study. Pope achieves his effects partly by the use of the exact epithet—as well as *chaste*, *grave*, *black* already mentioned, there is *golden* (with its suggestion of the power of wealth), *liv'ry'd o'er*, *thronging*; partly by the choice of verb—*lifts*, *draws*, *dragg'd*, *trails*, *dance*, the horrible *crawl*, *run*; partly by changes of pace and stress—*hers*, or the dragging effect of the run-on in sense from ll. 152 to 153; partly by the insistent pointing at the scene—*Lo!*, *See*, *Hear*. Above all, the effect is due to the nightmarish picture itself, which all these details help to present. Virtue is punished (*carted*, displayed on a cart) as if *she* were a prostitute; England's *Genius* is *dragg'd* behind like a criminal. There is a terrible perverted vigour and energy about the whole scene, summed up in the paradoxes of ll. 163-5.

page 145   DIALOGUE II

Published July 1738

'I take your second Dialogue', wrote Swift to Pope, 'to equal almost any thing you ever writ.' Pope had originally proposed, it seems, to bring out a Dialogue every year; but the opening lines suggest that he may have feared that the new Stage Licensing Act (1737) might be extended to the liberty of the press in general. Also, no doubt, he felt inspired to write, and thus published this only two months after the first. In it, Pope is on the whole more direct in his approach; the range of diction is similar, the metrical virtuosity unequalled. He is especially concerned here with the justification of particular, as opposed to

general, satire. The best commentary on this is in a letter to Arbuthnot
—see letter 11, p. 25. Most of the personalities attacked have already
been discussed—the Friend ranges over Pope's satires to bring up
examples of his methods; what chiefly distinguishes this poem, though,
is the number of people Pope singles out for praise. Even more than
a catalogue of his enemies, it is a roll-call of his friends, comparable to
that in *Arbuthnot* ll. 135 ff.

l. 1. *Paxton*, Solicitor to the Treasury, was employed by Walpole
to smell out libellous writings.
ll. 5 ff. Pope implies that one reason for his printing 'today' is that
the increase of Vice is too fast for him; note the surprising phrase 'sins
up to' in the context of l. 9.
l. 11. *Guthry* published the Memoirs of Newgate criminals, often
giving only their initials—unlike Pope, who prints names in full.
l. 15. *sowze*, to swoop down like a bird of prey; *all the Kind*, every
malefactor, without distinction.
ll. 16 ff. Notice the ironic juxtapositions and contrasts as Pope
mockingly warms up to his eloquent address. The rapid dialogue that
follows illustrates Pope's complete mastery of his form, his ability to
achieve any effect whatever within his basic iambic five-stress framework. Note the pace of l. 19, with its quick fire of monosyllables, and
the way the stress falls on *not*. Pope refers back, here, to the first
Dialogue, l. 112, and to allusions in earlier satires.
l. 31. *Beasts of Nature, feræ naturæ* ('of wild kind'), a legal term to
denote animals which may be hunted, etc.
l. 39. *Wild*: Jonathan Wild (see Fielding's novel), hanged in 1725.
He is relevant here because Opposition writers liked to draw parallels
between his career and that of Walpole.
l. 61. *Selkirk*, it is implied, hates the Prince of Wales, but will
change, out of self-interest, when the Prince comes to the throne.
ll. 65 ff. The Earl of *Scarborough* is described by Pope as of 'known
honour and virtue'; *Pelham* was the brother of the Duke of Newcastle;
his house at Esher was designed by William *Kent*; *Craggs*, Secretary of
State in 1718, had been a neighbour and friend of Pope; he died in
1721.
l. 71. *decent* has the meaning here of moderate, and is a term of
praise. *Secker* was Bishop of Oxford, *Rundle* of Derry, *Benson* of
Gloucester; *Berkeley*, the great philosopher, was Bishop of Cloyne.
Pope, as a Roman Catholic, need not have been expected to say much
in favour of the Anglican clergy.
ll. 74 ff. This eloquent paragraph of praise includes many admired

figures of Pope's younger days. Of them, *Sommers, Halifax, Shrews-bury, Carleton, Stanhope* and *Atterbury* were all dead. Most had been, or still were, friends of Pope, and opposed, in more or less degree, to Walpole. The list ends (l. 92) with an allusion to Pope's friendship with the Prince of Wales.

l. 81.   *End*, object.

l. 99.   *The Man of Ross*, see *Bathurst*, ll. 250 ff.; *my Lord May'r* is Barnard (see *Bolingbroke* ll. 85 ff.).

l. 97.   *Beaver*, a fur hat, or one characteristic of Quakers.

l. 111.   *Number*, Lat. *numerus*, the bulk of the population.

l. 117.   *Ammon* refers to Alexander the Great, who claimed to be the son of Jupiter Ammon.

l. 125.   Pope implies that his friends, whether they had resigned or been dismissed, had acted conscientiously.

l. 129.   *Arnall* was a Government journalist, one of the Dunces.

ll. 130-1.   More prominent Opposition members are catalogued here.

l. 143.   Warton records that this actually happened while Lords Bathurst and Burlington were dining with Pope at Twickenham.

l. 150.   *Turenne* was Marshal of France in the seventeenth century.

ll. 157 ff.   The Friend, asking why Pope should attack those who had never offended him personally (*Selkirk*, Judge *Page*, Dodington—*the Bard* of l. 160) supplies the key to Pope's replies. *Be-dropt* and *stained* suggest the excremental imagery of ll. 171-80; and the main point is dealt with in ll. 189-96, leading up to the fine statement of Pope's 'provocation' (l. 197). Line 161 is a quotation from a poem by Dodington.

ll. 172 ff.   The point of this deliberately unpleasant image, as of most of the imagery of filth in Pope and Swift, is put across sharply in ll. 182-4, after the Friend has expressed the reader's natural reaction. The physical image creates disgust, which is then to transfer itself to the moral failure implied behind the allegory: the courtly life is, to the satirist, utterly disgusting, and his reader must be made to share the disgust.

l. 187.   *Pindus*, a mountain in Thessaly associated with the Muses.

l. 194.   Alludes to the proverbial horns of the cuckold.

l. 205.   Again, Pope uses the device of the Friend to voice the reader's possible objections, so that they can be answered. What is the effect of the triplet at ll. 205-7?

ll. 212 ff.   It is worth contrasting the style here with that of the earlier, more colloquial passages. What is the difference?

ll. 220 ff.   Two of Pope's dominant images—insects, and the Sun—

combine here with superb effect. *Tinsel* suggests fragility, artificiality, and a superficial beauty; the *stains*, or markings, which might be beautiful on, say, a butterfly are here blemishes; the ineffectuality of the insect-courtiers is conveyed in the image of a cobweb spun to shut out the Sun—the light of Truth; and, in any case, the Muse's wing annihilates them. All the contempt Pope feels for these people is summed up here.

l. 227. *Address*, the formal reply to the King's speech.

ll. 228 ff. Pope implies that the Muse is powerless to cover up evil—for example, Waller's elegy on Cromwell does not atone for the *black Ambition* which brought about the Civil War, or Boileau's absurd flattery mitigate Louis XIV's conquest of the Low Countries (though see *Fortescue* l. 111).

ll. 237 ff. *Anstis*. Pope notes: 'the chief Herald at Arms. It is the custom, at the funeral of great peers, to cast into the grave the broken staves and ensigns of honour.' The asterisks probably denote *George*, and *Frederick*, Prince of Wales.

l. 239. This is obscure as well as rather bathetic. The Earl of *Stair* was a man of honour and integrity, and an opponent of Walpole. Lord *Mordington's* wife kept a low gambling house. Pope is evidently implying the worthlessness of worldly honours.

ll. 240-1. Bishop *Hough*, an opposer of James II, and Lord *Digby*, a supporter, are brought together here as men of principle and integrity, though on opposite sides.

l. 242. The imagery with which Pope makes vivid such abstractions as Envy, Honour, Flattery, etc., is worth noting.

l. 249. As in ll. 2-3, Pope glances at the threatened censorship of the press; one false step on the part of the satirist, and the Truth he upholds will topple over into the hostile pit of the law.

l. 255. Pope's plan for these is seen in the letter to Swift (letter 13, p. 26).

Pope's note at the end of this Dialogue includes the already quoted words about his protest against the insuperable corruption and depravity of manners. . . . 'This was the last poem of the kind printed by our author, with a resolution to publish no more.' He goes on, 'Could he have hoped to have amended any, he had continued those attacks; but bad men were grown so shameless and so powerful, that Ridicule was become as unsafe as it was ineffectual.' A further comment is provided by his letter to Fortescue, 8 September 1738: 'I for my part am willing to be Old in Disposition, so far as to seek Retreat and Peace. . . . I am as content to quit the clamorous Part of a Poet, Satire, as you could be to quit that of a Pleading Lawyer . . . *Quiet* is the Life of Innocence & Good nature . . . which is best? Honour, Title, or Quiet?'

page 152

THE DUNCIAD

Book IV

Published March 1742

It must be said straight away that Book IV is an independent poem, first published as *The New Dunciad*, which can be read without reference to the other three books. *The Dunciad* has a complicated history; as first published in 1728 it was Pope's first major satire after the *Rape of the Lock*, an attack on dulness, pedantry and the perversions of the intellect. It appeared anonymously, though no one was fooled by this. The following year, still in three books, an 'official' edition appeared— The Dunciad Variorum, with the Prolegomena of Scriblerus—with a full paraphernalia of notes, 'critical testimonies', addresses to the reader etc., all this being designed to simultaneously expand the attack by explaining the references to personalities, and provide in itself a further burlesque of pompous scholarship. The 'hero' of this poem was Lewis Theobald, who had attacked Pope's edition of Shakespeare. The 'action' was very simple: in Book I the Goddess Dulness is introduced, and chooses Theobald as her Laureate; Book II relates a grotesque 'poetic games' held in Theobald's honour; in Book III Theobald descends to the underworld, where his predecessor in dulness, the playwright Elkanah Settle, shows him in a vision the past and future empire of Dulness. The closing lines are an earlier version of the passage which now ends Book IV.

This version has many moments of greatness, but we are made too much aware of Pope's personal indignation and grievances: many of Pope's friends felt that it was unworthy of him. 'Employ not your precious moments and great talents on little men and little things', wrote Atterbury, Bishop of Rochester. But, although Pope does not always bring out his larger purpose, the concept of Dulness was an important one. Pope's note says she 'is not to be taken . . . for mere Stupidity, but in the enlarged sense of the word, for all Slowness of Apprehension, Shortness of Sight, or imperfect Sense of things . . . a ruling principle not inert, but turning topsy-turvy the Understanding . . .': she is introduced in Book I as 'Daughter of Chaos and eternal Night', and

Gross as her sire, and as her mother grave,
Laborious, heavy, busy, bold, and blind,
She rul'd, in native Anarchy, the mind.

When, in Book II, she 'summons all her sons', 'An endless band/Pours forth, and leaves unpeopled half the land'. They are by no means all just poor scribblers: they come 'from drawing rooms, from colleges, from garrets'—judges, churchmen, courtiers, patrons, pedagogues. Settle's speech in Book III, especially ll. 75-92, is a powerfully sombre evocation of the real extent of the empire of Dulness.

By 1742 the prophetic vision of 1728-9 was coming, it seemed to Pope, all too true. *The New Dunciad* is a poem of burning sincerity; all the way through we feel that this is something that really matters: Pope's world, the world of the Augustan ideal, is collapsing round him, and there is a *Götterdämmerung* atmosphere, particularly about the last lines. In this poem we are shown the award of honours, by the Queen, to her faithful Dunces; the satire is much more general, and, although persons are introduced, they are introduced as spokesmen for their whole class. They are influential classes, too: the genteel, polite, and learned world is here, all those who are supposed to have a hand in the formation of taste; and they are all corrupt. They are anti-art, and therefore anti-life: their values are throughout perverted.

In 1743 Pope gathered all his material together and, making necessary changes, published in October *The Dunciad* in four books. Theobald was by now out of date, and Cibber was enthroned in his place; the change does not affect things very much, as the hero is a passive figure throughout.

As the title suggests, *The Dunciad* is a mock-heroic poem, but it is in complete contrast to the *Rape of the Lock*. The earlier poem was a more light-hearted use of the form Pope revered above all others; it is a Lilliputian epic, a sermon written on a pinhead, perfect in form. *The Dunciad*, on the other hand, reads like a fragment of some enormous sombre epic; the style is still used to imply the contrast in values throughout, but this time the materials are all the things Pope found most baleful and, for all the comedy, despair is never far away. In such passages as the opening invocation, and the closing lines, all suggestion of satire has dropped: this is straightforward epic writing, as splendid and tragic as anything in English. As the ancestry of Dulness quoted above suggests, the main influence behind the poem is that of Milton (see particularly the description of Chaos in Book II of *Paradise Lost*); a second influence is Virgil's *Æneid*. Within this mainly Miltonic and Virgilian framework, however, Pope is able to employ a variety of styles: some of the most sensuously beautiful lines he ever wrote, for example, occur in the 'Grand Tour' passage (ll. 297-310), where Pope deliberately returns to the style of his early *Pastorals* in order to convey the combination of decadence, beauty and uselessness—for this is wandering in 'Fancy's Maze', and 'Truth' is far away. A similar delicate beauty is found in the speeches of the horticulturalist and the lepidopterist (ll. 403-36). Such writing contrasts with the prevalent atmosphere of murk and gloom, conveyed by such key-words as clouds, mists, lead, black, dim, dull, heavy. The diction is flexible enough to admit, in the midst of the 'grand style', such deliberately ugly words as lug, chew'd, stinks, bowzy, punk, skulking; it has been said that both style and subject-matter (in so far as these are separable) can be summed up by l. 400:

> 'A Nest, a Toad, a Fungus, or a Flow'r'.

l. 9 ff. As always in Pope, the sun is an image of intellectual and moral light, which is being blotted out by Dulness (the *Seed*—i.e. offspring) of *Chaos* and *Night*.

l. 16. *Saturnian* has a multiple meaning: Saturn identified with Time, devoured his children. In astrology, Saturn was considered to have a very evil influence; in alchemy he represented lead. Poets referred to his reign as 'the Golden Age', which is here, of course, seen ironically as an age of bribery and misused wealth.

l. 20. Cibber. What is the effect of *soft* here?

ll. 21 ff. This passage sums up the things Dulness is opposed to, and those she supports—the latter (e.g. Sophistry, Chicanery, Casuistry) being often perversions of the former. Thus *Billingsgate*—foul and abusive language—is a corruption of *Rhetoric*.

l. 28. i.e. the Judges (in *Furs*) and the Bishops (in *Lawn*).

l. 30. A pun on the name of Judge *Page*, the 'hanging judge'.

ll. 31 ff. Mathematicians, for Pope as for Swift, were considered as among those who misused their intellect by abstruse and absurd speculations, such as trying to square the circle or to determine the amount of matter in Space. Pope admired Newton, however.

l. 41. *Thalia*, the Muse of Comedy.

l. 43. *Chesterfield* eloquently opposed Walpole's Stage Licensing Act of 1737.

ll. 45 ff. This *Harlot form* is the first of those who approach the throne, and represents the spirit of Italian Opera. Notice the choice of epithets to characterise her. Her speech is full of musical puns. *Division* is the replacing of one long note by a number of short ones, to produce a florid effect.

l. 65. Italian opera sees *Handel* as an enemy of Dulness. This was true enough, but Pope had, in fact, little appreciation of music. Handel is like the mythical Giant *Briareus* because he used a large orchestra (*hands*), which made a great deal of noise (ll. 67-8).

ll. 71 ff. Notice the puns in this passage (e.g. *posterior, gravity*). Three classes of servants of Dulness are mentioned: those who are dull in their own right, those who are too weak to resist it actively, and those who, as patrons, encourage it.

l. 88. The *toupees* (wigs with top-knots) are worn by the men of fashion, the *gowns* by the scholars.

l. 100. *The Muse's Hypocrit*, is the poetic dilettante, mindless of the worth and dignity of poetry—e.g. Hervey, who is probably *Narcissus*.

l. 105 ff. *Montalto* the solemn and dignified Sir Thomas Hanmer, whose edition of Shakespeare came out in 1743-4. *Benson* commissioned (for his own glory, Pope implies) a translation into Latin of *Paradise Lost*, and an edition of a Latin version of the Psalms by Johnston, a minor Scots seventeenth-century writer—very *unequal crutches*.

l. 116. Refers to the Vice-Chancellor, and Heads of Colleges, at Oxford, who helped sponsor Hanmer's edition. The 'Gentleman Commoners' there wore gold tassels on their caps.

ll. 120 ff. The only editions of great writers (*Wits*) acceptable to Dulness are the 'mutilated' kind just mentioned.

ll. 121 ff. *Medea*, the sorceress, rejuvenated *Æson*, father of Jason, with a singularly loathsome magic potion; the process, however, involved slitting his throat and replacing his blood with the juices.

ll. 139-336. The passages which follow represent the corruptions of education. Pope told Spence, 'What was first designed for an Epistle on Education, as part of my essay-scheme, is now inserted in the fourth book of the Dunciad'.

ll. 139 ff. The first speaker is evidently Dr Busby, Headmaster of Westminster School. He is introduced by mock-heroic diction, with echoes of Milton's 'Moloch, horrid King'; his cane becomes a *dreadful wand*, he wears, appropriately, a *birchen* garland, dropping with *Infant's blood* from the beatings. The schools, in fact, are being seen as places of physical cruelty and deadening, pedantic routine, (ll. 157-160) with versifying learned mechanically (ll. 161-4). *Beaver'd* refers to his fur hat which, legend tells, he kept on while showing Charles II round the school, in case the boys should think anyone was greater than himself. *Winton*, Winchester; the *Samian letter* is Y, used by Pythagoras as an emblem of the different roads of Virtue and Vice.

ll. 166 ff. Busby looks across to Westminster *Hall* and the *House* of Commons, and at some of the eloquent Opposition statesmen. From *his* point of view they have degenerated by escaping from his narrow regimen.

l. 174. Dr *South*, a clergyman who had been educated at Westminster, had allegedly implied that a perfect Epigram was as difficult to write as an Epic.

l. 176. James I, considered the most pedantic of all kings.

ll. 182 ff. *Arbitrary sway* in schools such as that of Busby, seen as the repression of liberty, is extended to arbitrary sway in monarchs, such as George II; Pope opposes the Divine Right of Kings.

ll. 189 ff. The academic Dunces from Oxford and Cambridge now swarm in. Some of Pope's friends at *Christ Church*, Oxford, had opposed Bentley. The philosophers of both universities are shown as contemptible and dull, riding such 'horses' as *Crouzaz* (actually a Swiss), who had attacked the *Essay on Man*, and *Burgersdyck*, a seventeenth-century philosopher. The reading of Locke's *Essay on Human Understanding* was forbidden at Oxford in 1703. *Marg'ret* refers to St John's College, Cambridge; Bentley himself was Master of Trinity, Cambridge, from 1700 to 1742; he had quarrelled frequently with the college Fellows (hence l. 201). Pope has a favourite pun at l. 202. Bentley is called *Aristarchus* after a commentator on Homer; *Remark* (l. 204) probably refers to Bentley's often-used formula for the titles of his books—'Remarks on . . . etc.' *Walker* is the Vice-Master of Trinity.

ll. 210 ff. Bentley's speech sums up the scholastic pedantry of editors. He deserved a place in the poem for his absurd edition of Milton, but not for his classical scholarship, which was of the highest order. This complicated and indigestible passage includes references to Bentley's boasted restoration of the obsolete Greek letter *Digamma*; disputes about Latin pronunciation; his choice of minor authors such as *Manilius* and *Solinus* to comment upon, 'the more freely to display his critical capacity'; his habit of quoting fragments from obscure Greek authors, and from dictionaries such as that of *Suidas*. It concludes (l. 237) with a reference to three scholars whose very names seem to convey their dulness. All that it is necessary to grasp of this passage is the general context of pedantry, and the important conclusion of ll. 233-8. Such people, like so many of the Dunces, are so occupied with minutiæ that they miss the great harmony of things. See the Queen's speech at ll. 453 ff.

l. 243. The Head of a House is the Principal, etc., of a College (see *Augustus* l. 38); Dulness is the *real* Head of many.

l. 244. *Noûs* is the Mind, or First Cause, behind the Universe: Pope's note indicates that he is hitting at those systems of Divinity which terminate in blind Nature—see also l. 485.

l. 245. *Barrow* had been a Master of Trinity, *Atterbury* Dean of Christ Church; both are, of course, praised here, but are powerless to stop the anti-religious forces of Dulness, summed up in the pun on *Canon*. The *Pole* is the sky in general.

ll. 251-4. Notice the appropriateness of the rhythm of the first couplet, and the imagery (*clouds*) of the second.

ll. 255 ff. Bentley goes on to specify another way in which he serves the Goddess: by letting those with more talent pick up a smattering of everything, but a grasp of nothing—only sufficient skill to *misuse* knowledge, as in l. 260.

l. 267. The *Cement* (stressed on first syllable) is Authority.

ll. 275 ff. The next example of the misuse of Education is the young Fop who has made the Grand Tour. He is presumably too stupid to speak for himself, so his Governor presents him. The conception of travel as education was originally a noble one, but it has been perverted, as ll. 320-1 stress. Pope considered this speech one of the best things in the new poem.

The infant is *dauntless* because of his irreligious upbringing: he is not afraid of God. Line 286 means 'begged that she might be blessed by her son becoming a rake'. Lines 307-8 refer to Venice, now notorious for its licentiousness. Line 314 sneers at George II. The three mentioned in l. 326 were all notorious gamblers, the two latter being 'managers of Plays' at Drury Lane. Line 328 refers to the fact that M.P.s could not be arrested for debt—as the *glorious youth* undoubtedly would be sooner or later.

This whole passage is a fine example of Pope's ability to put the pastoral or Georgic style to satirical use: the *surface* of these lines is sensuously beautiful: note the sonorous effect (helped by nasal sounds) of *Convents, bosom'd, slumber, purple*, contrasting with the liquids of *Isles, lilly-silver'd vales, languor, love, lute*, and the lightness given by the participles *diffusing, panting*, etc. What lies beneath is despicable: this is suggested by such words as *obsequious, slaves, the smooth Eunuch, Stews* (brothels), and particularly by the contrasts—*Cupids* and the *Lyon, Vice* and *Christian, spirit* and *whor'd*. This last is made more effective by its rhyme position, a device which is augmented at l. 332.

l. 341. *Paridel*, a philandering young knight in the *Faery Queen*.

ll. 347 ff. The next supplicant to Dulness, *Annius*, is a cheating and forging dealer in ancient coins, sculpture, etc. The references in ll. 361-70 are mainly to images on coins. *Mahomet* (stress on first syllable) is said to have declared that a white pigeon which came to him was Gabriel bringing messages from God. As he forbade images, a coin with him on it would undoubtedly be a forgery; so, probably, are the others. *Otho* and *Niger* were Roman emperors of very short reign; hence their coins would be very rare. *Lares,* household gods.

ll. 371 ff. The story told by *Mummius* (who, as his name suggests, specialises in Egyptology: a *Sistrum* is an ancient Egyptian musical instrument) is alleged by Pope to be true. A coin collector, pursued by Moorish pirates (*Sallee Rovers*) had swallowed his coins; a physician friend, also an antiquary, had helped recover them from his stomach after bargaining for some of the best. Thus Mummius, who alleges that he has bought them (l. 385) claims the coins—the *horned race,* so-called because they bear the insignia of Jupiter Ammon, the ram's horns.

l. 392. Annius is already *cramm'd with capon* (l. 350); supping as well with Pollio will, he hopes, cause him to void the coins. In any case, a famous obstetrician, *Douglas,* will be there to help with the 'delivery'. The unpleasant suggestion given by the combination of *soft* with *obstetric* is, of course, deliberate: the Dunces are to be loathed.

ll. 397 ff. Next to appear are the 'Virtuosi', represented here by the obsessive florist and butterfly-hunter; as has already been said, the point of their appearance is stressed by Dulness' speech at ll. 437 ff. Virtuosi—those interested in trivial curiosities, antiques etc.—were frequent objects of satire. Contemporary gardening manuals give elaborate instructions—including the making of paper ruffs or collars—for protecting delicate blooms. Their distorted values are shared by those who applaud them—note *charming, divine,* and the rivalry with Nature suggested. The florist uses *promiscuous* approvingly of his own work, but insect *lust* of his rival. Calling the flower *Caroline,* after the Queen, is a nice touch of irony.

ll. 421 ff. The language recalls the description of the sylphs in the *Rape of the Lock,* with additional mock-heroic overtones given by the too-elegant epithets for the butterfly. *Heat and Air* perhaps conveys further irony; but it all seems harmless and charming enough, until one hears Dulness' approval. The *sleeping friends* (see l. 346) are excellent as they are, and are recommended as brothers; but people wake up—even the drowsiest brain is stirred by something. Her sons, then, must see that those brains are given trivial baubles to distract them: virtuoso studies are desirable—they keep people from the dangers of philosophy. *Wilkins,* a founder of the Royal Society, discussed the possibility of Man's flying.

ll. 459 ff. The last words of Dulness' speech suggest the (to her) equally attractive possibility that men may become Freethinkers by such studies. The next speaker is one of these: a foe to *Mystery,* i.e. to truth through divine revelation, and to such *moral evidence* as the historical record of Christianity. *A priori* argument is the inferring of certain effects from given causes: these arrogant thinkers, having formed their own conception of God, *reason downward* and, finding that the visible world does not fit in with their theories of God, decide that God does not exist. Instead, they postulate a universe of purely mechanical laws, or the Lucretian idea of Gods completely indifferent to mankind. The result of all this is the kind of thing condemned in the *Essay on Man*: proud Man makes himself the centre of the universe, self-interest is the only driving force, and too much faith is placed in the workings of reason. The Goddess Dulness (l. 485) is the epitome of all this. An alternative heresy is that of *Theocles*, in a dialogue by Shaftesbury, who worships Nature as a Goddess—'impow'ring Deity, Supreme Creator'. *Tindal* (l. 492) was a Deist, who held that a positive revelation was superfluous.

ll. 492 ff. *Silenus*, the drunken companion of Bacchus, here probably represents Thomas Gordon, a follower of Walpole and a harsh critic of the clergy. Pope gives, in Silenus' matter-of-fact words, a simple and devastating summary of the modern education and its results. In ll. 511-13 the allusions are not certain—Pope left asterisks. Kent is the 'Bug' of *Bolingbroke* l. 90, and died in 1740; Berkeley was First Lord of the Admiralty, and died in 1736. It is suggested that both men may have owed their advancement to one of George's mistresses (hence *Punk*, whore; and *Harlot's slave*). The dissipated young Earl of Warwick had died in 1721.

ll. 517 ff. The *Magus*, or Wise Man, of Dulness, the *Wizard Old*, acts as her High Priest. On the political level this is almost certainly Walpole, now 66 and at the end of his long reign (he fell from power in January 1742) but, when the poem was written, still formidable. His *Cup* is the potion of self-love; the *Star* and *Feather* part of the insignia of the Order of the Garter, for which men will abandon their principles. The effect of this cup is opposite to that of Circe's: hers transformed men to beasts, but they kept their human minds; here they keep their human *shape*, but their minds are bestial.

ll. 529 ff. Dulness, however, offers consolations—impudence, stupidity, shamelessness, etc. *Cibberian* because of Colley Cibber's proverbially brazen behaviour. The *Cimmerians* lived in perpetual darkness.

l. 538. Pope puns on parti-coloured and the political party.

ll. 541 ff. Opera and its patrons are again glanced at.

ll. 549 ff. This fine passage goes far beyond any mere attack on epicures: Maynard Mack has said that 'although light in tone, (it) carries a scathing indictment of the perversion of religious values in a money culture'. Note the number of religious allusions here, giving the pervading suggestion of blasphemy or sacrilege. *Seve* and *Verdeur* are French terms relating to wine. *Bladen* and *Hays*, both gamesters, and *Knight*, the absconding Cashier of the South-Sea Company, were, Pope's note tells us, living in luxury in Paris.

ll. 565 ff. The degree-giving ceremony, and the Queen's speech, is an opportunity for summing up the various categories of Dunces. Dabblers in Shakespeare studies; the foolish gentlemen who by their membership were making the Royal Society a standing joke among the wits; Freemasons, for having 'mysteries' of their own, and for being, like the disciples of Pythagoras, a 'silent race'—they, like the Royal Society and various others, held an 'annual feast', which was, no doubt, the sole reason for many people joining; *Gregorians* and *Gormogons* were other secret societies.

ll. 585 ff. This part of the speech mentions some of the frivolous behaviour of the high-born or learned sons of Dulness. There is evidence enough of all these things—of Dukes as amateur jockeys (l. 585), noblemen dressing up as footmen and running races (l. 586); an Earl driving a stage-coach (l. 587); an entomologist Baron producing illustrated works (l. 589); a lecture given to the Royal Society on 'The Usefulness of the Silk of Spiders' (l. 590); judges and serjeants-at-law engaged in a solemn ritual which looked rather like a dance (l. 591); cricketing peers; a famous gourmet as Bishop of Durham (l. 594)—note the satirical *Souls*. The *daring son* is Walpole, as First Minister; these lines were written before his fall. Pope probably means, by the *three Estates*, King, Lords, and Commons, though this usage is incorrect.

ll. 609 ff. The *Hall* is Westminster (the High Court); *Convocation* is the synod of clergy; the *Nation's Sense* (see *Dialogue* I l. 78) is here the House of Commons. *Palinurus* was Æneas's steersman, who went to sleep and fell overboard: here, Walpole.

l. 626. After this line the *New Dunciad* closed with the couplet:

> While the Great Mother bids Britannia sleep,
> And pours her Spirit o'er the Land and Deep.

ll. 627-56. This magnificent conclusion expands the original ending of Book III. Pope's note included the significant passage: 'Do not, gentle reader, rest too secure in thy contempt of the Instruments for such a revolution in learning, or despise such weak agents as have been described in our poem, but remember what the *Dutch* stories somewhere relate, that a great part of their Provinces was once overflow'd, by a small opening made in one of their dykes by a single Water-Rat.'

ll. 628 ff.   The Muse, bidden to *relate* at l. 619, herself goes to sleep, and Pope—the 'one dim Ray of Light' of l. 1 now expiring—has to carry on alone. Nearly the whole of this last passage shows the extinction of light of various kinds. Pope's favourite Sun image is present by allusion, because it is the sun that gilds the clouds (l. 631) and forms Rainbows (l. 632). The flashes of Wit, which may be independent of the Sun of Reason, are short-lived (l. 633). The Arts are like stars extinguished by cloud, like flowers fading off the plain of heaven, like the eyes of another watchman, Argus. What is implied by these comparisons?

Truth lies now in darkness: from her normal proverbial 'home' (the bottom of a well) one can at least see the stars, but Pope transfers her to a cave. The image of l. 643 is perhaps of a ladder, now shortened and useless. The First Cause is God; now, as in l. 475, mechanical natural laws have been thrust into his place. ll. 645-6 refer to various metaphysical speculations about the nature of Soul and Body, some thinkers attempting to deny reality to the body, others claiming that the soul is material and mortal: the result is the general confusion of l. 648. *Mystery* has the same meaning as in l. 460: Warburton's note says that this line refers to those, such as the Deists, who 'attempted to shew that the mysteries of Religion may be mathematically demonstrated'.

With l. 649 we return to the imagery of light being extinguished. Religion is presumably *blushing* because of the invasion of her mysteries, as well as through shame at the degeneration of the country. Neither the *human Spark*—the light man is able to give of his own accord—nor the *Glimpse divine* he has of God's light, is left; and the passage comes to its climax with a reversal of the 'Let there be Light' of the Creation.

SUGGESTIONS FOR FURTHER READING

Detailed discussion of the poems will be found in the various volumes of the Twickenham Edition. Most Biographies of Pope should be treated with caution, but the following are recommended:

Bonamy Dobrée, *Alexander Pope* (1951).

George Sherburn, *The Early Career of Alexander Pope* (1934).

Samuel Johnson, *Life of Pope* (1779-81), reprinted in Everyman's Library.

Peter Quennell, *Alexander Pope: the Education of Genius, 1688-1728* (1968).

The best brief introduction to Pope is by Ian Jack, No. 48 of the 'Writers and their Work' series published for the British Council (1954). Recommended critical and 'background' books are:

A. R. Humphreys, *The Augustan World* (1954).

James Sutherland, *A Preface to Eighteenth Century Poetry* (1948).

Ian Jack, *Augustan Satire* (1952).

James Sutherland, *English Satire* (1958).

F. A. Pottle, *The Idiom of Poetry* (1946).

G. Tillotson, *On the Poetry of Pope* (1938).

R. A. Brower, *Alexander Pope* (1959).

Aubrey L. Williams, *Pope's Dunciad* (1955).

F. R. Leavis, *Revaluation*, ch. III (1936).

Cleanth Brooks, *The Well Wrought Urn*, ch. 5 (1947).

James L. Clifford (ed.) *Eighteenth-Century English Literature* (1959): see particularly 'Wit and Poetry and Pope', by Maynard Mack.

James Sutherland (ed.) *Essays on the Eighteenth Century presented to David Nichol Smith* (1945): see particularly 'Pope at Work' by George Sherburn, and 'The Inspiration of Pope's Poetry' by John Butt.

Carrol Camden (ed.) *Restoratian and Eighteenth-Century Literature: Essays presented to A. D. McKillop* (1963): see particularly 'The Shadowy Cave', by Maynard Mack.